An interwoven History of...

TEA & TOIL
AT THE WOMAN'S CLUB

An Interwoven History of..

TEA & TOIL

AT THE WOMAN'S CLUB

By Bainy Cyrus

Paperback ISBN: 979-8-9894840-0-3

Hardcover ISBN: 979-8-9894840-1-0

Dedication

This book is dedicated to my late mother, Indie Bain Bilisoly, who taught me the importance of history and literature. And who instilled a love of reading and writing. I could feel her encouraging spirit over my shoulder as I wrote this book. You got it, Mom.

Saving the Martin Mansion began as such an enormous project to take on that it sometimes felt impossible. Since the Mansion was within a few months of bankruptcy, we had little time, no staff, and no funds but a lot of determination and a deep love for the house that grew stronger every day. This journey has been nothing short of a miracle, and we thank God daily. We envisioned this house as a respite for the community and a club our members can be proud of once again. We hope you enjoy this house as much as we have.

~~~~Suzanne Ott and Polly Peterson Jones

"You only learn patience when you need it most."

~~ Polly Peterson Jones
~~~~

About the Author

Bainy Cyrus is the author of five books. She was born severely deaf in Norfolk, VA, and learned to speak/lipread at Clarke School in Massachusetts. She graduated from Virginia Tech in 1985 with a bachelor's degree in landscape horticulture and worked as a landscape designer for nearly 20 years before deciding to change careers. In 2004, Bainy earned a master's degree in counseling from Old Dominion University. She worked as a job coach for people with disabilities for fifteen years until her retirement in 2021. Her first book, "All Eyes," was published in 2005 as an anthology titled "Deaf Women's Lives: Three Self-Portraits" and won the silver Eric Hoffer award in the memoir category. Then, "All Eyes" was published as a stand-alone edition in 2010 and won two silver awards in the autobiography/memoir category. Next, she self-published "Della on Facebook" in 2012, depicting her year-long daily posts on her Labrador puppy, Della, who passed away of old age in 2023. Bainy lives in Norfolk with her husband, Steve, and their lab rescue, Sydney. She enjoys hiking, biking, pickleball, gardening, and RVing.

Acknowledgments

It took me six years to write the first paragraph for this book after coming up with the idea in 2016 due to my job and then our RV travel across America immediately after retirement. I must thank Troy Valos, the special collections librarian at the Slover Library, for getting me started in September 2022 by showing me how to find old newspaper clippings, magazine articles, and related links. Then Nancy King, my relative, increased my motivation by loaning me the *Martin Family History* book, which has stories about Alvah Martin, the original builder of the Martin Mansion, later known as The Woman's Club. And I thank the amazing technology of newspapers.com for allowing me to collect over 700 clippings dating back to 1905. Hardy Everett was kind enough to show me his amazing collection of historical books, including John Parker's *Thirteen Blocks* (of The Hague neighborhood). I also show gratitude toward Cynthia Wise Smith and Joanna Church for taking the time to read my manuscript. Susanne Ott, Polly Jones, and Paige Rose were ever patient with my constant questions on text and visits about how they saved the Martin Mansion. The Woman's Club of Norfolk members are much appreciated for their support of my book. Most of all, this book would not have improved a hundredfold without the incredible professionalism of my editor, Barbara Noe Kennedy, who was not afraid to act like a drill sergeant for my book. Finally, I thank my husband, Steve, for managing the publishing process by phone and text with the staff. And my heartfelt gratitude to our late dog, Della, and then our rescue black lab,

Sydney, for sitting patiently next to me while I scribbled away on the keyboard.

Contents

Introduction

After speaking to several locals here in Norfolk, Virginia, in the past few years, I was astonished that many people knew next to nothing about the civic and volunteer services of the Woman's Club of Norfolk since its establishment in 1905. When locals hear of "The Woman's Club" on 524 Fairfax Avenue, they envision it as a party house or a wedding venue. They see only semi-formal guests mingling from room to room on the first floor or dancing in the auditorium, not middle-aged and elderly ladies in spiffy dresses and pearls ratcheting up a plan to serve the community or organizing a fundraising project. Yes, The Woman's Club is a party house but also a *business* house. One hundred years of meetings, elections, lectures, classes, debates, signatures, phone calls, writings, stampings, and even disagreements had occurred in that Georgian Revival home also called the Martin Mansion honoring the 1910 original builder, Alvah Martin.

I admit I was ignorant of all the incredible work accomplished by the Woman's Club of Norfolk, Virginia Federation of Women's Clubs, and General Federation of Women's Clubs—until I collected the firsts of hundreds of newspaper clippings and online articles. I typed the first Google search for this book, "How Woman's Club originated," which led to several articles and stories about Jane Croly's rejection by men at the Charles Dickens event that spurred her to establish the first woman's club ever. Just then, I was spellbound by the rapid multiplication of woman's clubs nationwide, leading to the formation of the umbrella organization, the General Federation of Women's Clubs (GFWC). And I stared admiringly at the GFWC founder Jane Croly's black-and-white photos, one of which showed her sitting sideways with a rigid posture and a resolved look on her face. Her attractive downward eyes gave a sharp look, giving an indication of power. That photo inspired me to research more on such formidable women in the fledgling woman's clubs during the Progressive Era. Women in the late 1800s were finally transforming from home confinement to a society where they could make a difference—a huge one.

My attention then turned to the Woman's Club of Norfolk (WCN). To my amazement, I found numerous clippings of *The Virginian-Pilot*, so many activities of this budding club were mentioned. In 1906, the first article on the WCN's action was the Clean Up Day, in which the new club asked Mayor Riddick to have everyone in Norfolk clean up their yards. I was incredulous to see how a woman's club could successfully affect an entire city with a simple request while it was only a few months old. *The Virginian-Pilot* published almost every WCN meeting or lecture, often specifying the department; for instance, there would be a brief article on the club members of the literature department reading Shakespeare. And I must thank Beverly Dozier, "The Archive Lady" and a current WCN member, for finding rare laminated yellowed articles of *The Virginian-Pilot* in cardboard boxes she had so delicately arranged up on the third floor of the Martin Mansion. Many of these fragile articles date back to the early 1920s, emitting a strong, musty smell. We sure got a whiff of the rich history of the Woman's Club of Norfolk.

This book has intertwining histories of the Martin Mansion, the Woman's Club of Norfolk, the General Federation of Women's Clubs, The Hague neighborhood in the Ghent Historic District, the city of Norfolk, and even America on a chronological basis with some flashbacks. I certainly hope you will enjoy reading *Tea and Toil at The Woman's Club*.

Bainy Cyrus

Prologue

December 2014

The ten-thousand-square-foot Georgian Revival mansion appeared to be sturdy with its tan bricks, showing resilience after eleven decades of parties and meetings. Thousands of people had stepped up on its wide concrete steps and then into an impressive foyer with a 360-degree view to attend a club meeting, celebrate a wedding, watch a school skit, participate in a fashion show, and even live in an apartment on the second floor. The Martin Mansion, belonging to the Woman's Club of Norfolk, seemed alive with its beautiful architecture, so unique that it had drawn curiosity and admiration from passersby. And the locals here in Norfolk, Virginia, never failed to reminisce about a debutante party or a Christmas caroling decades earlier whenever they drove by this stately home. I was one of the locals and often thought of my elementary school activities in the auditorium on the right side of the mansion and Thanksgiving family gatherings on the first floor.

Long after its 1910 construction, the Martin Mansion appeared to be gracefully aging like the Egyptian pyramids without any chance of toppling. But it only looked that way on the outside. No one knew the decrepitude of the mansion, much less what was happening underneath. The brick foundation had already begun to sink after over a century of sitting on Fairfax Avenue in a coastal city known to be prone to flooding and unleveled with soft, loamy soil. The foundation's extensive cracks could be seen through the arched openings under the wraparound porch but had not been checked for years. The mansion inched forward at a slight angle toward the street, a little more every year, and inside, the cornice areas on all three floors were noticeably bending down toward the front. But the mansion was too big to give a discernible sign of sinking to anyone standing on the sidewalk.

However, the interior showed otherwise, indicating that something was terribly wrong with this long-beloved Woman's Club. The walls were peeling. Hardwood floors were deteriorating. Dust balls were developing. The Martin Mansion was abandoned due to an elderly director in cognitive decline. It was eerily quiet except for a few tenants upstairs, unlike the boisterous atmosphere reverberating through the first floor in earlier years with a bride throwing her bouquet or chatty members of the Woman's Club of Norfolk. The mansion was on the verge of dilapidation.

***

It was during an evening walk with her husband in the early 2010s that Susanne Ott first stumbled upon the Martin Mansion, mesmerized by its grand porch. She did not see its current state but rather clearly what it could be, not fully recognizing the future parallels to the Tom Hanks movie, *The Money Pit*. It took several weeks for Susanne to muster up the courage to knock since she did not know who owned that house. An elderly lady came to the door and introduced herself as the director of the Martin Mansion. Those two began a conversation in which Susanne accepted the invitation to join the Woman's Club of Norfolk, a century-old organization that bought the mansion in 1925. The director gave Susanne a history book of the club that impressed the latter so much that she recruited a couple of friends to join the Woman's Club; one of them was Paige Rose.

After several weeks, Susanne and Paige found themselves among a handful of remaining active members of a club that boasted a buoyant seven hundred members in 1930. And the director appeared to be affected by age-related health issues. She was also living in one of the second-floor rooms at the Martin Mansion and ran the place. As soon as they paired up to investigate the condition of the mansion, Susanne and Paige noticed curiosities and irregularities all around. It was not only the mansion but also their Woman's Club as a dying organization.

The financial state of the Woman's Club of Norfolk was questionable since there was hardly any income from club activities and rental events in the mansion known for its popular wedding venue for many years. And the money from the second-floor tenants did not appear to flow in. A building structure and piece of the property had been sold by the director without board knowledge or approval – at far below market value. Worse yet, the Martin Mansion was at the point of bankruptcy.

Susanne asked the director questions about the financial state of the Martin Mansion, only to be rebuffed by the older lady who insisted, "We are comfortable." She was still in charge of the mansion and the organization; therefore, Susanne could not get precise answers on the monthly club income or outgoing bills.

Not one to give up, she persisted and repeated hard questions to the director, who became belligerent and irritable. That continued for two years as Susanne endured harsh words, sometimes personally insulting, while Paige watched with great concern. It appeared that old age had taken a toll on the director, who first managed the Woman's Club of Norfolk with no problems or abnormal behavior. She became unbearable and drove away club members but Susanne and Paige, who loved the mansion too much to relinquish it to disintegration or put it on the market.

They asked the director point-blank what would happen if the club ran out of operating funds. The director casually said, "Well, we would just give the house and contents to the General Federation of Women's Clubs or just sell it." That statement shocked Susanne and Paige, and it was when they also learned that their club had lost its hundred-year membership in the umbrella organization, based in Washington, D.C., because of non-payment. And it was interesting that the director said "she" would give the mansion back to the General Federation to surrender the Woman's Club of Norfolk altogether. Hearing that one statement from the director, Susanne and Paige felt their energies galvanized to save their club and the mansion, which were fading fast in front of their eyes. Time was running out, as was money.

Those two women later told me that there were times they felt like giving up but knew that the Martin Mansion was too valuable with its unique woodwork and rich history dating back to 1910. Paige had her wedding there in 2006 and could not bear handing the mansion to a developer who would likely gut it out and turn it into condos. And she and Susanne knew that locals would be heartbroken if the cherished "The Woman's Club" on Fairfax Avenue lost its historical value to the developer or even the bulldozer. I, myself, would feel the same way after growing up along with the mansion and attending a great many parties there.

Since the Martin Mansion has been owned by an organization for decades, it is known as "The Woman's Club" by the locals and out-of-town guests. However, the "Martin Mansion" name still sticks with some people today, especially a fundraising organization trying to save the mansion. And I intend to use that name throughout the book as well, depending on the situation. So, the Martin Mansion and The Woman's Club refer to the same Georgian Revival home on Fairfax Avenue, as those two should not be confused with one another in this book. And to make it less confusing, I am referring to the organization, not the mansion, as the "Woman's Club of Norfolk" or "WCN."

***

During the holidays of 2014, the director's family members arrived at the mansion and announced that it was time to save the mansion by removing their mother from her apartment on the second floor and taking her home. But not before the paperwork had been transmitted to the next person in charge of the Martin Mansion and the Woman's Club of Norfolk. Susanne knew the director would not take kindly to her request for the financial and bank statements transmitted directly to her. Therefore, all agreed Paige would handle the transition of papers between the departing director and the Martin Mansion. She and the director arranged to meet at the bank one afternoon, where documents, bank statements, and checkbooks would be exchanged. One of the older lady's family members would accompany her.

Believing there would be extensive stacks of paperwork to return to the Martin Mansion, Paige emptied her Mazda sedan, temporarily removed her six-year-old daughter's car seat and flattened the back seats. As a busy mother jostling between The Woman's Club and Natalie's preschool, Paige had to run against the clock to get the paper transition done before reinstalling the car seat and meeting the pick-up time for her daughter.

As soon as Paige walked into the bank lobby, she was roughly greeted by the director, who thrust the paperwork toward her. It was not even a stack, as Paige would have expected the director to possess after years of documentation for The Woman's Club. Instead, the tiny blue tote bag she found holding contained only ten pages of paperwork, accompanied by a checkbook and a few bank statements. Paige later imitated herself to me, holding up an imaginary bag by the handle with her index finger and expressing astonishment by such a measly amount of paperwork expected to cover decades of the mansion's records.

Ignoring her club associate's shocked look, the director showed Paige one page consisting of phone numbers of the mansion's electrician and other service companies. Next, she gave quick instructions for managing a twenty-one-room mansion with a reception hall that had hosted weddings, parties, funeral wakes, charity drives, and other events for nearly a century. The director's family member stood by, appearing uneasy, and urged it was time to leave. The older lady looked at Paige, smiled sheepishly, and said in a roaring voice, "GOOD LUCK!"

Paige was too stunned to speak as she stared at the lady who once sweetly complimented her at her wedding at The Woman's Club in 2006. The bride in her forties had decorated the reception hall with a garden party theme. The director told Paige she had seen many wedding decorations at the mansion over the years, and it was the prettiest one she had ever seen. Paige took that compliment as a unique token from the director of the Martin Mansion. But now she was a different person, affected by old age mentally and physically.

As the director turned to leave with her family member, Paige tried to stop her with a few more questions about how to take charge of the Woman's Club of Norfolk and the Martin Mansion altogether. The director stopped, turned to Paige, and exhibited slight remorse for thrusting all the untrained responsibilities toward a stranded lady thirty-five years her junior. Her face softened for the first time in a while, and she met Paige's eyes in genuineness. The director had always liked Paige for her innocence and possibly felt guilty for placing her in an enormous mess to clean up. She opened her mouth to explain further instructions, but her family member pulled her away and steered her toward the door. The family member knew Paige and Susanne, even without training, would repair what was left off by her mother, who was no longer competent to manage the mansion.

Astonished, Paige watched the director heading out the

door as she held a flimsy tote bag that would not yield much information for her unexpected new position. It was as if a massive jumble of confusing IKEA tidbits was heaped on Paige to put together a whole object. A ten-thousand-square-foot mansion in disarray AND a dying club with only three or four active members would not be a piece of cake. Paige realized she and Susanne were in for a difficult, unbearable job during the holiday season.

***

Susanne and Paige were left with the empty mansion except for the second-floor tenants and a handful of club members. To their dismay, these two women found only nine thousand dollars in the bank account of The Woman's Club, whereas it should have been in the five digits or more. Susanne and Paige learned that the tenants had been paying meager rent, if any. And nine thousand dollars in the bank account was not enough to maintain the then 105-year-old mansion and the Woman's Club of Norfolk. Worse yet, the mansion was in terrible condition. Now in charge and determined to revive their club by asking some members to return for help, Susanne and Paige inspected the mansion without being blocked by the director. They braced for the worst.

The downstairs, with the decorative foyer surrounded by handmade dark oak paneling and a landscape mural, might have looked normal to the untrained eyes. Still, there were obvious signs of scary, deferred maintenance. The two women were horrified to see water stains on the walls and ceilings, apparently caused by pipe and roof leaks. And there was a moldy smell all around. Susanne and Paige feared the Martin Mansion was dripping on the inside like a long-unopened jar terrarium.

The electric cords overloaded with appliances in the industrial kitchen were a fire hazard. Those two women immediately unplugged all the appliances, leaving a few intact. They knew water and electricity do not mix, much less dripping moisture. In addition, the kitchen had not been cleaned thoroughly for months; the countertops looked sticky with old spills, and the white cabinets had fingerprint smudges. The women dreaded looking down on the filthy vinyl floor, which felt spongy under their feet. Finally, Susanne and Paige looked at each other and figured they would have to go down to the basement directly under the kitchen since it had the potential for flooding during severe storms.

When they opened the basement door, the odor of urine, mold, and decay overwhelmed them. It was the site of a men's restroom, along with one large room and a few small ones. The basement windows seemed opaque, with no outdoor light because of their location under the wraparound porch, not the mansion's exterior wall. The women predicted a few inches of standing water in the basement. Then they opened the electrical panel on the wall and found no labels for the switches. That is not good, Susanne and Paige thought. With its horrid smell, the basement was so suffocating that the women had to escape back upstairs.

Before calling for assistance, Susanne and Paige figured there were bills to pay, so they opened a large stack of unopened mail neglected by the director. One stood out from the city of Norfolk regarding the inspection. The women learned from the phone call that the director had blocked the city inspector several times, insisting it was her house.

The Martin Mansion did not pass inspection in both home and fire safety. Not even one positive check on their list. Susanne and Paige were handed a thick folder of required repairs with a two-month deadline. The unpredictable gas stove was no longer permitted due to fire hazards. The electrical wirings were in shambles. Some water pipes were corroded. Worse yet, the roof leaked. That meant many expenses for the Woman's Club of Norfolk. And two months did not seem long enough to beat the deadline.

Susanne and Paige were despaired but wanted to save the Martin Mansion. The Woman's Club of Norfolk only needed more members, more dues, and a renewed membership to the General Federation. That was not unsurmountable, but the ten-thousand-square-foot mansion in the worst shape would be like a massive tangle of strings to untangle, albeit with a lot of money. The nine thousand dollars left in the checking account by the director was likely not enough at all.

Then, the situation at the Martin Mansion became worse. Susanne handed Paige a letter, and it was from the Internal Revenue Service stating the Woman's Club of Norfolk had not paid some required taxes in years and owed approximately eight thousand dollars. Paige dropped to her seat and looked at Susanne in despair. They then looked around the wall-paneled room and felt their hearts ache for the mansion that was once beautiful and bustling with hundreds of club members in the past, foxtrot dancers, wedding guests, Christmas parties, elementary school skits, and even the First Ladies of Virginia. But to Susanne and Paige, the Martin Mansion had come to a standstill like a ghost, with virtually no money to keep it afloat. Realizing there were no more options to bring it back to life, Paige turned to Susanne with a dreaded look and conveyed the worst possible idea. Susanne heard the message, shook her head, and said, “No, no, we cannot let it go. We must fight.”

Underneath these women, the aging foundation was also fighting to keep from sinking.

Chapter One

Let's imagine it is a clear, calm day in the late fall of 1920. "Edgar," the boater, feels the slightly rough currents of the Atlantic Ocean and sees the water's steely blue color.

On a solo mission, he is transferring his boat for the winter from his summer cottage in Virginia Beach's North End to his Norfolk home farther inland. Cautious not to venture too far into the open sea, "Edgar" stays as close to the beach as possible without being turned over by the waves. Heading north, he veers around the big corner bump of the mainland, a new military installation named Fort Story on Cape Henry. The Old Cape Henry Lighthouse appears, pleasing "Edgar" since it signals safety. His eighteen-foot-long varnished wooden boat with an outboard motor is no longer rocking from the ocean currents as "Edgar" enters the calmer Chesapeake Bay. With metal gas cans prepared for his Evinrude engine, he feels confident in motoring several miles alongside the concave-shape shoreline of Lynnhaven Roads and then up to Ocean View, a part of Norfolk County.

Moving northward toward the tip of Willoughby Spit, "Edgar" sees a peninsula in the distance with an island on the right, about seven miles away. That island "Edgar" knows is Fort Monroe in Hampton, the largest stone fort built in the United States. Now, he is on a channel between Hampton and Norfolk, and that channel is called Hampton Roads, where the water is even calmer but less blue. "Edgar" sees the large James River flowing southward between the peninsula and the Isle of Wight, but he has no intention of motoring upward. Instead, he turns around Sewell's Point, the site of Norfolk Naval Base, and heads south into a much smaller body of water, the Elizabeth River. That dark river enters the heart of Norfolk.

"Edgar" makes a stop past the entry into the Lafayette River, where he plans to store his boat at his home. He wants to see something farther south before returning to his house. So, "Edgar" carefully maneuvers his boat alongside Lambert Point and Fort Norfolk. And he views West Norfolk and Portsmouth across the river on his right. He then passes the Merchants and Miners Wharf, and veers left into Smith's Creek. "Edgar" waits for the turnstile of Smith's Creek Bridge to allow his boat farther into the creek, whose name was recently changed to The Hague.

He turns left, notices a hundred-foot footbridge on the right, and passes a row of newly built stately homes that skirt around the unusual, artificial, semi-circle shoreline. "Edgar" admires various architectural styles of tall, narrow homes nearly glued together, including Tudor, Queen Anne, and Colonial. The scene gives him a delightful illusion of being in Europe, not in a rundown wharf city known as Norfolk, Virginia. As he approaches the top left end of the Y-shaped Hague, "Edgar" picks up his bowler hat from under the steering wheel and places it over his head as a courtesy to a few other boaters resting in the water. Some wave back, and others holler welcoming words.

Only a few hundred feet wide with calm water, The Hague ends at a straight line of the stone landing in front of a park next to Christ and St. Luke's Episcopal Church, while the other end stops at a slightly curved line over 1,300 feet away in front of a museum.

The first end is where "Edgar" stops his boat, ties it to the post, and climbs up on the steps toward Mowbray Arch. The street unfolds into a neighborhood shaped like a semi-circle grid pattern with tree-lined avenues and large areas of green space. And, of course, there are upscale homes of different architecture, many of which are not even older than "Edgar" himself in his early forties. He enters Fairfax Avenue, the first block from Christ and St. Luke's Episcopal Church, strolls past the first two homes on the left, and finds what he has been looking for.

An 8,500-square-foot Georgian Revival mansion was built only ten years earlier, and that was before the addition of a 1,440-square-foot auditorium. "Edgar" has heard a great deal about this beautiful place, which was just sold this year to his organization, the Virginia Club, by the family of the original, deceased owner, Alvah Martin. Awestruck by the sharply symmetrical exterior with tan bricks, "Edgar" stands directly in front of the mansion, arms askance. He looks up at the concrete steps leading to the wraparound porch with thin white columns spaced evenly apart and admires the gigantic wooden door flanked by vertical, narrow, beveled glass windows.

Then "Edgar" knows he is at the right place as he notices above the door the narrow arch window featuring house number 524. Next, his wide eyes scan the front of the house, where the curved front section with two glass-blown windows is situated on each side of the door. The second floor, extending over the veranda roof, repeats those two curved sections. A small, railed porch in the center holds a narrow door flanked by small vertical windows. The three dormers on the third floor look striking, with their concrete tops resembling bat wings. "Edgar," thinks that the house must be the grandest and most proportional one he has ever seen, shaking his head in amazement. And its size is as massive as the Atlantic Ocean he just ventured from. Taking a deep breath, he braces for more surprises inside the mansion now owned by the Virginia Club, walks up the steps, and opens the door.

***

Long before the construction of the stylish homes in The Hague, that area in Norfolk, Virginia, was primarily farmlands. That was before the marshy waterway called Smith's Creek was reshaped into a neat semi-circle canal and renamed The Hague. Located in the southeastern part of the state, Norfolk was first inhabited and ruled by the Native American tribe called the Chesepian or Chesapeake several centuries before the English settlers took over in the 1600s. The Chesapeake tribe, which also occupied nearby Portsmouth, Chesapeake, and Virginia Beach, named the Norfolk area "Skicoak" and thrived on fishing and shell fishing right off the Elizabeth River and Chesapeake Bay. And they farmed on rich black soil that still exists in Norfolk today. The Chesapeake spoke the Algonquin language and stayed civil with the Nansemond tribe farther west in Suffolk. The Chesapeake were peaceful people and minded their business in Skicoak. Then, they faced a total wipeout by Chief Powhatan around 1590.

There was a great deal of reluctance on the chief's part

since the Chesapeake never caused any trouble. However, the Powhatan was one of the thirty tribes that formed an Algonquin civilization known as the "Powhatan Confederacy." This group numbered over fifteen thousand Indians that developed permanent settlements with good trade and one government covering eight thousand square miles in Virginia. The Algonquin priests informed Chief Powhatan that he must eradicate the Chesapeake tribe because they were evil and would likely destroy the Powhatan Confederacy by burning villages and killing them all. This prophecy frightened the Algonquin priests and religious men of various tribes, although they could not specify the timing of the possible ruination of their empire by the Chesapeake. Finally, after being pressured many times, Chief Powhatan reluctantly slashed the Chesapeake tribe of three hundred to four hundred members who lived near the mouth of Chesapeake Bay. The Chesapeake were extinct when the early English settlers arrived in Norfolk on separate occasions, beginning in 1607. They set up permanent inhabitance in a spattering of areas from the Chesapeake Bay shoreline to the western and eastern branches of the Elizabeth River. Henry Seawall, Thomas Lambert, and Thomas Willoughby were the settlers; therefore, their names (except Seawell's omitting an a) are seen today throughout Norfolk: Sewell's Point, Lambert's Point, and Willoughby Spit.

The British Empire saw great potential in Virginia after the first permanent settlement was established in Jamestown in 1607, despite the hardships of hunger, disease, and Indian attacks in the following years. The Virginia General Assembly was established in 1619 in Jamestown and comprised one governor, his council, and twenty-two representatives serving as burgesses. Then, in 1643, the House of Burgesses was launched in Williamsburg, seven miles from Jamestown, and served as America's first legislative and democratic government. It was the act of the House of Burgesses that established Norfolk in 1680 and then laid out the town in 1682, expecting this new port city to act as a trade and commerce center. They named the town after Norfolk County in England. Lastly, Norfolk was incorporated in 1736 and remains a hub for trading, shipbuilding, ship repair, cargo shipping, light industry, railroad, and coal. This coastal city is also home to the world's most extensive naval base and the North American Headquarters for NATO (North Atlantic Treaty Organization).

***

The history of The Hague, where "Edgar" the boater first saw the Georgian Revival mansion, began in the late 1800s when the two Dutchmen, J. P. Andre Mottu and Adolph Boissevain, eyed the creek as the potential for an upper-class neighborhood to enhance Norfolk as the industrial city. They worked for the Norfolk Company, a real estate firm connected with the Norfolk and Western Railway that transported coal from West Virginia as well as grain, chemicals, and automobiles from other states. The curvy Y-shape of Smith's Creek reminded Mottu and Boissevain of waterways in their native country, Holland, as the former had just immigrated to America in the same year. An idea lit over those Dutchmen's heads: That section of Norfolk would become a replica of the Dutch district with upscale homes of European architecture on the waterfront. Mottu and Boissevain began their project on the shoreline by filling the marshland with dirt and shaping it into a semi-circle pattern. However, it would not be until 1897 that a bulkhead was built to "reduce wind and water movement," protecting homes in the new neighborhood. Captain Bolton won the twelve thousand dollars (close to four hundred thousand dollars today) construction bid for the wooden bulkhead that spanned 1,380 feet, extending from today's Christ and St. Luke's Episcopal Church to the Chrysler Museum. Visualizing the future homes alongside the curved shoreline, Mottu and Boissevain decided to rename Smith's Creek "The Hague" after the capital city of the province of South Holland in the Netherlands.

The neighborhood on The Hague, which would become Ghent, sat on a large tract of farmland where the Chesapeake tribe must have planted corn or soybeans centuries ago. And that area was called "Pleasant Point," which eventually changed to "Ghent." The exact origin of that new name is unknown today, but either of these men chose "Ghent": Jasper Moran or Richard Drummond. Moran, a wealthy landowner and an early Norfolkian, bought the farm, built a home, and decided to name his neighborhood Ghent in honor of the treaty that ended the War of 1812 in which he fought. Or it could be Commodore Drummond who, too, owned a home there and picked the name Ghent after one of his ships carried the actual copy of the treaty across the Atlantic. Regardless of who chose the name, the Treaty of Ghent inspired them enough to name the historic neighborhood that continues its popularity among Norfolk locals and visitors today.

The construction of upscale homes of European architecture began in 1890, with most popping up between 1892 and 1907. The formerly quiet waterway became a bustling waterfront Amsterdam-like district. That helped the image of Norfolk as a not-so-clean city due to the coastal and coal industry. It was like opening an old, beaten-up chest and seeing the beauty inside with jewels. Development of the middle- and upper-middle-class homes intensified in speed, so much so that it spread to surround over thirty blocks, most of what is today's Ghent Historic District. The main street that skirted the shoreline, Mowbray Arch, soon became the ideal spot for stately homes. Apparently the most expensive created in the European style. Today, "The Hague" and "Ghent Historic District" are interchangeable; they both occupy the semi-circle, grid-pattern neighborhood. The locals, including myself, use just the term Ghent since it extends approximately a mile in two directions, north and west, and a half mile to the east – not only The Hague. Hence, there are "Historic Ghent," "West Ghent," "Ghent Square," and just "Ghent." Just all these sections that ended the War of 1812! I lived in three different apartments in Ghent for eight years before marrying Steve in 1994 - the first two apartments were only across the street from each other, and the third a half mile away. It was a delight to live in Ghent, which is one of the most popular areas in Norfolk with its abundant history.

***

Alvah Howard Martin, a prominent Norfolkian, saw potential in The Hague and would soon build two residences, one of which is the main subject of this book. Known as the "Norfolk's Renaissance Man," Alvah had several distinct careers in his sixty-year lifetime, and those around him greatly admired his dynamic energy. A tall, slender man with grace and orderliness, he was born on September 20, 1858, acquired his education through private tutors and public schools, and was valedictorian at the "Webster Institute," according to the 2001 family history book. I tried researching this school and found that there are many with the Webster name across the country; therefore, it is not known if Alvah's "Webster Institute" was of higher education. His remarkable intelligence naturally led him to study law under his attorney father, Colonel James Green Martin, while employed in the clerk's office. Before his law education, Alvah acquired his first job as a writer for the Clerk of the Norfolk County Court at the young, tender age of sixteen. He impressed everyone with his meticulous writing, full of credibility, and was officially appointed as deputy clerk in 1881. Because of his utmost patience, Alvah performed so well that he was re-elected repeatedly for thirty-eight years. As Lyon Gardiner Tyler, a Virginia biographer, stated, "None surpassed him in all that is desirable in a Public Officer."

Alvah was not only the county clerk but also served as president of the Merchants and Planters Bank, which he founded in 1899. He also owned extensive property in Norfolk and Princess Anne Counties and coal lands in West Virginia. But he was more versatile than that. Alvah was on U.S. President Taft's

Executive Committee and "used his influence with the President to secure the Port of Norfolk, the deepest water harbor on the U.S. East Coast, as the port of entry for the State of Virginia, a historic maritime decision that has led to significant regional, state, national, and global impact," the Visit Norfolk website states.

A staunch Republican with progressive thinking, Alvah was heavily involved in politics and often featured in *The Virginian-Pilot* articles for his political views and actions. Admittedly, he did not make friends with those of opposite opinions, especially in a Democratic Norfolk, as one report stated that some locals thought he had too much power. Alvah also led the Fusionists, a combination of black Republicans and white leaders, ostensibly Democrats, who opposed the straight-out Democrats or those who refused to work with blacks. He was always in a political storm. Still, Alvah was respected for his calm demeanor and effortless versatility.

He also directed the three-hundredth anniversary of the Jamestown Exposition on October 5, 1907, bringing together thousands of visitors to celebrate the first permanent English settlement over fifty miles north. Next, he oversaw the planning of Admirals Row at the Norfolk Naval Base, where thirteen state houses would be built on Dillingham Boulevard. Alvah's hard work in all distinct fields resulted in thousands of jobs for the Norfolk community, new neighborhoods, an improved economy, and a better quality of life for the Norfolk residents. This man takes credit for the revival of Norfolk's sleepy, ho-hum, gray city consisting of only blocky warehouses and dirty railroads; he brought color and zest to the state's third-largest city.

Alvah and his wife, Mary Eva "Mamie" Tilley, would bring their unique taste to their recently purchased lot at 524 Fairfax Avenue at The Hague. But he had first bought a house next door from Samuel T. Dickinson, who built it in 1902; this Queen Anne beauty of moderate size was attractive with pressed red bricks, terra-cotta detailing, and low-pitched roofs. The small, flat-roofed porch on the right side looked welcoming, with a central round arch supported by truncated white columns. The three-story octagonal tower and tent roof stood on the left half of the house. Over the porch and two windows on the second floor stood an eye-catching central gable wall dormer. The house exterior has stayed intact today after at least 121 years, like most other homes on Fairfax Avenue. Alvah and Mamie's second home of their marriage had a tiny front yard with garden beds and no grass. Today, the Queen Anne–style house is addressed as 518 Fairfax Avenue; however, in the early 1900s, it was presumably 222, according to the LocalWiki website under "Alvah H. Martin Residence." Several sources state that Alvah and his family lived there for a few years until their new home next door was completed in 1910.

The Queen Anne home was where Alvah and Mamie raised their six surviving children after five others had succumbed to infantile and early-age disease. Those unaffected by disease, three sons and three daughters had been born and raised in their previous home in the Berkeley section of Norfolk, four miles east of The Hague.

The Martin family was quite an interesting clan, with the oldest surviving child, Fay, exceeding the youngest surviving child, Dorothy, by nineteen years. Those two girls together eventually would produce one of the most influential persons in the media world: Frank Batten, who founded The Weather Channel in 1982 and chaired Landmark Communications (now Landmark Media Enterprises), which at the time owned more than fifty community newspapers and special-interest publications in eleven states. Dorothy and her husband, Frank Batten Sr., bore their only son, Frank, in 1927. Unfortunately, when Frank was only one, his father succumbed to pneumonia before the availability of antibiotics.

Having been close to her married older sister, Fay Martin Slover, the newly widowed Dorothy and her one-year-old son Frank moved into the Slovers' home. From then on, young Frank grew up with the two mothers and followed his uncle's footsteps into the newspaper business. Fay's Jewish husband, Colonel Samuel Leroy Slover, owned two Norfolk newspapers, *The Virginian-Pilot* and *The Ledger-Dispatch*, the last of which is now defunct. When the publisher of *The Virginian-Pilot* unexpectedly died, Colonel Slover took an enormous gamble of placing his twenty-seven-year-old nephew, Frank, in charge. That was when the young publisher, with excellent management and teamwork skills, began his fifty-year profound success in the media world.

Personally, Frank Batten and his wife, Jane, were great friends of my parents, Frank and Indie Bilisoly, for several decades. And I once skied with Mr. Batten in Aspen in 1987. He was a humble, friendly man, often letting others get on the ski lift line before him. He had overcome throat cancer that forced the removal of his larynx; however, he managed to speak understandably—and intellectually—while still working his way up to media outlets that were much more complex than newspapers, such as cable TV. Unsurprisingly, as a shrewd businessman, Alvah Martin gave his grandson Frank Batten the genes of humility and ingenuity, although those two had never met. Unfortunately, Alvah died nine years before Frank entered the world.

Because of his premature death at fifty-nine in 1918, Alvah never met several of his grandchildren who were born afterward. My aunt Frances Martin Lindsay was one of them, as her father, Alvah H. Martin, Jr., and her mother, Frances Perkins, bore their only child in 1929. Known as "Little Frances" to family and friends, my aunt married Robert King, a naval aviator, and delivered their first son, Bobby Jr., in Virginia Beach. When Frances was pregnant with her second son, Billy, a tragic event occurred in January 1954: Robert was killed in the Mediterranean while landing on the carrier on a moonless night. Two years later, Frances married Robert's longtime friend Harvey Lee Lindsay, my mother's brother. Frances and Harvey bore three girls together and enjoyed their sixty-two-year marriage until she died in 2018.

Always curious and motivated, Frances delved into genealogy and family history and often talked about her grandfather, Alvah Martin, whom she had never met. She and her first cousins, including Frank Batten, worked together in 2001 to print a coffee-table book, *Martin Family History*, with fascinating black-and-white photos dating back to the patriarch Alvah Martin as a two-year-old toddler in 1860. Now that I have mentioned Fay, Alvah Jr., and Dorothy, the three of Alvah and Mamie's six children who did not die in infancy or early age, I must ensure the rest are not forgotten: Mabel Martin, James Green Martin, and Howard Gresham Martin.

My aunt Frances was so intrigued by her family history, dating back to the birth of her grandfather Alvah Martin, that she organized Thanksgiving gatherings later in her life at the same place that has enamored the public and even the world with its unique beauty. And that has been owned by the Woman's Club of Norfolk for a hundred years. It is, of course, the Martin Mansion.

***

The vacant lots on the left of Alvah Martin's Queen Anne home must have encouraged him to buy them and build two houses in the early 1900s. Little is known about how he processed the lot sales or constructed a three-story Georgian Revival home, but he watched everything from his current home next door. He hired James W. Lee and H. Robert Diehl, the architects from Norfolk, who estimated thirty thousand dollars (close to a million today) for the "Classical Revival" home; however, Alvah ended up paying around fifty thousand dollars upon completion. It took a year to build on a vacant lot, as there was no need for demolition or tree removal.

Below the arched openings beneath the Martin Mansion's front porch, an observant passerby will notice how the house's bricks were laid to make a sturdy foundation. It is unknown if those bricks were set on the concrete footing, which the dirt may have hidden. With its watery setting, Norfolk suffers from soft, loamy soil and requires secure foundations. Being meticulous in every way, Alvah Martin must have ensured his brick foundation would withstand even an earthquake, although Norfolk is not prone to the shaking scenario.

When my husband, Steve, and I built our house in Norfolk in 2014, five miles north of the Martin Mansion, we had to be cautious about building a foundation. Our house would stand on a former creek on one side; therefore, the concrete trenches were built strong with the extension of their standard width and height by another foot. And, of course, we followed the building code of elevating our house seven feet off the ground. Unfortunately, Norfolk is highly prone to flooding—and foundation cracking. The architects of bygone days knew that when they designed homes at The Hague, especially on Mowbray Arch, which flooded now and then. Therefore, you hardly see any home lower than three or four feet from the ground in the Ghent Historic District, like most parts of Norfolk, for that matter.

Once the foundation was completed on 524 Fairfax Avenue, with the house elevated by approximately five feet, a subfloor was built and ready for framing. Observing from his next-door home, Alvah Martin emphasized symmetry in the first floor's design and watched the wooden studs erect like perfectly aligned domino blocks. A copy of the overview architectural plan by Lee and Diehl still exists in the office of the Woman's Club of Norfolk; however, it does not show the wraparound porch or the auditorium added several years after construction. Other than the eighteen-by-twenty-foot kitchen sticking out in the back, the future house looked like a thick-lined square from a bird's eye view.

The first floor's layout looks simple and proportional, featuring four main rooms measuring almost the same size. The foyer divides the first floor, separating the left and right parlors, both of which look identical, each with a fireplace. Then, the foyer stops at the staircase and a small hall leading to the butler's pantry. The library on the house's upper left side has a slight curve on its outer wall, as does the dining room on the upper right side.

Because of its symmetrical pattern, the first-floor plan is effortless to read. It is like peeking into a well-organized jewelry box, with four sections of the same size and one elongated section in the center. No one would ever get lost walking around in Alvah's new mansion. Better yet, the entire first floor is open for anyone entering the foyer from outside; every room lacks a wall or two. The east and west parlors each have only two walls. Alvah knew that a flawed architectural plan for a home would position a long flight of stairs or a blank wall greeting you at the front door. Instead, Alvah created an open, inviting foyer with a nearly 360-degree view of the entire floor. His future home would have a wow factor upon one's first step into the foyer—as it still does today. I have seen many gaping mouths whenever we serve an annual lasagna lunch for burly guys from the Norfolk Fire Department.

Then the second and third floors came up, the former

larger with more rooms. The open stairway occupied a fourth of the space on both floors, with suites leading to two rooms on each side. Three bedrooms, one of which was a primary bedroom, were placed on the second floor, while the fourth was set far to the back of the house via the hall from the suite. Alvah's office was on the second floor as well, its two walls adorned with attractive beveled glass bookcases from bottom to top. Next to the office, the primary bedroom enjoyed a water view of The Hague on the right and a small porch directly over the front door. That could have belonged to Alvah and Mamie.

The third floor is much smaller, with two bedrooms, a spare room, a closet, and an elongated attic. It is believed the youngest child, Dorothy, her nanny, and the servants lived on the third floor. Last, there is one convenient thing that made everyone happy: A dumbwaiter leading up and down to the butler's pantry, thereby avoiding having to climb the stairs.

It is not only the first-floor layout that has generated profound admiration for decades but also the mansion's unique handmade woodwork: wall paneling, ceilings, staircase, fireplaces, mantels, cabinets, bookcases, columns, and rails. Still intact and sturdy today, they are mainly of the same type of wood, oak, and of the same color, dark brown. That shows the taste of Alvah Martin as an outdoorsman; his wife, Mamie, must not have minded the masculine and stark look of the Tudor-style interior in their new home.

Most rooms have oak wainscoting, where vertical wood panels cover the lower six- or seven-foot portion of the walls.

That technique was common in England's country estates and manor houses during Alvah’s time. It would not be surprising if he discovered the paneling idea during one of his trips abroad. That oak wainscoting at the Martin Mansion continues alongside the stairway to both the second and third floors, aligning with the angle of the stairs and rippling around the mansion like an accordion music sheet.

On the first floor, six interior wood columns on pedestals define the entrance to each of the four rooms. All those columns were made in fluted Greek Ionic style, with their square tops curved on four corners. Each of the twelve-foot-wide entryways, edged and lined with oak trimmings, has two round columns abreast. The main entryway leads to the west parlor, the second entryway to the east parlor, and the third to the dining room. The fourth entryway leads to the library from the west parlor, sans the columns.

The columns are not the only impressive element of each entryway; an unusual design of moldings and trimmings tops each entrance. First, decorative crown molding with teeth and feet looms over the flat board with thin, scalloped, ribbon-like carvings and then ends with the trimming. All those wooden entryways, accentuated with fluted columns, give a taste of Roman architecture.

For an unknown reason, the West Wing Parlor (as it is called these days) is the only room on the first floor without a coffered ceiling with dark oak trimming (other than the kitchen in the back). Maybe Alvah and Mamie agreed to have one feminine room without bold woodwork. The West Wing Parlor does not even have wall paneling. And it may be because that parlor had more sunshine coming through the windows from the west, so why mess up the room's tranquility with dark wall paneling and trimmings on its ceiling? The East Wing Parlor has oak trimmings in a crisscross pattern on its ceiling, so it was destined to be a masculine room. Despite its smaller size, the foyer has more crisscross trimmings on its ceiling, creating twenty-one white sections, whereas the other rooms have fewer trimmings and larger white sections. It is declared that the foyer is the most heavily laden with woodwork, and Alvah may have intended it to have the most appeal and gaping mouths.

Every room in the entire Martin Mansion has dark wood molding along the floor and ceiling lines, giving a sharp contrast between white walls and dark brown wood. It may be helpful that the exterior of the Martin Mansion has tan bricks instead of the black-and-white Tudor style because exposing the same stark design inside and out would have been excessive to one's eyes. Therefore, it has always been a pleasant surprise to enter the quaint-looking Georgian Revival mansion, expecting to see dainty lace rooms and flowered wallpapers, and instead encountering such a beautiful Tudor-style atmosphere with all the handmade woodwork. Many visitors have expressed astonishment once they step into the foyer. I have seen a good number of wide eyes, dropped arms, and open mouths.

Alvah Martin added something rarely seen in other homes, considered the most captivating characteristic of the Martin Mansion. With a passion for nature and hunting, Alvah hired an unknown artist to create a mural above the oak paneling around the foyer, the front door, and the wooden archway before the staircase. As the mural remains today, the country and mountainside scenes envelop the foyer like Michelangelo's Sistine Chapel ceiling. Slightly worn with a few chips and wrinkles here and there, the mural begins at the small top corners of the arched front door and the first corners of parlor entryways, featuring tall conifer trees, lakes, and mountains in the distance under the whitish-blue sky with faint clouds. Those two corners are not the same since one has a log cabin, but they measure the same in width and length.

Then the left-sided mural, viewed from the front door, continues after the West Wing entryway into a much larger scene with more features in sequence: A bigger house made of wood and stones, a white-aproned woman sweeping the house pathway, an arched stone bridge over the lake, mountains in the distance, wooden rail fences snaking through the country land, a resting sailboat, a white-clothed farmer, and finally a massive deciduous tree with a snarled trunk. A part of that tree continues around the corner of the foyer toward the archway before the staircase. Then, behind the archway, the sky-topped mural morphs into a different landscape but still with mountains looming over the lake. The mural ends toward the butler's pantry under the slanting ceiling. This section has a log cabin in the center surrounded by tall brown and green conifer trees, and a blue-clothed farmer is seen tending to his garden in front of the cabin.

However, that is not all. The right-sided mural, measuring about six feet across, appears from the right corner of the archway to the East Wing Parlor entryway. Like the one in the mural directly across the foyer, another massive deciduous tree is the first feature, with its top left branches spilling over the corner of the archway. When you look at the archway ten feet away from the front door, it will look like a wedding arch with greens draping over its top corners. The interesting part of the right-sided mural shows the same features as mountains looming over the lake but with a cluster of tiny buildings and a steepled church; under that large tree stands a hunter with his long rifle over his shoulder and his dog behind him. Only a part of the hunter's profile under his wide-brimmed hat is shown looking up at the tree. Some people suspect the hunter was Alvah Martin himself. He had a fierce passion for bird hunting, so it could be. And he chose this mural that resembles a vast John Constable painting. If you want to find Alvah, he is depicted above the staircase by the dining room door.

The fireplaces in the Martin Mansion were beautifully built with wood trimmings and solid Italian tiles but kept to a modern size, not massive or extraordinary. The West and East Wing Parlors are almost identical, with rectangle mirrors over the wood mantels. However, there is something unique about the dining-room fireplace, which again shows Alvah's love for hunting: the three hand-carved, three-dimensional wood plaques over the mantle. Two small identical square plaques each feature two birds, assumedly American woodcocks, nestled together amid thick-bladed tall grass. One larger one between the bird plaques shows two large dogs, obviously Irish setters, surrounded by brush, including a cut tree trunk and rail fences. Close together, one dog is lying down at rest while the other stands, both looking in the same direction. It is unknown where Alvah obtained them or if he hired a woodcarver to make them. Or it could be the work of the world's renowned British sculptor and woodcarver Grinling Gibbons, who died in 1721. Highly versatile in his career, Gibbons created statuaries and church monuments in stone and marble, sculpted bronze statues, and carved wooden materials such as thrones. He even decorated Windsor Castle, Kensington Palace, and St. Paul's Cathedral. Alvah's wood plaques look too noteworthy for a local woodcarver or even an American one to master; therefore, it is believed he purchased them in England. Despite their eight-inch size, the dogs appear so unbelievably natural in 3D that you cannot resist the urge to reach over the mantle and pat them.

Alvah must have spent a great deal of time in the library, given its masculine look. Its dark brown oak wainscoting covers more than half of the room's lower half, making it dark and somber – perfect for reading a book or smoking a cigar. The library has a gracious wooden arch above the paneling, and thick trimmings and moldings adorn the entryway to the West Wing Parlor. Instead of the columns, it has two sliding pocket doors made of the same wood, which Alvah could shut tight for privacy or quiet. The three tall windows on the curved part of the room are edged with header caps, casings, and windowsills of dark oak. Like others in the parlors, those door-sized windows consist of two sashes, the upper one with grilles and the lower one without, just plain glass. Because of their curved settings, the lower sashes have slightly curved glass, likely to have been handblown.

Therefore, looking out the window at the Martin Mansion, you will see a somewhat wavy scene outside. If I am not wrong, it is a rarity to see handblown curved windows in other homes these days. And it would be difficult to find a replacement if one of them breaks!

In the library, a simple fireplace perches between two original bookcases with beveled glass doors. Each bookcase stands under a small oval beveled window edged with significant trimming. The size of quite large watermelons, those two windows bring rays of morning sunshine into such a dark room; it is like observing two strange egg-shaped objects in the universe! However, that room was not destined to be a library since the butler's pantry door in the right corner gives the impression it was originally the family dining room next to the kitchen through the solid wall. And a ring button used to call the servants is found on the floor, where the head of the table would have been. It is not known if Alvah changed the location of the dining room and made this room a library.

Today's dining room, located behind the East Wing Parlor, has a swing door to the kitchen and the butler's pantry. There is a ring button on the wall, which could have been used to call children down for dinner. Maybe Alvah and Mamie decided to use this room with the wooden dogs on the mantle for family dining so that the patriarch of the mansion could read or banter with friends in the library, surrounded by such a masculine design of woodwork. Undoubtedly, the library is the darkest room in the mansion, except for the two blindingly bright oval windows.

***

According to a few articles from *The Virginian-Pilot*, the Norfolk newspaper, the Martin family often entertained in their newly built home. Part of that had to do with the size of the Martin family and, of course, Alvah's prominence in the city. Unfortunately, little is known about the family's activities at the new mansion during their inhabitation of only ten years. It is unknown if all six children lived at the estate since the first four were over twenty years old. However, my aunt Frances' book, *Martin Family History,* confirms that the brothers, Alvah Jr. and James, lived together in a bachelor's pad a few blocks away in Stockley Gardens in 1912. The family book also specifies the age of every child of Alvah and Mamie at a particular time, and it turns out the youngest child, Dorothy, was only seven when they moved into the new mansion, and she was the only one growing up there. The fifth child, Howard, was sixteen at the time and likely lived at the estate in the following years until he married in 1918. Mabel, the second child, was twenty-three at the time of the mansion's completion and may have lived there until it was sold in 1920; she married late at age thirty-nine, six years after the mansion was sold. At any rate, the new estate with six or seven bedrooms would have accommodated the entire Martin family on the first night!

Fay, the oldest child, had married in 1909 and may be the only child who never lived at the mansion that was completed in 1910. However, Alvah gave Fay and her husband, Samuel Leroy Slover, a site next door to the estate, so the newlyweds built their own house at 530 Fairfax Avenue. As it still exists today, this simple, blocky Colonial-style house with red bricks and white trimmings was completed in 1912. When Fay and Sam moved in, they could have started a large family to occupy the seven-bedroom place, but they never had children. Then, sixteen years later, a one-year-old child, Frank Batten, would start his developing years in that house with the Slovers and his mother, Dorothy. Besides, the garage was built in the back between Alvah's and the Slovers' for sharing; its tan-brick exterior matched Alvah's mansion. It has been long understood that people of the past, apparently the age of innocence, shared a garage between their homes. So Alvah and his son-in-law Sam must have shared the benchwork or even a manly chat.

Alvah then sold his previous home at 518 Fairfax Avenue, next door to his new home, to his sister Maud and her husband, S. W. Lyons, in 1912. So now, the first block of Fairfax Avenue from Mowbray Arch had three related families living next door to each other, with Alvah's most prominent house in between.

The Virginian-Pilot occasionally published a brief personal update on the Martin family due to Alvah's rank in the city of Norfolk, and it was always in one sentence. For example, one article quoted: "Mr. Alvah H. Martin and family have closed their home on Fairfax Ave and gone to their cottage at Willoughby Beach for the summer." And another read: "Mr. and Mrs. Alvah H. Martin and daughter Dorothy returned to their residence on 524 Fairfax Avenue from a trip abroad." Alvah and his family appeared to stay at their beach cottage in Willoughby Spit on Chesapeake Bay every summer, only about ten miles up north from Fairfax Avenue. And since Dorothy was still in her prepubescent or pubescent years, she must have accompanied her parents on trips overseas and in the country.

***

One may be surprised that Alvah had put so much effort into decorating the mansion's interior with expensive woodwork and a mural and unintentionally left it after only eight years. The estate was destined to be his dream home, at least a permanent one, until he passed away at his beloved estate from a series of health issues at age fifty-nine on July 6, 1918. His health had been declining for several months; therefore, his death was not unexpected in the end. His death certificate, in indecipherable handwriting, stated he died from "(Unknown word), Cirrhosis, Blood vessels, kidneys, Liver TC." With his lifelong outdoor activities, it would be hard to believe that the tall and slender Alvah with a chiseled face succumbed to health issues, but medicine in the first quarter of the twentieth century was not well-advanced.

The Virginian-Pilot posted an article on July 9: "The funeral of Alvah Howard Martin, whose death occurred last Saturday morning, took place yesterday at his residence on Fairfax Avenue at 3 o'clock with an unusually large attendance, as numerous business organizations of Portsmouth [For non-locals, I want to clarify that this city is across the Elizabeth River from Norfolk] as well as Norfolk, the courts, municipal bodies, and county supervisors, were represented. The services were conducted by Rev. S.T. Senter, D.D. of Epworth Methodist Church. …There was a magnificent floral display consisting of offerings from Norfolk, Portsmouth, Norfolk County, and other sections. The casket was covered with a beautiful pall of white roses and smilax. …"

Imagine Alvah's casket in the center of his precious wood-adorned foyer surrounded by the mural that honored his alfresco character with its mountains, lakes, trees, cabins, and even a hunting rifle—before he was carried to and buried at Forest Lawn Cemetery not too far from his beach cottage at Willoughby Beach. If one were looking at the mural, Alvah would be envisioned in his final resting place between the emerald green mountains in western Virginia and the shimmering waters of Chesapeake Bay, notably during the fall hunting season.

His biography in *Norfolk County, Virginia: Genealogy and History* reads: "A gentleman of wide and varied interests, Mr. Martin's easy versatility makes him equally in his proper element in a gathering of sportsmen, financiers, politicians, or businessmen, and whatever the occasion he is fitted and prepared to speak with authority or to act with capability. It is the catholicity of his tastes that has gained him such a wide acquaintance and such a vast number of friends who recognize the worth and merit of the man. However, they may be associated with him."

***

Another unexpected tragic event occurred in the Martin family thirteen months later: Alvah's wife, Mary Eva "Mamie" Tilley Martin, died of health issues related to high blood pressure, and the children were left with the mansion, occupying only the youngest child, Dorothy. Devastated by her parents' deaths a year apart, the sixteen-year-old Dorothy was taken in by her sister Fay and her husband, Sam Slover, next door. Dorothy would forever be appreciative of Fay and Sam, considering them her guardians, and remain with them at 530 Fairfax Avenue for the rest of her life, except for one or two years in which she married Frank Batten, Sr., moved into their own place, bore a son, faced the detrimental loss of her new husband, and indefinitely moved back with the Slovers with her one-year-old son Frank.

Next door, the Martin Mansion was suddenly empty or had only one inhabitant, the yet-to-be-married Mabel Martin. The three Martin sons, James, Alvah, Jr., and Howard, had their own places. Mabel may have continued to live at the estate after college, or maybe she moved away independently.

Regardless of whether or not one person lived there at the time of the tragic events, the Georgian Revival home at 524 Fairfax Avenue was now devoid of livelihood. The library sat unused without the patriarch reading books or smoking cigars; the West Wing Parlor was idle without the matriarch entertaining her friends with tea; the East Wing Parlor was listless without the children playing games in front of a roaring fireplace; the dining room sat hushed without the large family clinking glasses and sharing current events.

Within a year, in 1920, the Martin Mansion was sold.

***

The Virginia Club, a gentlemen's organization in Norfolk incorporated in 1873, bought the Martin Mansion for seventy thousand dollars from the executors and three sons of deceased

Alvah H. Martin. That seemed more than what Alvah had paid for upon the completion of the mansion; however, he had added extensive woodwork, a mural, chandeliers, bookcases, and other attributes for the décor. Having moved several times, the Virginia Club had residence outside downtown Norfolk for the first time. Unfortunately, their original building, along with others, including the adjacent Atlantic Hotel downtown, was destroyed by an inferno in 1902. Afterward, the Virginia Club stayed at their temporary quarters on Granby and Freemason Streets until a new building on West Freemason Street was ready for occupancy. Then, the new building became a bit expensive during World War I, and the Virginia Club had to reduce expenses by moving away from downtown. Thus, the club decided to purchase a mansion in a cheaper section and moved to 524 Fairfax Avenue in the fall of 1920 and began its activities, primarily parties and dances.

To celebrate the formal opening of their new residence, the Virginia Club threw a reception and dance on November 27, 1920. After a year of stagnation, the Martin Mansion was revitalized with three hundred boisterous guests and a string orchestra. Palms, ferns, and cut flowers adorned the first floor. This reception would be one of the countless parties the gentlemen threw there over the next five years, some quite rowdy and others subdued. The Martin Mansion welcomed gentlemen of high rank from all over the state: The University of Virginia Alumni Association often had their meetings there; the Virginia Bar Association brought their prominent local and state lawyers in for receptions; and Mr. William Cameron, the ex-governor of Virginia, stayed there as a longtime guest.

The Virginia Club was kind enough to hold women's activities as well at its residence, so the women, devoted to the card game, were delighted to host bridge tournaments and luncheons in the West Wing Parlor or the East. It is believed the club also hosted debutante parties, with college-age girls arriving in gowns and gloves, mingling with their parents and guests. The Virginia Club knew females helped enlighten the atmosphere with stirring compliments on the beauty of their clubhouse. It had to be a comprehensible showplace for the Virginia Club, which otherwise would have rented a hunting lodge or a church reception hall.

But the Martin Mansion was not without incident. According to *The Virginian-Pilot*, an attempted robbery occurred in the mansion during the Virginia Club ownership. On April 19, 1923, E.P. Davis, the club bookkeeper, was alone there, and at around 10 p.m., he was accosted by "a young white bandit, his face concealed behind a blue handkerchief … and dressed in a dark suit …wore a cap." The bandit held up his .45 caliber revolver to the bookkeeper's face and threatened to shoot unless he passed over the cash. He then showed a slip of brown paper written in pencil: "Money or your life." The bookkeeper was calm as ever and said to the bandit, "Come along and help yourself," preparing to show him the way. Instead, the bandit demanded his paper slip be reread, and the bookkeeper invited him again to follow him. Still, the bandit must have been intimidated by the extensive size of the Martin Mansion—or the dark oak paneling all around. So, he quietly slipped out "without getting a dime."

As their time at the Martin Mansion went on, the

gentlemen of the Virginia Club continued throwing boisterous parties that fitted the contemporary era of the Roaring Twenties as both men and women hammered on the floor with their foxtrot dances. And the parties became so congested that the Virginia Club hired a contractor to add an auditorium on the right side of the mansion for fifteen thousand dollars. That auditorium would measure thirty by forty feet and consist of regular double-sashed windows all the way around except the left side wall, where people gained access from the dining room and kitchen. That wall was the site of the sun porch that was demolished to make room for the auditorium. The stage for the orchestras or speakers would be situated in the back of the auditorium. Then, the Virginia Club would throw even larger parties, squeezing in half a thousand guests. The new addition would vibrate like a giant phonograph, possibly arousing complaints from residents on the entire block of Fairfax Avenue.

But … when the auditorium was partially completed, the Virginia Club went bankrupt and had to move out at lightning speed, leaving the mansion back in the hands of the nonplussed Martin heirs. This men's club did not become homeless, specifically, as it merged with the Norfolk Boat Club to make its facilities more attractive and financially efficient. Lastly, the Virginia Club settled at the Merritt T. Cooke residence at the foot of Bute and Freemason Streets. It was described as "admirably suited to its purposes," with lofty ceilings, vast halls, and graceful staircases combining to make a beautiful structure, just like the previous residence on Fairfax Avenue. The Virginia Club, to its relief, was back in its true home: Downtown Norfolk. Its leader,

N. H. Bundy, revived and reorganized the once-bankrupt organization with the help of former members. And the Virginia Club is existent today, still downtown. A description on its website recounts the whirlwind history and countless relocations: "Throughout the Club's existence, there runs a strong and steady pattern of conviviality and good fellowship, in itself an enviable attainment for any club and one that deserves meritorious comment and prideful acclaim. While we may not go back to the 'old table/young table' setting, we are confident that those who follow will continue to be bound by the objectives and traditions that have carried the Virginia Club so admirably since 1873."

***

Now, the Martin Mansion sat empty again, but only for a short time. An organization celebrating its twentieth anniversary in 1925 had been eyeing this mansion for its permanent residence. It was the Woman's Club of Norfolk.

Chapter Two

The Woman's Clubs might not be here today if it were not for Charles Dickens. Known for his numerous influential novels, including *Oliver Twist* and *A Christmas Carol*, this nineteenth-century British author had spurred the interest of a female newspaper journalist, Jane Cunningham Croly, enough to lure her into his speaking engagement at Delmonico's in New York City. In 1868, the year the Fourteenth Amendment was ratified to the U.S. Constitution, Jane walked to this popular upscale steakhouse on Beaver Street, expecting to buy a ticket to listen to the lecture of Charles Dickens, whom she greatly admired, only to be turned away because she was a woman. The fiery Jane Cunningham Croly would have none of it.

Born in England in 1829 and transplanted to America as a teenager, Jane was a blue-eyed, brown-haired, petite woman with an elegant manner—and fiercely independent. During her childhood, she used her pastor father's library to educate herself with books, edited the school's newspaper as a student, looked after her Congregationalist minister brother's home in Worcester, Massachusetts, and helped with his popular church newsletter. After being raised in Upstate New York during the second half of her twenty-five years, Jane moved to Manhattan in 1855 to seek journalism work. She endured several unsuccessful attempts and finally found a position at *Noah's Sunday Times* as a women's columnist. At that time, female journalists were forbidden to write about art, literature, music, science, or theater. Instead, Jane was required to write about gossip. She was paid three dollars a week to write for "Gossip with and for the Ladies," which would later become "Parlor and Sidewalk Gossip" under the pen name Jennie June. It is unknown how intelligent Jane felt about writing about trivial things such as marital affairs instead of classic novels for which she had a fervent passion. Hence, Charles Dickens lured her into Delmonico's to apply for a ticket to his dinner lecture.

Delmonico's had long been known to cater to a male-dominated society and hold meetings for all-men clubs, especially the New York Press Club. Women were forbidden to attend by themselves but would have to accompany their male counterparts if they wanted to dine in such a fancy restaurant. Any unescorted woman deliberately entering Delmonico's would be scorned as a sex worker. Nevertheless, the members of the all-men New York Press Club were frequent patrons of this nation's first white tablecloth restaurant, where they discussed literature and journalism.

Invited by the Press Club to speak at Delmonico's, Charles Dickens agreed on the date, April 18, 1868, squeezing it into his hectic schedule while traveling in America to give lectures. The local press members were invited with the stern instruction not to report on the Dickens event until after it occurred. But the word got out, and people rushed in to apply for tickets priced at fifteen dollars each. Jane Croly was one of them, along with other female professional writers and editors in NYC—only to be rejected by the Press Club.

Outraged, Jane turned to Horace Greeley, the prominent editor of the *New-York Tribune*, for support, as she had written articles for that newspaper. Greeley conferred with the Press Club, of which he was a member. The club finally caved in three days before the Dickens dinner and announced the women would be allowed on one condition: "They must sit behind a curtain, unseen by the gentlemen in the audience and unseen, as well, by the guest of honor, Mr. Dickens," author Catherine Gourley wrote in *Society's Sisters*.

But Jane was not having it. Her unsurprised brother described her as a "volcanic force" in action. She had a better idea and announced to her allies in journalism: "We will form a club of our own. We will give a banquet to ourselves, make all the speeches ourselves, and not invite a single man." By 1868, Jane was no longer writing gossip and had accomplished many milestones only an unshakable working mother of three with an incoming baby could manage. She had already published two books, *Talks on Woman's Topics* and *Jennie June's American Cookery Book*. She organized meetings for women to learn and discuss issues surrounding their societal roles. Most of all, Jane was now a respected and successful author, editor, and journalist; better yet, she was the first woman to syndicate her column in cities across the country.

The all-male New York Press Club should have seen it coming. Not only Jane's impressive feat but also a brand-new all-woman's club explicitly unheard of in New York City or anywhere else.

***

Jane's organization was born two days after the Dickens dinner;

she named it Sorosis (the Latin prefix "soro" means "sister"). And that name has another meaning: A multiple fleshy fruit, such as pineapple or mulberry, formed from flowers clustered together on a fleshy stem. Those two different definitions of Sorosis relate to each other, as the sisters resemble flowers connected to the foundation of their club; that is, a stem! And alas, the name Sorosis rhymes with liver disease. But Jane did not mind. Associated with like-minded journalists, authors, and editors of the same sex in Manhattan, she invited the children's author Josephine Pollard and the columnist Fanny Fern to join Sorosis. Within a few hours, Sorosis expanded to include more women: journalist Kate Field, *New York Ledger* writer Anne Botta, magazine editor Ellen Louise Demorest, and sister poets Alice and Phoebe Cary. All those new members certainly would know how to put articulation on their lips and in their hands to launch Sorosis. But how would they make their new club known to the male-dominated New York City?

Not surprisingly, Jane had an idea: To persuade Delmonico's to allow Sorosis to have an all-women luncheon in its white tablecloth dining area, in the same spot where the New York Press Club had dined for years without a single woman. So, with their progressive thinking, the Delmonico brothers agreed to host their restaurant's first all-women "power lunch" in its private dining room on April 20, 1868, two days after the Dickens event.

At that first Sorosis gathering, Jane declared that every meeting would not be a tea party; Sorosis was to be all straight-down business on gaining "collective elevation and advancement" of its female members. Once these fourteen ladies sat at a large table, they were destined to break down gender barriers in New York City and across America. They were not created to stay home and do chores every minute of their lives. Instead, they were to become less inhibited in family life, education, employment, religion, business, and government. They would no longer be holding only spatulas; they would also hold pens. And they would finally use their tongues for advocacy, not only for taste cooking. The women, enjoying their group meal without male escorts for the first time at Delmonico's, would change American society's perspective of their gender. As member Margaret M. Merrill put it, Sorosis "is of women, by women, and for women."

The Delmonico brothers had made a brilliant decision that would significantly increase their revenues in the upcoming years. The first Sorosis luncheon with Jane Croly and a dozen professional upper-class and middle-class women was so successful that the next luncheon added more club members. One black-and-white photo, discovered on the Internet, is believed to depict one of the power lunches in the dining room at Delmonico's, where the well-dressed and hatted club members sat close together at each round table covered with a white tablecloth. The number of club members in that photo appeared to be over a hundred. It is impossible to count all the women in that room; there were so many that anyone wanting to leave could not push her chair back away from the table. The Delmonico brothers must have known they owed Jane Croly an enormous favor for increasing their business a hundredfold. The first sentence of a 2016 article on the Timeline website by writer and history junkie

Stephanie Buck reads: "Deny her a seat. She will fill hundreds."

For Jane Croly, Sorosis's main goal was to promote basic housekeeping to "municipal housekeeping," which involved legislative and social reform for issues including education, regulation of foodstuffs and medicines, sanitation, and health. A well-educated woman could practice that type of housekeeping, also known as social or civic housekeeping; she could bring awareness of municipal problems to the public. Since there was no running water, electricity, or central heating in the nineteenth century, cleaning was much more arduous than cooking. If not done correctly, disease and contamination could envelop the home and the public. For instance, women had long known that coal smoke trapped in homes could cause health issues for the inhabitants, especially babies; therefore, those housekeepers spent hours scrubbing soot from kitchen gadgets and walls. There was so much the public did not know about the danger of contaminated foods, indoor emissions of coal smoke chemicals, unfiltered water, and lack of medicine. Sorosis would fix all that by having its members advocate for better home conditions—and cleaner cities. These women would also fight for water sanitation.

Jane and her members also hoped the club would inspire confidence in women and bring "womanly self-respect and self-knowledge." And educate women on their rights, community involvement, citizenship, and civic duties. But, more critically, it inspired women to become sophisticated and no longer subservient. This was the club where women should feel free to share deeper and broader ideas, voice opinions, and even oppose ideas with explanations, right here at Delmonico's, which had become the go-to spot for the Sorosis meetings. If a woman wanted to join Sorosis, she had to be recommended by another club member. Then, she would have to pass inspection, take a loyalty oath, and pay an initiation fee of five dollars ($104 today).

Sorosis expanded to eighty-three members within a year, many of whom were accomplished writers, artists, historians, scientists, teachers, and philanthropists. And they were primarily middle-aged, white, and middle or upper-middle class. Sorosis was incorporated in January 1869, and Alice Cary, the poet, became the first president. The membership meetings occurred on the first and third Mondays of each month at, of course, Delmonico's.

The New York Press Club and its male counterparts were flummoxed by the success of Sorosis but took it with amusement. These men saw the acute coordination and professionalism of this new all-woman's club, so they asked if *they* could join. But a clear, sharp response from Sorosis ensued:

"We willingly admit, of course, that the accident of your sex is on your part a misfortune and not a fault, nor do we wish to arrogate anything to ourselves because we had the good fortune to be born women. ... Sorosis is too young for the society of gentlemen and must be allowed time to grow. By and by, when it has reached a proper age, say twenty-one, it may ally itself with the Press Club or some other male organization of good character and standing. But for years to come, its reply to all male suitors must be, 'Principles, not men.'"

For harmony, the New York Press Club invited Sorosis

members to a fancy breakfast at their expense. The men spoke and sang to the women but had requested that the women stay quiet without ever uttering a single word and sit still throughout the entire meal. That was not taken kindly by the guests. So, the Sorosis Club invited the New York Press Club members to their tea, where the women spoke and sang to the men but also imposed the same stay-quiet and sit-still rule on their guests. And footed the entire bill for the tea. That settled it. From then on, men and women intermingled socially at Delmonico's and paid their way. Later, at an unknown date, the New York Press Club accepted women and still exists today as a powerful, diverse organization after falling apart during the Great Depression and then revitalizing after World War II.

Sorosis and the New York Press Club's intermingling scene at Delmonico's reflected the progress of the women's rights movement that began in 1848 when the nation's first women's rights convention occurred in Seneca Falls, New York. Over three hundred attendees fought for women's social, civil, and religious rights. On July 19, 1848, Elizabeth Cady Stanton, one of the organizers of the Seneca Falls Convention, gave a speech on its goal and purpose:

"We are assembled to protest against a form of government, existing without the consent of the governed—to declare our right to be free as man is free, to be represented in the government which we are taxed to support, to have such disgraceful laws as give man the power to chastise and imprison his wife, to take the wages which she earns, the property which she inherits, and, in case of separation, the children of her love."

This July convention also launched the women's suffrage movement (the right to vote) and slavery abolitionism. Elizabeth Cady Stanton and the other organizers put forth the Declaration of Sentiments asserting women's equality in politics, family, education, jobs, religion, and morals. The History website on "Seneca Falls Convention" states: "The declaration began with 19 'abuses and usurpations' destined to destroy a woman's 'confidence in her own powers, to lessen her self-respect, and to make her willing to lead a dependent and abject life.'"

Then, the declaration listed resolutions that called for women to be treated as men and their equal rights within the church and access to jobs. Only one resolution did not pass at the convention and would take seventy-two more years to do so: The right to vote. Therefore, the women's suffrage movement would be one of the main topics among women in New York City and across the country.

But…Sorosis preferred avoiding politics since this organization focused on encouraging "womanly self-respect and self-knowledge" for its members. The report on The Rutherford B. Hayes Presidential Library and Museums website states, "While no member or guests of Sorosis Clubs are permitted to discuss religion or politics directly, the idea of Sorosis was monumental in its purpose. It allowed women to socialize, serve the community, and create club politics. It was popular for the local Sorosis division to discuss topics such as poetry, travel, war efforts, and the welfare of citizens." It made sense because, with the help of Sorosis, the women were achieving mental, emotional, cognitive, psychological, and moral strength. They were learning to think for themselves, choose their political views, and even take part in activism. Jane Croly added the explanation of Sorosis in her 1898 book, *The History of the Woman's Club Movement in America*: "The outlook upon the world, the means of education, the opportunities for advancement, had all been denied her." Education was vital to politics and religion, and Sorosis was wise to focus on teaching the long-inhibited women to speak for themselves first before diving into those more complex topics.

***

While Sorosis prospered in New York City, another woman's club had formed over 225 miles away: The New England Woman's Club (NEWC). Its first public meeting took place in the back of Boston's Tremont Hall forty days after Sorosis's first meeting at Delmonico's. The founder of NEWC, Julia Ward Howe, introduced the purposes of the club with the help of Caroline M. Severance, the first president, and another member, Harriet Hanson Robinson, who was the founder of the National Woman Suffrage Association of Massachusetts. The NEWC aimed to provide a meeting place for women to gain knowledge and inspiration for their roles at home and outside, work together on social causes, listen to guest speakers, and even take part in debates. The NEWC's main goal was to help its members learn about and discuss sensitive topics such as slavery, politics, and education for children. But most of all, encourage them to become proactive.

The main difference between the two landmark woman's clubs, Sorosis and the New England Woman's Club, was the intensity of politics discussed in their beginning phases. The NEWC was more vocal about suffrage and slavery abolition, as Harriet Hanson Robinson advocated for women's right to vote while Julia Ward Howe backed the freedom of enslaved people. Jane Croly of Sorosis, on the other hand, pushed for the education and empowerment of women so they could learn and think for themselves when facing public issues and politics.

So, it was all groundwork at Delmonico's and all take-charge at Tremont Hall. However, the strong similarities between Sorosis and NEWC included strengthening the mentality of women, relinquishing inhibitions of being a woman, and encouraging women into societal roles. More woman's clubs across America would follow suit in the following decades.

***

Now, it was the twenty-first anniversary of Sorosis. In 1889, President Grover Cleveland signed a bill admitting Washington, Montana, North Dakota, and South Dakota to statehood. By that time, over ninety woman's clubs had formed since the founding of Sorosis and the New England Woman's Club. The credit goes to the connection between New York City and Boston: Jane Croly and Julia Ward Howe worked together as the representatives of their clubs and traveled the country to promote the value of a woman's club in general. Those two resilient, middle-aged ladies, ten years apart in age, endured long train and horseback rides to unfamiliar places in America to inspire thousands of women to fight for better education, social reform, and voluntary community service.

The older Howe must have been better equipped to travel in rough conditions than Croly because she had served in the Civil War for the U.S. Sanitary Commission, promoting clean and hygienic conditions for soldiers and hospitals. In 1862, *The Atlantic Monthly* published Howe's famous poem, "The Battle Hymn of the Republic," which is considered the Union's Civil War anthem. She was also a fierce opponent of slavery. The photo of the sitting Howe before her death at ninety-one shows years of courage and perseverance, as her obviously blue eyes pierced through the camera; her lips stayed closed in a pensive way, and her right hand held the walking cane firmly.

Emily Faithfull, the British women's rights activist, was impressed with the woman's clubs in America during her visit in 1884, especially Sorosis. She wrote: "Sorosis ... was organized ... to promote 'mental activity and pleasant social intercourse,' and despite a severe fire of hostile criticism and misrepresentation, it has evinced a sturdy vitality and demonstrated its right to exist by a large amount of beneficent work. ... These ladies pledged themselves to work for the release of women from the disabilities which debar them from due participation in the rewards of industrial and professional labor ... I believe it has been the stepping-stone to useful public careers and the source of inspiration to many ladies."

To celebrate Sorosis's twenty-first anniversary, Jane Croly and Charlotte Emerson Brown, the president of the Woman's Club of Orange (New Jersey), invited ninety-seven woman's clubs throughout the country to attend a conference in New York City. Not all the clubs could make it, but sixty-three of them and their delegates could. The primary purpose of the convention was to initiate an umbrella organization for the woman's clubs. On April 24, 1890, those sixty-three clubs officially formed the General Federation of Women's Clubs (GFWC), with Charlotte Brown as the first president. They ratified the GFWC's constitution and bylaws to prompt the U.S. Congress to charter this international organization in 1901. Jane Croly explained that the unity of women's clubs would enhance community service by volunteers worldwide. "We look for unity, but unity in diversity" became the GFWC motto, first spoken by Ella Dietz Clymer at the 1889 gathering, at which point she was president of Sorosis.

Once the GFWC was formed, the woman's clubs' membership skyrocketed nationwide. First, I would like to explain the reason for using lowercase and singular terms for the general woman's clubs. It is noticeable that the General Federation of Women's Clubs has a plural for the gender as well as capitalization for the entire name (except for "of"). But then, when woman's clubs are mentioned in general without formal names, they should be in lowercase as well as in singular terms. In contrast, if there is an official woman's club with its own name mentioned in this book, then it should be capitalized. The Woman's Club of Norfolk is an example. However, I have noticed from extensive research on woman's clubs across the country that *some* clubs use the plural term, so it does depend on each club.

Soon after the establishment of the GFWC, some woman's clubs joined this umbrella organization directly, but then state federations became effective in the early 1890s, further increasing membership. By 1906, approximately five thousand clubs belonged to the GFWC and embraced its international agenda. Some pre-GFWC woman's clubs focused on community work, while others were religious in the foundation. And some long-existing and new clubs had shifted to community improvement. Not all these woman's clubs were the same, even if they belonged to GFWC, but they shared the GFWC's goals: The establishment of an eight-hour workday, ending child labor, and reforming civil service, public health, and conservation. One of the organization's early successes was a massive letter-writing campaign that contributed to the passing of the Pure Food and Drug Act.

In the early 1900s, the GFWC was the largest women's organization in the country – *only before* suffrage became the hottest topic that this umbrella organization attempted to avoid. The GFWC had long desired to keep politics and religion out but paid a price, just temporarily. It then lagged in membership in the following years behind the National American Woman Suffrage Association. Upon realizing that every woman's right to vote was astronomical, the GFWC finally agreed to support the suffrage movement. As a result, its national membership grew to around 1,700,000 at its peak in 1914.

Even before the end of slavery, there were numerous black woman's clubs across America, especially in Philadelphia. Black women were keen on looking after their community's welfare and organizing self-help efforts. They often worked with churches to ensure the communities were cared for. And they even raised money to launch an anti-slavery newspaper, *The North Star*. So, indeed, black woman's clubs existed long before Sorosis and expanded northward between 1880 and 1920 due to the Great Migration, a movement of black people from the rural South to urban areas in Northern, Midwestern, and Western states. This flight began in the 1910s and ended in the 1970s, resulting in approximately six million black people settling in the North.

The newly formed GFWC faced a dilemma over whether to include black woman's clubs in the Federation or even support the membership of black women in affiliated clubs. The Women's Era Club of Boston, headed by African-American activist Josephine St. Pierre Ruffin, was given admission by the GFWC executive committee in 1900. But southern women objected and forced the cancellation. In addition, African-American club woman Fannie Barrier Williams had been admitted to the Chicago Woman's Club and then to the GFWC in 1894 but was removed because of objection by southern women. However, all that did not deter black women from continuing to organize themselves and work through the National Association of Colored Women (NACW) rather than the GFWC.

***

Jane Croly remained as busy as ever and stayed steadily involved in the GFWC for many years after launching Sorosis. She often traveled as "The Mother of Women's Clubs" in the press, leaving her husband at home to look after their family. Jane had made a gracious comeback after being woefully rejected by the all-male New York Press Club at Delmonico's and missing her lifelong dream of ever meeting the world-renowned Charles Dickens: She founded the New York Woman's Press Club in 1889. Sure enough, forty women joined on day one, followed by over sixty more by 1893. Jane was right in proving that women were dead serious about literature and journalism, and these women could use assistance from other members in preparing their articles for the press. Social chats were allowed, bringing women together and developing friendships. Headquartered on East 23rd Street in Manhattan, the New York Woman's Press Club continued until it disbanded in 1980. But there is still the New York Press Club today admitting women, no longer rejecting them.

Chapter Three

Woman's clubs were forming across America, as well as in other countries, at the turn of the twentieth century. However, the coastal city, undergoing extensive revitalization with new upscale homes at The Hague, did not have a woman's club. Norfolk had long desired to establish one after being impressed by the Woman's Club Richmond, two hours away. (Yes, that club is capitalized and is now called The Woman's Club at The Bolling Haxall House). Nestled on the James River in the center of the state, the capital of Virginia saw a woman's club established in 1894 by fourteen women in the parlor of Jane Crawford Looney Lewis' downtown home on West Franklin Street. The club's website states, "These women had established a literary and cultural association designed for 'the delightful friction of well-trained minds.'" Norfolk wanted the same for its female inhabitants; fortunately, one ambitious woman made it all possible in 1905 - in a hotel room.

Virginia Gatewood, the daughter of an Episcopal clergyman, was a born leader and organizer. In November 1905, she summoned a group of women to a room at the Atlantic Hotel in downtown Norfolk and announced her proposal for a woman's club for Norfolk. Her allies immediately accepted it and elected Gatewood as the first president. Next, they sent out five hundred invitations to Norfolkians, and two hundred responded with a resounding yes. Thus, the Woman's Club of Norfolk was formed—but not on Fairfax Avenue. It would be twenty years before the WCN permanently settled at the Martin Mansion.

This hotel event organized by Gatewood was so enthralling that *The Virginian-Pilot* published an article on November 12, 1905:

"The Woman's Club of Norfolk is an assured success, for on Thursday afternoon, when two hundred women assembled in the Atlantic Hotel by invitation from Miss Virginia Gatewood, it was plainly seen that the call had appealed to them, and they wanted to help establish such a club at once. Much enthusiasm was displayed, and the temporary organization was effected."

Under Gatewood's leadership, the women decided their new club would first comprise three departments: literary, music, and art. They would then work on a broader basis after the club was well-established. This is the creative process that goes into establishing a club of any kind: Start slowly and build slowly. At that first meeting at the Atlantic Hotel, the woman drew up a plan for the constitution and bylaws, following the instructions of the GFWC. They scheduled the next meeting with three purposes: to adopt the constitution, consider bylaws, and possibly elect department officers.

***

A month after its launch, the Woman's Club of Norfolk was now a fully established organization with a home at the Thom residence on Freemason Street, which they were renting at a reasonable rate. Not much is known about the rental agreement, but at least this new club had a place to work in. The woman added several new departments to the club, increasing the number to six: literary, music, art, social, civic, and current events. A large committee would control each department with its own chairwoman. There would be a separate meeting for each department committee where the members would discuss and carry out the plans. Lastly, each committee would show its proposal to the entire organization for approval. Barely a few weeks old, the Woman's Club of Norfolk (WCN) was well-tuned, with its two hundred members itching to empower themselves and enhance the community as a whole. Jane Croly would have given her nod of approval—and beamed at the WCN's first project in town: Municipal cleaning in Norfolk.

Most members had opted for the civic department since they considered the beautification of their industrial city pivotal. And they desired to prove their dedication to improving community matters. Sure enough, *The Virginian-Pilot* announced on April 11, 1906, that the mayor of Norfolk, Dr. James G. Riddick, wholeheartedly agreed with the suggestion by the civic department of the Woman's Club: a call for every inhabitant of Norfolk to set aside a day for cleaning their yard, both back and front and all around, and even their street. The paper's title read in bold, large letters: "TODAY THE DAY TO CLEAN CITY." So, the Woman's Club of Norfolk started "Municipal Cleaning Day," which included not only residences but also public buildings and streets. Even the sewer and drain department agreed to handle all the extra garbage and urged residents to place their trash in front of their doors instead of in their yards so the collectors could sweep them off and throw them into the truck quicker than a vacuum cleaner. In addition, the street department agreed to clear the long-lain dirt and stubborn weeds off the streets, exposing the clean asphalt and red bricks—all in one day. The Woman's Club of Norfolk had undoubtedly brought about a cleaner Norfolk.

***

Then, the fledgling Woman's Club of Norfolk faced an issue: an overload of membership applications, more than it could handle. One member told *The Virginian-Pilot* that the WCN was "pretty near overwhelmed" and needed to take steps to admit new members instead of picking them up off the street if they showed only enthusiasm. From then on, every applicant would need to be investigated like a microscope. Skills, interests, and attitudes were now the main considerations for screening. Miss Gatewood, the club president, declared a special meeting to change the constitution, allowing the board of governors instead of the club itself to handle the new membership matter. Since the WCN launched exactly a year earlier, the constitution had required that the vote of two-thirds of the club members accept new members. But with an overwhelming number of applicants, voting could no longer be done in one meeting. Instead, more sessions would be needed. By receiving many more applications, the membership of the WCN numbered precisely 260. The club would undoubtedly get more extensive, but there would always be a limit.

***

The members of the Woman's Club of Norfolk were keenly interested in history of any kind, especially American history. They were enthusiastic about the landings of early settlers at nearby Cape Henry, in the northeast corner of today's Virginia Beach, about twenty-five miles east of Norfolk, and at

Jamestown, about fifty miles west. Many historians understand that over a hundred English settlers spent three months sailing across the Atlantic and made their first landing at Cape Henry on April 26, 1607. They erected a wooden cross in gratitude for their safe voyage at sea and then moved farther inland to Jamestown for permanent settlement.

Therefore, the Woman's Club of Norfolk and the GFWC eagerly hosted activities for the 1907 Jamestown Exposition held in Norfolk for six months. According to the WCN's minutes, the club was intensely involved in the three-hundredth anniversary celebration, entertaining celebrities and dignitaries, giving large receptions, and bringing in noted speakers. The General Federation of Woman's Clubs held its annual meeting in the Administration Building of the Jamestown Exposition (now the Norfolk Naval Base).

***

While the Woman's Club of Norfolk delved into monthly and special meetings, most of which took place usually on Mondays, Tuesdays, or Thursdays at 4:30 PM, one department would take charge of each afternoon meeting, which all the WCN members were encouraged to attend. On December 6, 1906, the literature department, interested in reproductions of historical work, read a paper on the "Revolt of Sudan" and "Fall of Khartoum," in which Egypt and Sudan fought each other in 1884–85. Egypt had held the city of Khartoum for some time. Still, the independent army known as the Mahdists broke into the city. It killed the entire garrison of Egyptian soldiers and four thousand, mostly male

Sudanese civilians. And they enslaved women and children. Some sources had stated that the attackers killed and beheaded British general Charles Gordon, the commander of the defenders, delivering his head to the Mahdi. It is unknown how these

spiffy club members took this horrid story, but it was the choice of the literature department for reading!

Five years later, the literature department made a significant show of Shakespeare, where three members read a paper they had written about one of the noted dramatist's books. Mrs. Sparks Melton read hers on "The Soliloquy in Shakespeare"; Mrs. F. C. Steinmetz's topic was "Psychology in Shakespeare's Tragedies"; and Miss Teresa Martin identified "Garrick and His Followers." The following month, Ben Greet, the well-known Shakespearean scholar and actor from London, was invited by the WCN to speak at their meeting about his love for "The Bard of Avon" and his dramatic plays. Greet strongly suggested that women, in general, cared greatly about culture and education. The WCN members should form an organization to study Shakespeare and encourage his dramas on the stage instead of poorly performed or written plays that appealed to theatre lovers. That night, Greet performed in his favorite Shakespearean play, "The Tempest," at Fort Norfolk, not too far from the Martin Mansion. That white stone fort on the water helped protect the city during the War of 1812. Then, during the Civil War, the Confederate army seized and used the fort to defend Norfolk and Portsmouth across the river.

When the art department hosted the WCN meeting on

November 22, 1906, the topic was "Leonardo and His School." First, several women read their papers on the renowned Italian artist Leonardo da Vinci. Next, Miss Gatewood gave a lecture on her definition of the "High Renaissance," explaining the artistic styles in Rome and Florence. Mrs. Walter Adams and Mrs. Alice Jenkins then read their papers on Leonardo and Bernardo Luini, the famous Milanese painter, followed by Mrs. Henry Baker's reading of William Wordsworth's poem "The Last Supper, by Leonardo da Vinci, in the Refectory of the Convent of Maria della Grazia—Milan." Later, at another meeting, the chairman of the art department, Miss Leta Serpell, gave a lesson about the history of Italian art.

The music department of the WCN invited local musicians and singers to perform in its concert programs over the years. Yet, there were talented WCN members who were encouraged to sing or play an instrument as well, while there was a piano at the Martin Mansion. Emma Young, one of Norfolk's most gifted singers, performed vocal selections early on while the talented musicians took turns giving a piano recital. *The Virginian-Pilot*, becoming more entertaining than just seven long columns with serious news in fine print, would announce an upcoming or completed "musicale" at the Woman's Club of Norfolk's rented home on 612 Colonial Avenue in Ghent, even radiantly identifying the performers and their instruments.

In 1922, the WCN entered a new music program: inviting out-of-town musicians to perform solo and receive press releases beforehand. That helped raise more funding for the WCN and civic causes. The soprano-pianist duo from the Cincinnati

Symphony Orchestra, Elizabeth Langhorst and Lillian Plogatedt, attracted a large crowd at the Ghent Club on October 24, 1922, and that financially benefited the Woman's Club of Norfolk, as the club members sold tickets with a percentage to the WCN fund. The Ghent Club was a Jewish social organization to which many members of the Ohef Sholom Temple belonged. That synagogue was built a few blocks away from The Hague, of course, in Ghent, and still exists today. Later, there was a joint recital from Baltimore, local bands, and a twenty-first-anniversary celebration for the WCN in which Governor Harry Byrd delivered an address, and Mrs. Edwin Feller sang "Carry Me Back to Old Virginny," accompanied by Mrs. Samuel Ferebee playing an instrument, presumably a piano. Music was a large part of the Woman's Club of Norfolk for several decades.

***

Virginia Gatewood, who was elected six times as the club president in fifteen years, had a personal interest in current events, reading newspapers, and collecting local news; therefore, she added the current events department to the WCN. Committee members discussed whatever topic was garnering public attention at the moment. The Aldrich-Vreeland Act of 1908 was one topic that the members shared their views on in response to banking panics and economic instability that stemmed from the Panic of 1907. This act created the National Monetary Commission. Imagine all these Woman's Club ladies discussing a complicated financial situation instead of being confined to home life and cutting up coupons on the kitchen table!

The current events department also invited guest speakers to discuss national and global events; some came from Asia. According to the November 21, 1906 article in *The Virginian-Pilot*, Captain Richmond Pearson Hobson enraptured the audience with his lecture on "America—the Peacemaker Among the Nations." Then, in December 1907, Professor Fukushima of the Imperial Art Academy in Japan impressed the WCN members with his lecture on "Japan and Her People." Next, the WCN's Virginia Gatewood spoke about her trip to Turkey in 1909, sharing its present conditions and political changes. In 1921, Dr. Robert E. Blackwell, president of Randolph-Macon College, lectured about the "Modern Mind." That certainly fits the current events department!

From the day the Woman's Club of Norfolk was established, the civic department was favored over other departments since the members wanted to contribute to society. Women knew the necessity of thrusting their can-do and can-help attitudes into homes and the community. They wanted a spotless city, so the Norfolk residents were repeatedly urged to rake and remove trash from their yards. The city employees were nudged to sweep and shave dirt off residential and public streets; the lawn and maintenance workers were persuaded to protect trees during mowing. According to articles in *The Virginian-Pilot*, the second club president, Mrs. Leta Serpell, and her allies requested that special attention be given to the enforcement of anti-spitting laws and the regulation to make women more secure in the streets from "reckless walking." That was provoked after "a very old woman was knocked down and seriously hurt by the carelessness of which the club complained."

The word "civic" also prompted the WCN members to not only encourage others, such as city residents and employees, but also the WCN members to help financially or physically. For example, the WCN donated in 1908 to the new YMCA building in downtown Norfolk. In 1917, when World War I broke out, the club members participated in activities for war relief by taking Red Cross classes, making surgical supplies, and knitting sweaters in preparation for the harsh winter out on the battlefields. The WCN also participated in the 1919 WSS Campaign (War Savings Stamps) for the US Government by selling unwanted items in their homes, building sentiment, advertising, and having the Boy Scouts assist with the posters. That campaign not only raised money for war supplies but also encouraged Americans to learn wise methods of saving and buying. In addition, the WCN sponsored a legal aid clinic, pushed for prison reform, and marched for women's suffrage. Later, in 1928, the WCN was dismayed to hear that Norfolk was one of the most expensive cities in the nation and launched "The High Cost of Living" lectures to address housing issues.

I collected more than two hundred clippings from *The Virginian-Pilot* featuring the WCN's work in the civic department and other departments during the first twenty-five years of its existence—and there's much more that I didn't include. The civic department won the most articles on the WCN's activities; however, one other department followed closely: Entertainment.

It was the phenomenal Gatewood's idea of monthly

entertainment after a long dry spell during World War I. She was eagerly involved in war work issues, the War Camp Community Service, and the Woman's National Navy League. Miss Gatewood figured night dances were what tired, war-torn WWI service members needed while stationed at the Norfolk Naval Base. She announced the plans for the Tuesday evening dances at Red Circle Club and the Saturday evening dances at the City Armory Hall for uniformed men of the Army, Navy, and Marine Corps. And Miss Gatewood chose an uplifting live band for each dance. Much to everyone's delight, those dances were hugely successful—and a respite for both men and women affected by one of the deadliest conflicts in world history.

The entertainment department of the WCN grew broader with plays and cabarets, which kept *The Virginian-Pilot* busy with uplifting articles and dashing headlines, apparently in gratitude to women. It even dedicated a section for women's interests and activities, as on one front page, the large bold headline at the top read, "A REAL WOMAN'S PAGE FOR REAL WOMEN," and on another front page, "WHAT'S GOING ON IN THE WORLD OF WOMEN," showing formal portraits of woman clustered together underneath. *The Virginian-Pilot* now offered more flair and named its Sunday section "Society," of course, with more female portraits squeezed into its page. More newspaper coverage for women reflected the victory of the women's movement and suffrage.

Mrs. Frantz Naylor, the third club president, was credited for her profound dedication to the entertainment department. She encouraged a dramatic performance by a group of Norfolk actors once a year, drawing a huge audience. Mrs. Naylor originated the cabarets later held at the WCN's new residence on Fairfax Avenue, which was, of course, the Martin Mansion, and brought the fashion show to popularity for many years. Those lively cabarets also included dances and bands, lighting up the city of Norfolk. Mrs. Naylor also was involved in bringing comedy and drama to the community, as the plays "Nathan Hale," "Adam and Eva," and the most notable "Squaw Man" were directed by the local director and actor William H. Starkey, the last of which was performed at the Wells Theatre in downtown Norfolk, which opened in 1913. Constructed in a steel-reinforced concrete structure with ornate decoration still visible today, that brand-new theatre was equipped with 1,650 seats, twelve boxes, and three balconies. Doubtlessly, the WCN was delighted to host the plays at such a fancy theatre at a reasonable rental rate. Thanks to Mrs. Frantz Naylor's enthusiasm, entertainment was a big moneymaker for the organization.

***

Since its establishment in 1905, the WCN's social department had offered teas, receptions, subscription card games, Christmas parties, and bridge tournaments. While the club members spent most of their time in meetings and lectures, they also interacted with each other socially and formed friendships. Every time a new season began for the Woman's Club of Norfolk, the members held an elaborate tea party with flower arrangements, even described in *The Virginian-Pilot.* And when a club president was elected or planned to retire, a reception party was thrown in her honor. It would not be surprising if the six-time-elected president Virginia Gatewood or the nine-time-chosen president Frantz Naylor were likely given more salute parties than birthday ones in their lifetimes.

Most WCN fancy parties included over three hundred women and men, an orchestra band, palm fronds, and a floating sea of lace and taffeta gowns. The younger generation was included at the debutante parties, the first of which honored Miss Lora Crump in November 1908. A more solemn reception was given in honor of the Secretary of the Navy, Curtis D. Wilbur, on February 28, 1928, following his lecture on "The Navy of the United States." The Woman's Club of Norfolk knew that the military deserved such high recognition; therefore, it hosted several talks and parties for them. And don't forget that the world's largest naval base was nearby.

In that same year, 1928, Fanny Washington, a descendant of George Washington, gave a speech to the spellbound Woman's Club about a newly published, three-volume series, *The Rebel and the Patriot, 1762-1777*, by Rupert Hughes. Fanny Washington professed the author grossly slandered her great-great-great uncle, calling the cherry tree story a myth and questioning his natural traits. To many readers' horror, Hughes called General Washington "profane, irreligious, a great flirt, and a prodigious rum drinker." Insisting on truth or whatever that was in history, the author had met controversy and scorn among those dedicated to the founder of America. Fanny Washington's speech at the Woman's Club inspired three hundred guests in the auditorium, as she described her ancestor as "intensely human, of a distinctly religious nature, generous to a fault, hospitable to the point of extravagance, and a good sportsman." Fanny indeed came to dispute Rupert Hughes' book and won the hearts of the club members.

Professors from the nearby College of William & Mary were invited by the Woman's Club of Norfolk to speak on diverse topics. One spoke about the government of Virginia; the other lectured on the education needs of public schools, and another talked about women's studies. A literature professor provided enlightening details about Shakespeare. Art and history were lectured as well. It was not only the College of William & Mary that brought their professors into the Martin Mansion; many other state colleges contributed their instructors. Interestingly, the Woman's Club of Norfolk expressed appreciation toward the professors by giving them gold coins. At that time, in the 1920s, people used St. Gaudens gold coins featuring Miss Liberty on one side and an eagle on the other side. Each of those beautiful coins was valued at twenty dollars, which would have been close to $350 today. However, if one wants to collect a 1920 St. Gaudens gold coin on eBay, it will cost thousands of dollars.

***

In 1909, the WCN did something unique to entertain the wives of the visiting delegates of Deep Waterways, the board of engineers inspecting waterways between the Great Lakes and the Atlantic Tide Waters. The guests took a tour around Norfolk Harbor, the Navy Yard, and the Newport News shipyard aboard a tugboat named "Virginia." The boat then landed at Old Point at the tip of Fort Monroe in time for the Deep Waterways wives to witness the drill at that stone fort, followed by WCN's gracious lunch picnic on the boat. *The Virginian-Pilot* stated that the Woman's Club of Norfolk had done a splendid job hosting a "tug party."

The year 1925 gave the Woman's Club of Norfolk a permanent settlement that would provide enlightening activities and parties for the next hundred years up to today. They purchased the Alvah Martin Mansion after brief consideration with the Board of Governors. Since its establishment in 1905, the WCN had had three previous rental residences that matched none of the Martin Mansion's grandeur, size, and beauty. So, when they heard the mansion owner, the Virginia Club, was planning to move back downtown, the Woman's Club of Norfolk grabbed the opportunity to discuss the possibilities of purchasing the Martin Mansion. It turned out the Virginia Club had taken off so quickly that the Martin heirs were left with the position of selling the mansion, so they and the WCN board members had been considering it for several months before announcing it to the WCN members. Mrs. Frantz Naylor, the long-lasting president, explained the advantages of owning such a great place at 524 Fairfax Avenue, one of which was an almost completed auditorium capable of occupying four hundred people. Hearing this, the club members immediately approved the purchase.

The Woman's Club of Norfolk bought the Martin Mansion for forty-five thousand dollars, about two-thirds of what the Virginia Club had paid. In addition, it was agreed between the club and the Martin heirs that the current and third residence of the WCN at 603 Westover Avenue, valued at thirty thousand dollars, would be used as part of the payment. So, the fifteen-thousand-dollar initial payment deal was put on the table. The moving date would be on October 26, 1925, with the celebration open to the public. *The Virginian-Pilot* published several articles, the last of which congratulated the club in bold headlines across the top of the page: "WOMAN'S CLUB TO DEDICATE NEW QUARTERS TOMORROW."

The WCN discussed ways of raising the initial payment for their new residence. Mrs. V. G. Culpeper, the finance chairman, reminded the members that when the last house was bought, each member was asked to donate ten dollars (close to $160 today) or obtain a new member. That could be repeated for the new place, and the three hundred members immediately contributed to the funding. The result was a direct cash payment of three thousand dollars, not much of a contribution toward a forty-five-thousand-dollar mansion. Due to the larger size of the Martin Mansion, the WCN would increase membership during the year and receive extra dues. Furthermore, the WCN could defray some of the debts by renting rooms on the second and third floors of the Martin Mansion.

The musician Bristow Hardin, who had rented a room in the previous WCN residence for years and helped with the mortgage, agreed to move his music studio to one of the rooms at the new place. The entire first floor, with the stunning woodwork, hand-blown windows, landscape mural, dogs on the mantel, and soon-to-be-completed auditorium, would be taken over by the Woman's Club of Norfolk's activities and parties. The WCN members knew that they would immediately finish the incomplete auditorium after moving in. Miss Virginia Gatewood's painted portrait, in which she sat with a stern look, would be hung in the West Wing Parlor. She would undoubtedly spend the next hundred years watching and ensuring that her beloved Woman's Club of Norfolk stays intact with decency and grace, even today.

The opening ceremony on October 26, 1925, at 3 PM, was attended by more than three hundred people, some of whom were from other women's organizations and several men. It began with a devotional service by the Rev. William E. Callender. Next, Mayor Heth Tyler and former Mayor Barton Myers congratulated the Woman's Club of Norfolk on their new quarters and twenty years of dedicated work in the community and beyond. Next, Judge W. W. Dey of the Juvenile Court expressed profound gratitude to the Woman's Club of Norfolk for their legal aid committee that had made his work easier among children and mothers. Finally, Robert M. Hughes, a prominent admiralty lawyer and one of the founding pioneers of William & Mary College (now Old Dominion University), praised the WCN's literary committee for extending literature to the community.

The WCN's current president, Mrs. Frantz Naylor, gave a speech about her goal to increase club membership in this large, welcoming residence. She and her members considered the purchase of the Martin Mansion their most significant achievement of the year, possibly in the WCN's lifetime, and it would give them more meaningful community service opportunities.

The Virginian-Pilot called the mansion "perhaps the finest clubhouse of its kind in the South." It now belonged to the proud

Bainy Cyrus
Woman's Club of Norfolk.

Chapter Four

Once, a bronze tablet, twenty by fifteen inches, was nailed to the tan brick wall on the right side of the front door, with its upper arch window featuring house number 524. Then, the Martin Mansion had been stamped with proof of ownership for all the world to see and marvel at, which continues today. The Martin Mansion is now called the Woman's Club of Norfolk or just "The Woman's Club." The last term still resonates in Norfolk and beyond; in the past ninety-eight years, those four syllables have rung the exact answer for the location of an upcoming wedding, a speaker's event, a memorial service, a school skit, or a fortieth birthday party. The bronze tablet, now tarnished sea blue from oxidation over the years and edged with dark brown borders, reads in bold, brown letters in five lines:

THE

WOMAN'S CLUB

OF

NORFOLK

FOUNDED 1905

The tablet viewer may think the Martin Mansion was constructed in 1905, whereas it should have been five years later. However, the tablet relates to the organization, not the mansion, since the Woman's Club of Norfolk was founded that year a few miles away at the Atlantic Hotel in downtown Norfolk, where

Miss Virginia Gatewood summoned a group of women with her idea of initiating the club. After installing the fifty-five-dollar bronze tablet by the front door in May 1926, the club hung a painted portrait of Miss Gatewood inside the mansion to honor her as the first club president. At the cost of a hundred dollars, the 2.5-by-3-foot portrait in a gold frame was assumedly hung where it is today, in the West Wing Parlor. Miss Gatewood is shown from the waist up in a surprisingly loose white dress or top that exposes her sternum and shows a corsage of purple flowers, believed to be orchids, down her cleavage. It is quite puzzling that the stern lady would allow her outfit to look like an unmade bed, but her facial pose was formal enough, exhibiting outstanding professionalism. With her long blonde hair pinned to the top in a French twist, Miss Gatewood would remind viewers of George Washington's unsmiling pose in a Gilbert Stuart painting seen in school textbooks. Only Miss Gatewood posed slightly to the right while George posed the other way. Her portrait, which cost a fortune at the installation, displays discipline and formality despite the haphazard outfit. As I have witnessed over the years, when many visitors and club members acknowledge Miss Gatewood on the wall in the West Wing Parlor, they realize the Martin Mansion is not the place to misbehave. They look as if a high school principal is approaching in the hall, and they stiffen their backs. Miss Virginia Gatewood was not one to horse around with.

When the Woman's Club of Norfolk moved into the Martin Mansion in October 1925, they had the contractor finish the auditorium abruptly left by the previous owner, the Virginia

Club. Approximately the size of a volleyball court, the auditorium had a coffered ceiling but was painted all white, unlike the dark oak trimmings in other rooms. The red oak hardwood floor in an overlay pattern from front to back was laid down to tolerate the heavy foot traffic of high heels, scraping of tables and chairs, and even lively dancing with men. Since the new addition was on the mansion's east side with hardly any afternoon sunlight, the windows were installed on the south side, the front of the mansion, where the trees and shrubs thrived in full sun. Hence, those three windows brought much-needed light into the auditorium. Six windows were installed on the east side, although the view would not be significant, facing a narrow alley and brick walls of the adjacent home. But it was better than a solid wall. Finally, four windows and a door in the middle were installed behind the stage at the back of the auditorium. That would bring in the morning sun and a beautiful view of the tall, four-stage, pinnacled tower of Christ and St. Luke's Episcopal Church, built in Gothic Revival architecture in the distance. That backside would lead people outside to the garden in front of the attractive red-brick wall on the property line. Finally, the auditorium's left wall was devoid of windows because of its connection to the dining room and kitchen. A swing door was added there for access to the kitchen.

With the advantage of an auditorium at their new residence, the Woman's Club of Norfolk could now add more members to fill such a large room for meetings or receptions. According to Earlye Lee Miller's book on the WCN's 102-year history, there were 680 club members, with 455 active ones, in

1928. So, it was indeed an extensive club, now with a new auditorium!

***

The year 1930 marked the twenty-fifth anniversary of the Woman's Club of Norfolk. The earliest departments still existed by the end of the WCN's twenty-five-year duration: art, literature, civic, social, music, and current events. But now, there were three additional departments: entertainment, education, and legal aid. According to one *The Virginian-Pilot* article in the WCN's annual report, legal aid had been added to the department list in 1930. Education had a lot to consider as the Woman's Club of Norfolk grew more concerned about the illiteracy rate of local adults and children. The WCN asked Norfolk County to investigate the illiteracy issue and find ways to resolve it. The speakers on educational needs were invited to speak at the WCN meetings. Most of the club members were mothers and knew the importance of parent-teacher interaction, so they conferred with the branches of the Parent-Teacher Association to ensure that girls would finish high school with the support of both parents and teachers.

Whatever the Woman's Club of Norfolk saw as a problem in the community, they spoke up and acted for the community. They used their minds, words, and hands to make lives better for their city counterparts.

Given all the activities of the Woman's Club of Norfolk in its first twenty-five years, this organization was no tea party, although that favorite beverage of bygone times was indeed poured at the end of each event. The Woman's Club of Norfolk provided an unbelievably extensive dose of education for the members, engulfing them in different cultures and energizing them into community projects. The departments of the WCN, each well-organized with its committee and president, were all rolled into one vast educational and motivational tool for the members, club guests, and even newspaper readers. One could not sway from those departments without thinking for one minute about how they had positively affected the Woman's Club of Norfolk. Those diverse departments were hugely beneficial for the members since women before the early twentieth century had long been restricted to their homes and deprived of liberties in a much broader, diverse world. Jane Croly fought her way out of a male-dominated society that forbade her from seeing Charles Dickens in person. Fifty years later, the literature department of the WCN would have torn the wall down if ever prohibited from attending *The Great Gatsby* author F. Scott Fitzgerald's lecture.

***

The neighborhood along The Hague, formerly called Smith's Creek and a branch of the Elizabeth River, remained beautiful and serene forty years after the first homes of European architecture were constructed on Mowbray Arch and other nearby streets. First, a private contractor built a wooden bulkhead along the artificial semi-circular shoreline in the late 1800s. Then, the city of Norfolk completed a sturdier retaining wall, using stones, around the water by 1919. Finally, more homes had been added to the grid pattern of the Ghent Historic District since the construction of the Martin Mansion. Approximately forty years after the first home was built on Mowbray Arch in 1890, the neighborhood along The Hague was pretty much settled, with hardly any room for further development.

By 1930, The Woman's Club stood two houses from the corner of Fairfax Avenue and Mowbray Arch with a partial view of The Hague. The West Wing Parlor on the first floor and the primary bedroom on the second floor had the same water view through the front windows in the curved sections, one section directly over the other separated by the veranda roof. In addition, one could glimpse the calm creek between the Slover home next door and the massive red-brick home belonging to the Bruces, catty-corner from The Woman's Club. It might not be a big deal to have such a small view of The Hague, but the best part about it was the sunset sky, which sometimes turned into a bright hue of red and orange. And despite the additional buildings blocking the view over the years, the sunset sky is still spectacular these days. So, that first window in the West Wing Parlor offers an evening show of orange and red skies with silhouetted black buildings. The window also has shown significant changes in the neighborhood along The Hague and beyond in the past century.

The red-brick home, catty-corner from The Woman's Club, was built for Frederick and Natalie Bruce in 1928, nearly two decades after Alvah Martin built his mansion. With its massive size and thirty rooms, the Bruce home still takes up most of the view from the West Wing Parlor window but is a pleasant sight thanks to its Colonial Williamsburg style. In the 1930s, the Bruce home was one of Norfolk's most expensive private homes with a full view of The Hague. It would later become a "Tidewater Academy" school in 1959 before changing its name to

"Douglas MacArthur Academy." Then, the school closed for good in 1969, and this building reverted to a private home.

While The Woman's Club and the Bruce home dominate over other homes on the 500 block of Fairfax Avenue, those two homes have the advantage of being close to The Hague, where people picnic, read, sunbathe, and chat on a grassy area along the bulkhead like Georges Seurat's world-famous painting, "A Sunday Afternoon on the Island of La Grande Jatte." That romantic scene can continue a quarter of a mile around the curve from the west end to the east end of The Hague, with a splendid row of European-style homes. And Mowbray Arch, despite being flooded now and then, is popular for walkers, runners, and cyclists. It is believed that back in the 1930s, this wide street had changed its surface from oyster shells to asphalt.

The Y-shape of The Hague remained the same twenty years after The Woman's Club was constructed, and the turnstile bridge was still leading yachts and sailboats into the creek from the Elizabeth River. Today, it would be virtually impossible to see a single boat on The Hague since that waterway was permanently closed in 1960, and an impassible one replaced the turnstile bridge. But The Hague was heavily dotted with yachts and sailboats back in the past, close to the east end, where the new Norfolk Museum of Arts and Sciences dominated the view with its limestone architecture resembling an Italian Renaissance palazzo with its open arcade on the ground level. It was founded in 1933 as the "direct result of the efforts of Irene Leache and her companion, Anna Cogswell Wood, who in 1873 founded a women's seminary that bore their names. The arts were a central part of the curriculum. Upon the death of Leache, Wood established a small collection in her companion's memory, which eventually (around World War I) became the Norfolk Society of the Arts. Through the efforts of Florence Sloane, a site and operational funding were secured from the city, and the first wing of the Norfolk Museum of Arts and Sciences opened in 1933, at the height of the Great Depression," as stated by the website of Society of Architectural Historians. That museum would be renamed the Chrysler Museum of Arts forty years later, in 1971. As it still does today with its renovations and additions over the years, the Norfolk Museum of Arts and Sciences made the east end of The Hague strikingly attractive.

At the west end of The Hague, across Olney Road, Christ and St. Luke's Episcopal Church was built and completed in 1910 at the same time as the Martin Mansion. As it still exists today, this large church is in the Early English Perpendicular Gothic style with granite and limestone. The four-stage, 113-foot bell tower, topped with battlements and pinnacles, holds Norfolk's oldest bell and can be seen across Ghent and from Portsmouth across the water. One peering through the back windows of the WCN auditorium or from Alvah Martin's bookcase-filled office could see the tower. Amy Waters Yarsinske, a well-known local author of many historical and regional books, wrote one titled *Ghent*, which depicts rare, fascinating, black-and-white photographs of Christ and St. Luke's bell tower in the distance, taken in the first half of the twentieth century. Because of its striking beauty surrounded by the lower city landscape, I would call it the Eiffel Tower of Norfolk; it is eye-catching and spellbinding.

Christ and St. Luke's has quite an interesting history. It was named Christ Church upon completion on Olney Road, and Bishop A.M. Randolph officiated the first worship service on Christmas Day 1910. Then, in 1935, Christ Church consolidated with its sister church, St. Andrews in West Ghent, and was renamed Christ and St. Luke's. A mile away, St. Andrews was and still is a charming Tudor-style red-brick church on Graydon Avenue. It then became an independent parish with financial security in 1940. In the mid-1950s, Lloyd Hall was added to Christ and St. Luke's, which, in turn, made this church the leader in the community today, serving the homeless and working poor in its soup kitchen and outreach ministries and abroad. The exquisite beauty of the church today encourages the frequent use of concerts by local and international musicians who bring the sound ripples across the calm Hague.

At the time of The Hague's development in the early 1900s, two additional religious buildings emerged on one side of Stockley Gardens, the shady park with three elongated sections. Ghent United Methodist Church was built in 1902 before Christ and St. Luke's emerged next to it eight years later, and then Ohef Sholom Temple next door went up in 1918. So that short block of Stockley Gardens began to show the diverse architecture of two churches and a synagogue: The Gothic style of Christ and St. Luke's, the Ionic Greek of Ghent Methodist, and the Greek Revival of Ohef Sholom. The last two look similar but have differentiating details, such as columns and porticos. And from the day they began existing side by side in 1918, all these three buildings have exhibited religious tolerance and support for each other. I remember attending a large bar mitzvah at Ghent Methodist in 2004 because its next-door neighbor, Ohef Sholom, was under a major renovation; it went beautifully, giving us a sense of tolerance in the neighborhood.

The Drummond Bridge, leading across The Hague to the neighborhood from downtown, was built closer to the east end, providing plenty of room for boats to anchor or linger in the larger part of The Hague toward the west end. Norfolkians entered the neighborhood by the Drummond Bridge, using the trolley car that turned left onto Mowbray Arch after passing the bridge and vice versa. And the Drummond Bridge could be used for walking as well.

There was a twenty-eight-bed hospital in the neighborhood, across from Drummond Bridge, named Sarah Leigh Hospital. Dr. Southgate Leigh founded it in 1903. A red-brick colonial-style facility with long white columns at the entry, it remained a hospital until 1977, having changed names a few times. Sadly, this historic building was torn down after a devastating fire in June 1986. When living in an apartment in Ghent as a single woman, I was dismayed to see the inferno during my run. I watched the fire department unsuccessfully trying to keep the blaze under control for hours.

Also across from the Drummond Bridge, close to Sarah Leigh Hospital, stood Holland House Apartments, an attractive red-brick, Dutch-style building with four floors. It was constructed in 1905 to become a residential hotel for the 1907

Jamestown Exposition but changed to apartments afterward. Holland House was the "earliest example of apartment building in Ghent," as stated by Amy Waters Yarsinske in her book *Ghent*. She explains that the construction of apartment buildings increased with the expectation of housing those planning to attend the six-month-long 1907 Jamestown Exposition held in Norfolk. This type of building was relatively new in the city because most of the buildings had been single-family residences since 1890 and included European-style homes along The Hague. And, of course, the Martin Mansion. Thus, in 1904, new apartment buildings appeared with the Jamestown Exhibition visitors in mind. Holland House was one, followed by Pelham Place, Raleigh Square, and others beyond the west end of The Hague. Most of those apartments still exist today, surrounding the Stockley Gardens next to the Christ and St. Luke's Episcopal Church and along West Olney Road.

The Woman's Club found itself in an impressive historic neighborhood in the shape of the half-moon on a super-calm canal, with a massive Gothic Revival church at the west end of The Hague and an Italian Renaissance-style art museum at the east end. And with rows of Dutch-style homes in between, giving the entire neighborhood an eclectic European taste. It is a delight that The Woman's Club has stayed there for a century, belonging to such a beautiful, historic district that has garnered more garden and walking tours than any other area in Norfolk.

***

Mrs. Frantz Naylor, whose real name was Lillian, remained the president of the Woman's Club of Norfolk for eleven years, having served nine terms since 1920. She was a slender, attractive lady with striking eyes, and every portrait of hers seen in *The Virginian-Pilot* (a lot of them, impressively) and the WCN archives shows her beauty inside and out. Her radiant personality brought in many interested members, increasing by the hundreds, and she was not as stern as Miss Virginia Gatewood but serious about keeping the club aloft financially. In addition to Miss Gatewood, Frantz was a long-lasting, highly respected president and had to accept the tenth term because of the short-timed need for financial arrangements, although she looked forward to retiring.

The club members insisted Frantz stay a little longer because of the two things she excelled at: Entertainment and the annual pilgrimage to Cape Henry. From the day she became a member of the WCN, Frantz managed many plays, cabarets, and recitals, generating a large amount of money for the club. With the auditorium at the Martin Mansion, she was enthusiastic enough to bring in as many plays as she could. And she was fond of comedy shows as well.

But she was best known for her meticulous planning of the annual pilgrimage to Cape Henry to memorialize "The First Landing" of the English settlers there in 1607. It started with her connection to the Assembly of Tidewater Virginia Women, which focused on the awareness and restoration of historic sites around Southeast Virginia, including the College of William & Mary (but the assembly's work was made unnecessary when John D. Rockefeller stepped in to restore Colonial Williamsburg, including the college). The assembly turned its attention to Cape Henry. They felt it was not getting the national attention it deserved.

It was Mrs. Frantz Naylor's idea of instigating an annual pilgrimage every April 26 from The Hague to Cape Henry, twenty miles apart. She even asked for crape myrtles and azaleas to be planted along the route, insisting that the azaleas be in full bloom during the pilgrimage, which was possible in Virginia, thanks to its seasonal April bloom. Mrs. Naylor led the flag presentation at the commemoration service; the Cape Henry flag had the Cross of Saint George, believed to be a reproduction of the wooden cross the first English settlers set on the ground at Cape Henry in 1607.

Every pilgrimage was well-planned, beginning as far back as the day after the previous one. And Frantz was so eager that she invited the U.S. presidents for years to participate in the pilgrimage, even traveling to the White House. Unfortunately, not all the presidents could make it. But one did show up… Back in 1928, Mrs. Naylor invited President-elect Herbert Hoover to join the annual pilgrimage. Unfortunately, Hoover could not attend the pilgrimage but promised to do so the following year. He did finally appear at Cape Henry in 1931, but a lightning storm appeared and had ten thousand people running for cover. Sadly, President Hoover never spoke at the abruptly called-off commemoration service. Instead, he had to sprint over the dunes in the torrential rain and speed away in his motorcar.

In the WNC report compiled by Grover Franklin in 1994,

"A Day in the Life of Lillian W. Naylor, April 26, 1929," the story reads:

The ceremonies of the Pilgrimage to Cape Henry began in Norfolk shortly after noon when Governor Harry F. Byrd and the official party sailed into The Hague to receive the official welcome to the city. The dignitaries had arrived by automobile at Campbell's Wharf, where they boarded the barge of Rear Admiral Guy H. Barrage, commandant of the Fifth Naval District, which brought them to The Hague Landing at Olney Road, across from Christ Church (Christ and St. Luke's).

The landing place had been elaborately prepared. An escort of sailors from the Naval Base, troops of Boy Scouts, and a delegation of city officials awaited them. The Assembly of Tidewater Virginia Women, under whose auspices and by whose arrangement the pilgrimage has grown from year to year, had a large delegation of its committee women there as well.

A band from the Naval Base was performing when the barge scraped alongside the landing place. Flags were fluttering in the sharp April breeze. And a rousing cheer went up from the crowd as the visitors debarked.

Mayor Tyler of Norfolk, Rear Admiral Watt T. Cluverius, commandant of the Norfolk Navy Yard, and a large delegation of naval and civilian authorities were waiting to extend the official welcome to the guests.

Mayor Tyler presented the official "Key to the City" to Governor Byrd, whereupon Governor Byrd gave keys to the State of Virginia to Governor O. Max Gardner of North Carolina and

United States Senator Frederick H. Gillett of Massachusetts. Mayor Tyler was accompanied by a Guard of Norfolk policemen there to display Norfolk's Mace; this is one of the rare occasions when the mace is allowed to be taken from its vault in the National Bank of Commerce.

After the party had landed and the Governor's Salute had been played, the official party marched the short distance to the Woman's Club for an informal reception and luncheon.

At the Woman's Club, Mrs. Frantz Naylor, president of the Club and speaker of The Assembly of Tidewater Virginia Women, explained that it had been decided to hold two meetings annually, the spring pilgrimage to Cape Henry and a fall meeting in Williamsburg. After the luncheon, the party moved by automobile to Cape Henry.

This was what the Martin Mansion saw annually on April 26: A throng of guests from all over Virginia and other states preparing the pilgrimage to Cape Henry. And the mansion's occupants, especially Mrs. Naylor, started it all. In 1928, she traveled to Richmond for the presentation of Senate Bill 201, created the "Cape Henry Memorial Commission," and defined its powers. That commission would later install a huge permanent granite cross where the wooden cross was planted in 1607. In 1937, the painting "The Landing at Cape Henry," done by the Scottish Stephen Reid, was given to the Norfolk Museum of Arts and Sciences in memory of Alethea Serpell, who died two years earlier. The Organizations and Citizens of Norfolk had held the painting for a while. Miss Serpell, known as "Leta," was the second and fourth WCN president in sequence, an art collector, and a lecturer on art and history topics. Her friends and relatives presented the 50-by-62-inch oil on canvas painting in her memory to the museum at the east end of The Hague. That 1928 painting depicts Reverend Robert Hunt praying to the wooden cross on the dune, surrounded by the colonists he had sailed with. It is still hung at what is now called the Chrysler Museum.

***

Nearing her retirement after eleven years of presiding over the Woman's Club of Norfolk, Mrs. Frantz Naylor wrote a report for *The Virginian-Pilot*, detailing the expansion and success of her club since 1920. The first paragraph of the February 22, 1931, article provided surprising data on the club's progress: "The Woman's Club of Norfolk 11 years ago had 56 members and property of no character. Today, it has 700 members and property valued at $90,000."

I am a bit surprised myself because the Woman's Club of Norfolk, at the time of establishment in 1905, was overwhelmed with such a high number of applications and ended up with two hundred members. How the club had been reduced to a mere fifty-six members in 1920 is unknown; however, it is typical for every club of any kind to lose or gain members annually. By the time Mrs. Naylor ended her presidency, the club had made an enormous jump to seven hundred members in only eleven years. Therefore, Mrs. Naylor had to take credit for it because she was a powerful president with exceptional skills in raising revenue for the club—and making it much more interesting for all members and even non-members.

Or maybe the Martin Mansion attracted members and guests alike with its beauty and its large auditorium. Before the WCN purchased it as a permanent residence, the club had to move at least three times since its establishment in 1905. All those previous houses, close to each other, might have needed to be more significant to hold over two hundred members. Then came the fancy ten-thousand-square-foot new home on Fairfax Avenue, encouraging the colossal increase in club membership. And better yet, the WCN was no longer renting; it now owned the mansion. As a result, the Martin Mansion was an actual "property of character," unlike the previous residences of the WCN.

By 1931, according to Mrs. Frantz Naylor's report, the total cost of the Martin Mansion from 1920 to 1930, without estimation of interest on notes in the bank, was $59,580. The WCN had already made cash payments on the property of $33,580, which is impressive for an all-woman's organization that did not step into the working world. All the money came from the club's activities. Again, the credit went to the shrewd, long-time president, Mrs. Naylor. She brought in dozens of plays, cabarets, quartets, and many other types of entertainment into the spacious auditorium of the Martin Mansion for years. Thus, the revenue skyrocketed, enabling sufficient mortgage payments each time. In addition, the increasing number of members brought in more revenue with their dues.

The Martin Mansion gained so much attention, thanks to Mrs. Naylor's brilliant invention of the annual pilgrimage to Cape

Henry. Celebrities began filing into the foyer to be captivated by its woodwork and mural. Alvah Martin, in his grave, must have raised his head and pursed his lips downward in an impressed gesture. However, he entertained one celebrity of the country's highest rank when he was living in this mansion: U.S. President William Howard Taft. Alvah was a member of Taft's executive committee and persuaded the president "to secure the port of Norfolk as the port of entry for the state of Virginia." But still, Alvah would have been impressed with Mrs. Naylor bringing in a variety of celebrities: Governors of Virginia, governors from other states, city mayors, college presidents, noted authors, foreign musicians, famed playwrights, and even a George Washington descendant into his elegant mansion for three purposes—The Cape Henry Pilgrimage, entertainment, and lectures.

***

The city of Norfolk underwent drastic changes in the 1930s, due to two unfortunate events: one financial and the other natural. After sweeping through the frivolous Roaring Twenties, the nation stopped on the gloomy days of October 1929 as the Wall Street crash caused millions of Americans to lose jobs and be rendered penniless. Like many other cities, Norfolk fired teachers, reduced salaries, and closed city kindergartens. Soup kitchens, itinerants, and shantytowns appeared in the urban landscape, according to the encyclopediavirginia.org article on "The Great Depression in Virginia." Yes, things were unbearable for Virginians, especially for the farmers and urban people hard hit by such a lack of adequate clothing that they had to make garments out of flour bags. Farm income had been cut in half, machinery was now futile, crop fields sat barren, and farmers bartered eggs and whatever crop existed for necessities. Rural people depended on neighbors and relatives for food, whereas urban people of low economic status depended on soup kitchens.

I must compare my husband's rural grandmother and my urban grandmother during the Great Depression. Della Whitten lived in a cabin near Lynchburg, and Katherine Lindsay was living in an upper-scale home in the Algonquin neighborhood in Norfolk. Both grandmothers were affected by the Depression, but Della faced more difficulties and had to walk several miles to the country store to trade eggs and milk for flour and oil needed for her cooking. I do not know how my grandmother Katherine handled the Depression, but she had food. Unlike Della, she did not have to barter or depend on chicken and cows for trade goods. Like most other urbanites, Katherine must have had to put away her automobile in the garage and resort to walking. When Della's daughter Jeanette later handed my husband the only Christmas gift his grandmother had received as a young girl, I knew it was worth keeping and placed it in our china cabinet to be reminded of such hardship Della had to endure before, during, and after the Great Depression. Della only received a brownish-gold Fire King mug filled with hard candies for Christmas; my mother-in-law's note states it was given in 1922 to Della at age nine. Yes, that was long before the Depression, but Della and her family could barely get by, like many other rural people in Virginia. However, Della's struggling background did not dampen her life spirit. She prayed every night with gratitude and talked excessively with enthusiasm until she passed away at age eighty-seven in 2000.

Although my grandmother Katherine did not face as much severity as Della did, she was touched by the Great Depression, remained a devout Democrat, and fought for the betterment of impoverished Virginians, particularly the black ones. Her brother Colgate W. Darden, Jr., shared her sympathetic views and became the Democratic governor of Virginia in 1947 and then president of the University of Virginia for twelve years. Her other brother, Joshua Pretlow Darden, was mayor of Norfolk in 1950, committed to educational opportunities for black Virginians, and supported a site for the future Norfolk State University, a predominantly black college. I will never forget when, on March 22, 1982, my grandmother and I watched the space shuttle Columbia launch on TV, and she ranted, "What a terrible waste of money blasting people off to space instead of helping the poor!" With a heart for the impoverished white and black, my grandmother would have been infuriated if the shuttle take-off had happened during the Great Depression.

The black Virginians, with a large population in Norfolk, were the hardest hit; they were "last hired, first fired" and faced continual discrimination when searching for jobs and relief. Interestingly, they were not as impacted by the crisis as the rest of the population because their poverty had existed for so long that the blacks were "used to hard times anyway." Even so, the Great Depression was bad enough for the starving black children in Suffolk, twenty miles away, to skip school because they had no clothes. The Norfolk Naval Base provided food leftovers to help these children in Suffolk and Portsmouth within proximity.

The state of Virginia was not as severely affected by the Great Depression as the rest of the nation. Therefore, it recovered more quickly because it did not produce automobiles and steel, which took the brunt of the financial meltdown. The economy in Virginia relied on the balance of agriculture, industry, and commerce, the last two of which financed Norfolk. A large portion of the industry was consumer-oriented, producing necessities such as food, clothing, and cigarettes. In addition, Virginia had plenty of fertile lands to grow soybeans, cotton, and tobacco; if that state were in a hot, arid part of the country, the Great Depression would have had a more significant impact on this Commonwealth state, with none of these crops providing relief. Therefore, Virginia saw its recovery already by the middle of the decade.

The Woman's Club of Norfolk must have had to curtail its entertainment and reception activities during the Great Depression; the noise of the Roaring Twenties was now gone, with no foxtrots or melodies emanating from the auditorium. However, the club still had low-key recitals for buoyancy, not the blues. The literature department continued its monthly "Literary Round Table" meetings in which members discussed essays and books for positive mental health, not a letdown. The Junior Woman's Club of Norfolk, which had started in 1928 with daughters and granddaughters of the WCN members, was still active during the Great Depression and continued to sponsor entertainment events, such as a cabaret dance and fashion show on the same night. The Woman's Club of Norfolk knew it had to keep up with the extravaganza even if there was not enough money to spend; it only wanted to maintain high spirits among themselves, juniors, guests, and the community. The one significant thing the club was able to keep was the Martin Mansion, as many woman's clubs across the nation were forced to give up their club homes during the Great Depression. Even so, money was extremely tight for the upkeep of the Martin Mansion. Therefore, on June 24, 1932, the WCN produced and hosted a farce, "44 Flappers," at Blair Junior High School to accommodate as many seats as possible at a low price. That play promised the spirit of "Laugh and the world laughs with you." The farce was successful enough to bring money into the WCN's building fund, as it told an amusing tale about the changing status of women through the ages and as far into the future as 1944.

The Woman's Club of Norfolk was fortunate enough to keep its beloved mansion with the appealing foyer and spacious auditorium; it made a clever financial decision to continue hosting plays, preferably comedies, and to have the Junior Woman's Club of Norfolk take charge of fashion shows, which were becoming increasingly popular. As a result, money still flowed in, although not as much as in the 1920s. But the Woman's Club stayed on 524 Fairfax Avenue instead of being forced to move to a smaller place without an auditorium. As a result, the WCN survived the Great Depression.

All was well with The Woman's Club, with its mortgages being paid, its second-floor tenants staying put, and its occupants continuing club activities. But … there was one thing the mansion would soon have to fear: The major flooding of The Hague after the hurricane.

***

On August 13, 1933, a storm began brewing near the West Coast of Africa and then intensified into a tropical one, packing winds of 70 MPH. A nearby ship signaled the storm, but no advanced technology prepared the inhabitants for its treacherous path. Radio by shipping was the only wind speed report long before the Saffir-Simpson hurricane wind scale began measuring hurricanes into five categories in 1971. However, in 1933, the ships could report the wind speed at 135 to 140 MPH, which would have been classified as Category 4. The powerful hurricane took several days to continue its northwest course, fortunately south of Bermuda, and then weakened somewhat toward the East Coast. Then, on August 23, the Outer Banks in North Carolina, particularly Nags Head, took landfall with 90 MPH winds. A few hours later, this Category 1 hurricane made another landfall on the mainland after crossing the Albemarle Sound. And it continued northwest away from North Carolina, its eye aiming for Norfolk, Virginia, for the first time since 1821. While it could have been worse, the Chesapeake-Potomac Hurricane, as now it was called, did not linger for hours over Norfolk as the 2003 Hurricane Isabel did; it passed over the city only briefly and continued northward near Washington, D.C., Pennsylvania, and New York, weakening into a tropical storm.

It was a miracle the hurricane lost its intensity over the Atlantic Ocean before reaching the East Coast. Imagine Norfolk being pummeled by a Category 4; the city would have been obliterated and submerged entirely. Two days earlier, the Weather Bureau issued a warning to areas from Cape Hatteras to Boston, enough so to encourage the Norfolk Naval Base to secure its ships at port and under shelter. In addition, people were advised to evacuate from Ocean View, Willoughby Spit, and Virginia Beach. Unlike the 1900 Hurricane Isaac in Galveston Bay that went without adequate warning and killed over eight thousand people in its path, the Chesapeake-Potomac hurricane caused only forty-seven fatalities in total. The Norfolk and the Hampton Roads areas (Portsmouth, Virginia Beach, Chesapeake, Suffolk, Hampton, and Newport News) lost eighteen people at most.

The beach cottages in Ocean View, Willoughby Spit, and Virginia Beach were destroyed or swept to sea. The boardwalk at the Ocean Front in Virginia Beach buckled; the wooden amusement rides in Ocean View crashed; barracks in Fort Monroe were lifted off their foundations and banged into each other; and crops in the Suffolk fields were swiped off. The 70 MPH winds, when the hurricane passed over Norfolk, caused severe damage, splintering buildings and uprooting trees.

These days, people say the 1933 hurricane created Willoughby Spit. Not exactly. The massive hurricane in October 1749 raised the Chesapeake Bay by fifteen feet, built up the sand bottom, and made a large sandbar to become a 7.3-mile-long beach. It was where Alvah Martin and his family stayed in their summer cottage 150 years later. Ever since 1749, Willoughby Spit and Ocean View have seen their contours change over the years by coastal storms, northeasters, and hurricanes. The 1933 hurricane caused catastrophic damage to Willoughby Spit, as water reached the ceilings of homes and undoubtedly changed the shape of its beach, but it did not create it, as many people speculate these days.

That hurricane set a record high tide for the Tidewater area: 9.69 feet above normal. Sure enough, downtown Norfolk sustained severe damage and flooded by five feet, as well as The Hague. Someone wrote a part of "The Great Storm of 1933" article for Virginia Commonwealth University:

Huge plate glass windows in downtown Norfolk crashed under the pressure of the wind, showering the walks and streets with glass; awnings and signs were ripped, and large shade trees (easy prey after the record-breaking rain of 6.5 inches the Sunday before) blew over, in many cases carrying electrical and telephone wires with them...The downtown business area was flooded as never seen before. Stores on Granby Street were flooded on the west side, from Atlantic Hotel to Tazewell Street (about four blocks) and for nearly the same distance on the east side, the water being four feet deep on the street floor of many businesses, damaging stocks of goods and fixtures, as well as the structures. Damage to merchandise stored in the warehouses and piers also suffered heavy damage...

There are many photographs of the flooded downtown Norfolk where people sat in their rowboats, kayaks, and canoes, including the one in front of the Monticello Hotel. Black Ford sedans appeared to be stuck with water up to their hoods. One common thing with these people posing for pictures was that they all wore bathing suits. Robert Kelly, the historian for Casemate Museum, wrote, "The uniform of the day was bathing suits. The officer of the day reported in a rowboat."

There is only one photograph showing the flooded Hague about a mile away from downtown Norfolk; it shows evidence of the Elizabeth River pushing all the water into the former Smith's Creek, strong enough to make the semicircle neighborhood unrecognizable. The water overflowed into the Norfolk Museum of Arts and Sciences and Christ and St. Luke's Episcopal Church, making The Hague's west and east ends undetectable. Hence, the neat, curvy Y-shape of The Hague turned into a giant Rorschach blot with water creeping into areas that had been refilled with dirt upon the neighborhood's building in 1890. Stockley Gardens was one, now flooded with trees and shrubs uprooted and blown off.

That only photograph of the flooded Hague shows three women in bathing suits standing waist-high in the water on what appeared to be Mowbray Arch; the young tree trunks submerged about a third of the way up; the water lapping up against the walls of the homes just under the porches. It is unlikely that any of those European-style homes were ever flooded inside the first floor because they were smartly built at least five feet off the ground. Basements, of course, were flood victims, but it could have been worse, especially for The Woman's Club, which was dangerously close to the flooded Hague by only several yards.

Fairfax Avenue had to be soaked, but its rows of homes appeared high enough to avoid such damage. The minutes or any paper written by the members of the Woman's Club of Norfolk did not mention the 1933 hurricane; therefore, it is assumed that their mansion did not sustain any extensive damage. There are a few maybes: One or two trees went down in the yard, the basement flooded by a few feet, and a few windows were broken.

At least the Martin Mansion stayed intact. And the club members must have worn bathing suits for a few days after the storm.

Colonel Samuel Leroy Slover, who lived next door with his wife, Fay, her sister Dorothy, and her son, Frank Batten, must have been extraordinarily busy as a publisher and an owner of *The Virginian-Pilot* and *The Ledger Star* (the evening paper), covering pages with articles and photos on the Chesapeake-Potomac hurricane. Colonel Slover was also busy as a one-year mayor, refinancing the Norfolk economy affected by the Great Depression and then handling the hurricane damage in the city.

The Slover house on Fairfax Avenue was empty at the time of the hurricane since the family was living at their beach cottage in Virginia Beach. Still, they had to endure the unexpected high tide after young Frank Batten, six at the time, alerted everyone at dawn to the ocean surrounding their cottage and its waves breaking against the second floor. Frank and his family escaped to the Cavalier Hotel on the hill. Miraculously, the Slover beach cottage survived because of its foundation on clay, while many other places on flimsy sand were destroyed. Young Frank Batten must have been inclined to remember that terrifying hurricane every single day of his life, leading to his launch of The Weather Channel forty-nine years later! And the Slover's Norfolk house stayed unscathed, much less flooded on the first floor. It helped their home and the Woman's Club to be elevated several feet above the soggy ground while only a few yards from the overflowing Hague. It must have taken many days for the water to recede from Mowbray Arch and expose the semicircle bulkhead again.

***

The Woman's Club of Norfolk began its annual opening season, this time in celebration of its thirtieth anniversary, on October 28, 1935. The guest of honor was the WCN founder, Miss Virginia Gatewood, and she was now in her mid-seventies, still as keen as ever. After ending her WCN presidency in 1920, she moved to the Oceanfront. Over the years, Miss Gatewood had given talks on the "Club Foundation," as she also took charge of the War Camp Community Service and Navy League activities during World War I. She originated armory dances for the war soldiers and veterans at the Norfolk Naval Base.

Then, Miss Gatewood engulfed herself in founding the Women's Municipal League of Virginia Beach, which resembled the WCN in many ways, such as raising money for the fire department or YMCA, hosting benefit dances, and inviting guest speakers. This beach organization primarily focused on beautifying the Oceanfront streets with flower beds, eradicating mosquitoes, and making "a spotless town." So, both Norfolk and Virginia Beach had similar projects and activities, as did other nearby cities. Portsmouth, Suffolk, and Chesapeake had their woman's clubs following the WCN. None of the clubs would have existed if these women were still prohibited from all their liberties, such as voting, and confined to their homes. Jane Croly changed everything for the nation and the world, and Virginia Gatewood changed everything for Norfolk and Tidewater (which is the same as the Hampton Roads since it contains seven cities: Norfolk, Portsmouth, Chesapeake, Suffolk, Virginia Beach, Hampton, and Newport News).

Being the guest of honor at the reception of her former club, Miss Gatewood must have felt honored to see her portrait on the wall, painted a decade earlier. And she was likely impressed with the mansion she had never presided or taken part in since she left five years before the WCN bought it. So, while the WCN was celebrating its thirtieth anniversary, it was celebrating the tenth anniversary of its purchase of the Martin Mansion.

Nothing had changed at the mansion, although furniture and décor came and went. When the WCN moved in, some of the furniture must have been hastily left by the bankrupt Virginia Club. The WCN likely brought in their furniture from the previous residences, and they did move in a group of oil paintings loaned by their owner, Charles Barnett, in 1908. It is believed that many of those paintings depicted landscapes and flower vases. Mr. Barnett was the chairman of the Chesapeake & Ohio Coal and Coke Company and an agent for the Norfolk shipping company. He was often out of town and did not have a permanent residence in Norfolk. When in town, he and his family stayed on Fairfax Avenue with their good friends, Mr. and Mrs. John B. Jenkins. Mr. Barnett had a place at the Old Donation Farm in Virginia Beach and made it clear that the WCN would return his paintings when he felt permanently settled there as a retiree. It would not be until 1938 when the paintings were finally returned to Mr. Barnett after they adorned the walls at the WCN's previous residences for seventeen years and then at the Martin Mansion for thirteen years.

Those oil paintings must have been valuable to where the WCN started paying for fire insurance. Therefore, the club drew up a legal paper to protect itself from future claims. At first, the WCN was dismayed to return Mr. Barnett's paintings after many years of enjoying them and paying fire insurance. And it would be inconvenient to deal with the painting removal marks on the walls, which would require some work. Despite all this, the WCN agreed to return the paintings to the rightful owner, along with a letter of gratitude. Mr. Barnett even paid the expenses of fire insurance and hung his long-loaned paintings at his Old Donation Farm residence. At least Alvah Martin's 360-degree landscape mural was not going anywhere, rightfully owned by the Woman's Club of Norfolk.

When Alvah Martin completed his mansion in 1910, there was little electricity, and all light fixtures, including chandeliers, relied on gas. Since Norfolk had coal shipped to its piers daily, this combustible deposit must have been used to turn into lighting gas at the Martin Mansion. Therefore, the landscape mural eventually would darken due to coal and smoke, only to be cleaned and revamped decades later. When the Woman's Club of Norfolk bought the mansion in 1925, the gas chandeliers were converted to electricity and installed with Thomas Edison's little inventions. Then, by the 1930s, electric light fixtures became the norm. These wise club members would not ever use open candles during one of their large shoulder-to-shoulder parties, much less accidentally burn down Mr. Barnett's paintings. They would now feel safe with the light bulbs over their heads.

The WCN also purchased a much-needed icebox for $250 and agreed to pay five dollars a month in increments. That would have been over $5,400 today, not the money we pay for ours in our modest homes. But the WCN needed a heavy-duty refrigerator for their industrial kitchen that sometimes whipped up three hundred dinner plates at a time. So, the club had to be satisfied seeing their money go into stocking large bulk foods in their new icebox. And that cooking room was no dainty lace little kitchen; Alvah Martin built it quite unattractively, measuring eighteen by twenty feet to accommodate the foot traffic of chefs, butlers, and servants. And maybe he intended for the kitchen to get messy with the laying out of his hunted ducks on its large island table. However, his kitchen did not have to be pretty if it was built to be strictly industrial, and it suited the Woman's Club of Norfolk just fine since this club fed more people than Alvah Martin did—with their countless receptions and luncheons. The WCN had used the kitchen for many of its cooking classes, as in 1929, they hosted a class called "We Serve on a Maid's Night Out."

The one thing the WCN abandoned was the dumbwaiter, or what they called an "elevator," next to the kitchen. The club would not deliver dinner or tea to the tenants on the second floor. The WCN minutes said without offering a reason, "In July 1926, we closed the elevator," not too long after the club moved in. The door to the dumbwaiter was closed on both floors, and the wheel above the shaft rusted. It would be much later when the WCN found a new use for that second-floor alcove by installing a regular refrigerator for the tenants who were not allowed to cook in the kitchen. However, the tenants could still use the kitchen to prepare meals and wash dishes. Only cooking was forbidden, possibly in fear of a gas stove fire. The kitchen had a stairway next to it, and tenants were required to use it during events. This still applies today. Just sneak down the stairs, unseen, past the kitchen, not interfering with the event staff, and finally venture out the back door.

There were five bedrooms on the second floor for tenants, with one room set far back via a long hall and each one of the four rooms on a corner of the square part of the floor. Alvah Martin's office, first on the right from the grand stairway, was the smallest rental, while the other rooms were more extensive. There was a large bathroom between the two rooms; tenants had to share the lavatory, which was common in the old days.

When the WCN bought the Martin Mansion in 1925, the noted pianist Bristow Hardin moved in from the club's previous residence and settled in the most significant room, possibly Alvah and Mamie's bedroom, with a small porch over the front door. Hardin used that room as a music studio, and at one point, he objected to his pupils paying five dollars for an evening piano recital and said there would be no charge if the recital were in his studio. But the WCN board members insisted that some money was needed for electricity, to which Hardin reluctantly agreed. He lived at the WCN's previous residence and then at the Martin Mansion for a long time before opening his music school in downtown Norfolk and then Virginia Beach.

Next came the club members at different times, renting rooms on the second floor for themselves. It is unknown if all the rooms were rented simultaneously, but renting a room or two was an excellent idea for two reasons: Night watch and club revenues.

When building the mansion, Alvah Martin had made a puzzling decision not to have a bathroom on the first floor. Instead, he installed a butler's pantry in a place that would have been perfect for a powder room. Maybe he intended for men to use the toilet in the basement and women to powder their faces up on the second floor, where they would have to walk through his impressive bookcase office to the bathroom. All that changed when the Woman's Club of Norfolk, with a better sense of feminine needs, installed a toilet in the butler's pantry so that members and guests with high heels would not have to worry about trampling down the narrow steps to the basement or climbing up two long sets of stairs to the second floor. From then on, men still had to go down to the cellar, and women straight to the former pantry on the first floor—until in 2018, when the Martin Mansion savers (or heroines, for that matter!) cut the women's restroom in half and graciously offered the other sex its own restroom. Older men would certainly appreciate that.

The Woman's Club offered its auditorium for events unrelated to the club. In 1930, the Cotillon Club rented the auditorium for three nights each month from October to April, paying fifty-five dollars a month and furnishing their maid while the WCN allowed them to use the dishes. John Garland Pollard, governor of Virginia, taught a public affairs course and spoke in the auditorium, eventually leading to the 1933 birth of the Norfolk Forum, a public lecture series. According to the Forum's website, the idea of this nonprofit community organization was to bring to Norfolk four speakers a year "to present to potential members (assumedly the Forum members) a series of lectures from eminent individuals covering cultural, literary, and governmental issues before the nation." Although those quarterly lectures occurred elsewhere, such as the Smith & Welton lobby and the Blair Junior High School auditorium in Norfolk, the WCN auditorium could have been the ideal spot for the Norfolk Forum if not for so many people buying one-dollar tickets, which would cause an overwhelming crowd.

Still, vibrant ninety years later, the Norfolk Forum has obtained notorious speakers such as Gerald Ford, Margaret Thatcher, Art Buchwald, Ken Burns, Sanjay Gupta, and many more. The website says: "The Norfolk Forum is now the country's oldest publicly subscribed speakers' forum. The formula remains simple. It's still the best ticket in town." Still, the WCN's forum back in the 1930s had prominent speakers like Governor Pollard, who focused on history, culture, literature, and government; therefore, it likely generated the idea for the Norfolk Forum.

The Woman's Club of Norfolk offered the city of Norfolk the use of its auditorium for its Night Traffic School for automobile offenders. It is uncertain if the city accepted that offer; if so, the auditorium would have been spacious enough for traffic offenders to practice on the hardwood floor by foot, visualize red lights, and avoid bumping into each other. Then, the WCN extended its offer to the Norfolk community to use the auditorium at a reasonable cost. Unrelated events would take over club activities in that large room: School skits, school dances, nurse graduations, funeral wakes, birthday parties, private cocktail parties, youth religious concerts, and most of all, wedding receptions.

***

The day after Easter 1937, the Woman's Club of Norfolk realized they needed help washing stacks of dishes in the kitchen. Hence, they hired Kinchen Anthony, a jovial thirty-year-old African-American man. It is unknown whether he was asked off the street or by recommendation. Mr. Anthony did the dishwashing job accordingly and was paid promptly. It was uncertain to this young man whether that job was temporary or permanent, but then he realized no one ever told him to leave, so he stayed to greet members and guests at the door almost daily.

Years later, *The Virginian-Pilot* identified him as "Kinchen Anthony" since it was his legal name; however, the WCN minutes did it the other way around. Therefore, he was known as "Anthony" at the mansion and did not seem to mind that. He became a butler with a clean white shirt, black bow tie, and black trousers. The WCN members let Anthony do whatever he wanted to keep guests content and the mansion in tip-top shape. It was unlikely that the ladies ever gave Anthony a list of chores since he took it upon himself to correct a lopsided painting, wipe the missed corner of dust off the table, empty an ashtray, and fluff a smashed bridal bow. Anthony was his own boss and did a magnificent job at The Woman's Club—for thirty-eight years. He became known as "Anthony the Butler" to the Norfolk community.

So, on that post-Easter Monday, a young man from the small town of Tarboro in North Carolina began his quickly acquired job of unknown status, temporary or permanent, in the kitchen with stacks of dirty dishes in a house full of ladies who did not even think of telling him to come back or not to come back. However, those ladies would eventually embrace Anthony as their own, so that job was permanent, a very long one.

Chapter Five

In 1940, the Woman's Club of Norfolk reached its thirty-fifth year, having survived the Great Depression and keeping the Martin Mansion. This decade would give the WCN more involvement with the General Federation of Women's Clubs, which has done a tremendous job of making the world a better place in the past 133 years. When I joined the Woman's Club of Norfolk in 2016, it was my first time learning of this umbrella organization known as the "GFWC" in all the WCN documents and brochures. Honestly, for a while, I did not pay much attention to the GFWC or what it did as a general federation until I began researching it for this book in the fall of 2022. Indeed, I was floored by the incredible power of this international organization, which, at its height in the 1950s, consisted of 12,000,000 members and over 16,000 affiliated clubs in America and in sixty countries. Therefore, the General Federation of Women's Clubs will be mentioned here frequently from now on. But first, I will explain the histories of GFWC and the state federation, which have been a crucial part of the Woman's Club of Norfolk as well.

The Woman's Club of Norfolk joined the General Federation of Women's Clubs in 1914 after several years of belonging to the state federation of Virginia. There was a difference between the national and state federations of women's clubs regarding politics. In 1907, the GFWC Council met in Norfolk to coincide with the Jamestown Exposition, joined by several woman's clubs from Virginia. That prompted Alice Kyle, president of the Woman's Club of Lynchburg, and Elizabeth

Gish, chairman of the club's State Federation Committee, to develop an idea of forming a federation of clubs in Virginia. The Woman's Club of Lynchburg, about 190 miles away in the mountains, invited existing clubs in Virginia to attend a convention on May 16, 1907, at the Lynchburg YMCA—to form the Virginia Federation of Women's Clubs with a membership of ten clubs and almost seven hundred women. The Woman's Club of Norfolk became a member right then but had not joined the national federation since that fledgling club considered some of the GFWC's policies too liberal. It took seven years for the WCN to finally join the GFWC while it stayed with the state federation, now known as the GFWC Virginia.

Founded by Jane Croly in 1890 and chartered by Congress in 1901, the GFWC acted as an umbrella organization where woman's clubs could gather and discuss common issues and work together to implement social and political changes on the local, state, and national levels. Twenty years after its establishment, the GFWC had more than one million members in affiliated clubs on the local level and in state federations of women's clubs. Miss Virginia Gatewood, Mrs. Frantz Naylor, and other presidents of the Norfolk organization traveled to the GFWC's biennial conventions in different locations, particularly in Washington, D.C., and New York City. Then, these presidents came home to lay out new ideas to improve or resolve matters such as civil service reform, public education, pure food and drugs, child labor, juvenile justice, and public health.

The GFWC had done quite a bit in the 1920s and 1930s for the entire nation by "supporting the work of the Women's

Bureau within the Department of Labor, backing passage in 1921 of the federal Sheppard-Towner Infancy and Maternity Protection Act to promote the health and welfare of mothers and infants, creating an Indian Welfare Committee, and protesting the New Deal's National Recovery Act that allowed lower wage rates for women workers and exempted handicapped and home workers from its protections," as stated by the GFWC entry on the Encyclopedia website.

Besides President Theodore Roosevelt, the GFWC was a driving force behind founding America's first national parks and supported the creation of the National Park Service. As early as 1896, the GFWC became an advocate for green spaces and created the Forestry Committee, which eventually became what is known today as the Conservation Committee. When trees were cut down in magnitude for timber, the three women from the GFWC became leaders in fighting deforestation and securing the legislation that formed the National Park Service (NPS). Mrs. Lovell White spearheaded the fight to protect California's Big Trees and collected 1.5 million signatures petitioning Congress to save those majestic redwoods, garnering interest from President Roosevelt. Secondly, Alta McDuffie of New Hampshire led the GFWC fundraising campaign to raise ten thousand dollars that preserved over six thousand acres in the White Mountain National Forest and saved Franconia Notch from development. Lastly, Mary King Sherman, known as "The National Park Lady," advocated establishing the NPS and was dedicated to preserving the American wilderness. Sherman also lobbied for the creation of Rocky Mountain National Park in 1915 and campaigned for

Grand Canyon National Park.

Concerned for human rights, the GFWC encouraged federal support for the United Nations and campaigned for seatbelts in all cars, lights on neighborhood streets, and accurate labeling of food and medications. America could and can never do without the GFWC and all the woman's clubs affiliated with that umbrella organization. In the 1930s, the American Library Association credited the GFWC with establishing 75 percent of America's public libraries, as those woman's clubs founded 474 free public libraries and 4,655 traveling libraries. Indeed, the GFWC is credited for the idea of bookmobiles and continues today to support America's public libraries.

In 1934, the GFWC began a ten-year study to review the question of the Equal Rights Amendment (ERA), which was first drafted in 1923 by two suffrage movement leaders, Alice Paul and Crystal Eastman. Now that the Nineteenth Amendment had been ratified in 1920 to allow women to the ballot, the ERA was "a proposed amendment to the U.S. Constitution that would invalidate many state and federal laws that discriminate against women; its central underlying principle is that sex should not determine the legal rights of men or women." However, the GFWC was cautious not to delve too much into politics while dedicated to community improvement by enhancing women's lives through volunteer service; therefore, it did not adopt a resolution supporting the Equal Rights Amendment until 1944, after completing a ten-year study.

Likewise, the GFWC had been hesitant to include suffrage in its efforts at the turn of the twentieth century, and it lost members to the National Women Suffrage Association. In 1910, the GFWC finally supported this hottest topic within its organization, and its membership tremendously increased. The same applied to the long-delayed adoption of the Equal Rights Amendment by the GFWC, which began to see heavy membership by the mid-1940s.

Admittedly, not one woman's organization can do without politics unless it is knitting or cooking. Neither can the GFWC. After fighting so hard for their rights since the progressive movement, the women knew it would not be wise to stay silent toward any poignant (or important) issue on a local, state, or national level if they could now speak for themselves without being forced back into their kitchens.

Now that it was the beginning of the 1940s, which were expected to be turbulent due to World War II, it was fortunate that women already knew the importance of including politics in their organizations. They had learned valuable lessons from World War I and its effects on their communities. Of course, we understand that Jane Croly first did not want to include politics, including suffrage, in her Sorosis club since the empowerment of women and volunteerism were the main goals. But then, as time went on, a little bit of politics was thrown into obviously every woman's club across the nation on separate occasions. World War I seemed to have pushed the inclusion of politics in the feminine world, mainly the Woman's Club of Norfolk.

For instance, the WCN knew it could not only knit wool caps for the soldiers but also had to fight for better care of injured war veterans. No wonder the WCN invited politicians and professors to lecture on politics affected by World War I. And no wonder it had its current events department bring up the condition of the U.S. economy, the severity of child labor, the high costs of living in Norfolk, and many, many other serious issues that could not be silenced. The bottom line is that women HAD to get involved in politics if they wanted to fight for the betterment of society affected by war, poverty, disease, crime, and repression. Not only that, but also for improving conservation and nature, which were political topics. According to The UnCommonwealth website, when World War I was only two months into action, Robert Walton Moore, a member of the National Council of Defense, stated that in Virginia, the women were "much more completely aroused than the men are" and credited Virginia's women with the patriotism, economy, and energy necessary to win. He said, "We should unhesitatingly give them our emphatic approval and support," considering how much women contributed to their state and country.

So, women were more prepared to deal with politics, this time around with another world war. Undoubtedly, they would push harder in the 1940s and even get involved *physically* if they had to. It all started on December 7, 1941, when Pearl Harbor was attacked, and President Franklin Roosevelt declared war on Japan. Of course, the entire nation would be affected in every aspect. Still, one town in America would be hardest hit by World War II: Norfolk, Virginia—the site of the world's most extensive naval base. Clearly, the Woman's Club of Norfolk, the GFWC, and other women's organizations would be very busy in the next few years.

***

The history of Norfolk Naval Base started with the Jamestown Exposition in 1907 when highly ranking naval officials visited Norfolk to celebrate the three-hundredth anniversary of the English settlement in America. They looked at the site of Sewell's Point and thought it had the potential to be a naval base. That site was sheltered from the Atlantic Ocean but still had wide, passable channels for the ships to maneuver back and forth between Norfolk and the ocean. The same applied to planes that could fly over Chesapeake Bay straight out to sea and vice versa. The convenience of the site motivated visiting officers to encourage funds to purchase 474 acres, and they succeeded two years later. Thus, the Naval Station Norfolk, as it was called back then, was born. Even today, the base names could be more precise since some insist on the original name, Norfolk Naval Station, while others call it Norfolk Naval Base. A third name exists as well: Norfolk Operating Base (NOB), referring to the airfield. As a native Norfolkian, I call it "the naval base" or just "the base."

World War I first activated the world's most extensive base, with thirty-four thousand enlisted men and a new airfield at its site. Then, the base expanded in the next thirty years. At the time of the Pearl Harbor attack, Norfolk and San Diego were the nation's only two naval supply depots. Norfolk had everything needed for the base on its abundant land on the water, including existing facilities, long piers, runways, and fields. Thus, the Norfolk Naval Base had the potential for further expansion, a significant boom this time.

By 1941, ten thousand recruits were trained, sixteen thousand officers were enlisted on the site, and fourteen thousand sailors departed on ships from Norfolk. Then, after Pearl Harbor, the base added another 5,500 sailors and provided a variety of Allied forces. What turned Norfolk Naval Base into the largest naval base in the world was the existence of seventy-five ships alongside fourteen piers, 134 airplanes, and eleven aircraft hangars, as they still exist today. The base was prepared for four years of a brutal war on both sides of the world, the Pacific and in Europe—by air and sea from the hangers and piers on the Chesapeake Bay.

WWII caused Norfolk's sudden increase twofold in its population in a short period. Hundreds of sailors, military families, defense workers, and construction workers moved into the city. Because the naval base needed a rapid rise in employment to accommodate its overwhelming military population, Norfolk became a nonstop working machine with expanding industries and shipyards. Its people became so congested that new residences, apartment buildings, and barracks were quickly built across Norfolk and other Hampton Roads cities. Even the open area across The Hague from Mowbray Arch had temporary barracks. To meet the increasing demands, the U.S. Housing Authority (USHA) spent nearly two million dollars on its project to house military families at the Norfolk Naval Base. Those newly built five hundred units in Merrimack Village included single-story detached dwellings, two-family homes, two-story group houses, and apartments. The construction workers, many of whom came from North Carolina and other states, began living in campers and trailers in Ocean View, not too far from the naval base.

The sudden rise of industry and occupation might have helped Norfolk's economy during the wartime boom; however, this city had one thing to worry about: Its reputation as a dirty vice city teeming with brothels, tattoo parlors, and run-down bars. These were what sailors wanted for respite from their supposedly suffocating ships at the Norfolk Naval Base. The growing economy first drew blue-collar workers, merchants, and women from other areas to Norfolk to earn a better living. However, it would not be easy for some women to find regular employment; therefore, many resorted to prostitution. The Hampton Roads Naval Museum history website states that prostitution in the city meant that "Norfolk became nationally known in the early years of the war as a city of rampant vice with few redeeming qualities." The rise in prostitution put pressure on local law enforcement enough to gain attention from national media outlets. The federal government recognized this problematic vice in Norfolk, called it a "crisis," and offered aid to curtail rising prostitution. But it was still not easy for the Norfolk police to catch all the unlawful activities because the vice was widespread throughout the city, in hidden dwellings, slums, and desolate hotels.

***

As the war loomed, the Japanese fought to control Asia and captured some colonies, such as Malaya (now Peninsular Malaysia) and the Dutch East Indies (now Indonesia). That was unfortunate because those two colonies were leading rubber producers, and the Japanese takeover decimated America's rubber supply by over 90 percent. South America, also a rubber producer, could have supplied America to compensate for the loss, but cargo ships were needed for military purposes. Hence, there was a severe rubber shortage across America, affecting not only car drivers but also homemakers. There was not enough to make gloves, raincoats, baby pants, girdles, hot water bottles, bathing caps, garden hoses, and toys. The military had to take the remaining rubber for vehicle and aircraft tires, pontoon bridges, gas and oxygen masks, medical equipment, boots, raincoats, shoes, and even erasers.

Since civilians could purchase only five tires during the four-year war, they were encouraged to drive less. This brought in nationwide gasoline rationing to protect tires. Tires tended to wear out at 60 MPH; therefore, a "Victory Speed" of 35 mph was instituted to reduce the wear by half. Slow and steady turns were instructed to avoid wear on treads. Everyone was encouraged to use public transportation, share rides, and avoid rough roads. My mom, Indie Bain Lindsay, had to relinquish daily transportation to Maury High School, five miles away from her home, and began to stay every week with her aunts Annie and Mamie in Ghent, within walking distance of the school. She returned to her neighborhood, Algonquin Park, every Friday afternoon for the weekend. That suited Mom perfectly well because she had friends in Ghent and The Hague. She graduated from Maury in 1944, a year before the war ended, and majored in history at Sweet Briar College, four hours away. She later recounted the story to my brothers and me many times, calling the gas rationing the "smartest thing that ever happened in America."

***

The Woman's Club of Norfolk continued its usual activities during World War II, inviting college professors, authors, and politicians to speak at their meetings. In addition, the club continued recitals, card games, dances, and other events in the auditorium. However, an increasing number of poets, primarily from Norfolk, spoke at the WCN. John Richard Moreland, a local poet, explained that poetry was needed at the time since it was an emotional phase for everyone affected by World War II. As the John Hopkins Medicine website points out, poetry is "the healing word" and "can provide comfort and boost mood during stress, trauma, and grief. Its powerful combination of words, metaphor, and meter helps us better express ourselves and make sense of the world and our place in it." Moreland read his war poems that resonated with both defeat and victory; some of these included "Sea Burial," "I Know a Valley, Green and Wide," and "How Victory Will Come." *The Virginian-Pilot*, still industrious since its establishment in 1898, published short articles about poets reading at the Woman's Club of Norfolk, among many other war stories.

Like other clubs across America, the Woman's Club of Norfolk became heavily involved in the civilian defense program, which coordinated state and federal measures to protect civilians in a war-related emergency. The WCN did not act alone; it cooperated with other woman's clubs to meet goals. For example, Mrs. R. G. Boatwright, the president of the General Federation of Women's Clubs of Virginia (GFWC Virginia), urged all the members across the state to donate fifty cents to buy one ambulance for the Red Cross. The response exceeded the goal, and two, instead of one, ambulances were purchased! The club members were also encouraged to prepare for air raids, especially over Norfolk Naval Base. They learned the method of blackouts that suggested heavy black curtains, cardboard, or even black paint to cover windows and doors at night. All this prevented any glimmering light that might help direct the enemy aircraft.

The Virginian-Pilot stated in April 1943 that Mrs. J. D. Odell, the president of the WCN, encouraged members to work with the War Price and Ration Board by agreeing to reduce common goods in their homes, such as butter, sugar, and canned milk. These goods needed to be diverted to the war effort. Mrs. Odell organized card games to raise war bonds and encouraged members to sew for the Red Cross. The WCN members also filled 150 Christmas stockings for the U.S.O service, opened its Martin Mansion to the servicemen for reading, writing, and other relaxing activities, and served supper to service members at the U.S.O. building in downtown Norfolk. Club members were encouraged to collect wedding dresses throughout the city for brides before their loved ones went off to war. They planted fruits and vegetables at their private residences and public parks for the Victory Garden program, using rationing stamps and cards to reduce pressure on the food supply. The Woman's Club of Norfolk did everything it could to help the service members and the community stricken by the four-year war.

Three weeks after the Pearl Harbor attack, Congresswoman Edith Nourse Rogers of Massachusetts introduced a bill to establish a Women's Army Auxiliary Corps (WAAC). President Franklin D. Roosevelt signed the bill and set a recruitment goal of 25,000 women for the first year. But that goal was unexpectedly exceeded, so Secretary of War Henry L. Stimson increased the limit by authorizing the enlistment of 150,000 women volunteers. These women worked in various positions much needed during the war: medical care professionals, welfare workers, clerical workers, cooks, messengers, military postal employees, chauffeurs, and telephone and telegraph operators. Just then, the blue-and-yellow posters began popping up everywhere: Rosie the Riveter showed off her bicep and said, "We Can Do It!"

Two years later, the Women's Army Auxiliary Corps changed its name to the Women's Army Corps (WAC). That was after Mrs. Edith Rogers introduced additional bills to allow the enlistment and commissioning of women in the U.S. Army, or Reserve forces, instead of regular enlistments in the U.S. Army. That would drop the "auxiliary" status of the WAAC, allow women to serve overseas, and "free a man to fight," as the history section of the U.S. Army website states. The positions in WAC expanded to airplane and radio mechanics, weather forecasters, electrical specialists, sheet metal workers, and many others left by men. The women, many in uniform, were so productive that

General Douglas MacArthur called them "My best Soldiers," saying that the women serving in the Women's Army Corps “worked harder, complained less, and were better disciplined than many of my male Soldiers.”

Early on, the Woman’s Club of Norfolk recruited women for the WAAC after being encouraged by Mrs. J.L.B. Buck of Richmond, the vice president of the state federation. There was an urgent need for WAACs all over the country, and Virginia’s goal was thirteen hundred. So, the WCN set up a committee for the WAAC recruitment and had members volunteer at department stores, which proved to be the perfect place to find competent women. The voluntary duty was to find a shopper, put a stethoscope or a telephone connector in her hand, and encourage her out the door with the promise of self-empowerment.

There was an incredibly admirable action the General Federation of Women’s Clubs undertook for the war efforts: It initiated a “Buy A Bomber” campaign that succeeded exponentially—the entire nation was astounded that a woman’s organization would even consider supporting planes that dropped treacherous bombs. Mrs. John Whitehurst, the GFWC president at the time, applauded the idea for a “Buy A Bomber” campaign and quoted, “The women of the country are alarmed because we haven’t gotten after Japan. We want to go after Japan and give her a good bombing.” The campaign took off like a rocket. The GFWC clubwomen assisted with war bonds, as did the state federations. The Woman’s Club of Norfolk also helped raise bonds through card games. GFWC sold war bonds worth $101,617,750 to buy bombers and $154,459,132 to purchase planes—enough money for 431 planes! Next, $90,794,182 was raised for Victory Loans. State federations provided $234,834 in scholarships and $46,601 in loans to train nurses. The Federation recruited over six thousand young women for the Cadet Nurse Corps. Over 4,500 Juniors enlisted in the various services established for women. Such an impressive feat of all the woman's clubs!

The Junior Woman's Club of Norfolk took credit for raising plenty of war bonds and stamps by selling in booths at department stores and hosting fashion shows. *The Virginian-Pilot* was impressed enough to publish an article titled "Junior Women Go Over the Top" and explained that preteen and teen members had already sold bonds and stamps worth almost five thousand dollars, exceeding their goal. Along with the other Junior Woman's clubs in the state, the Norfolk club was selling bonds to buy a fighter/pursuit plane for seventy-five thousand dollars, which was spectacular for such young girls who were not even old enough to drive.

The U.S. military was so grateful for all the women raising money to buy its much-needed fleet of planes and bombers that it emblazoned the names of women's club federations on these aircraft.

***

My mom, Indie Bain (later shortened to just Indie), felt that something about the war in Europe was nagging at her mind: the severity of the Holocaust. Like many other Americans, she had known about the kidnappings and murders of European Jews since 1942 from news reports, but not of such enormous magnitude. Although the intelligence had early on learned of the Nazis' plan to eradicate all the Jews, the American people could not imagine Germany committing mass murder of Jews and other civilians. In late 1944, most Americans finally realized that the German atrocities at concentration camps were not "rumors." At the war's end, the world learned the truth about six million Jews being murdered. But my mom had a strange feeling all along that the news reports were not telling as much as they should. She would disagree with a newspaper article that considered the Holocaust a rumor and ask her mother if the Nazis were carrying out their plan of Jew eradication at concentration camps. My grandmother, Katherine Lindsay, did not believe in the Holocaust's severity because of the lessons she learned during the First World War, when atrocity propaganda was widespread. Stories of German soldiers mutilating Belgian babies were fictionalized by the British belligerents who wanted to provoke anger and promote the war effort. The allegations of such atrocity propaganda were proved by the postwar investigations in Europe. My grandmother never forgot that. Ironically, she was the same age during World War I as her daughter, Indie Bain, during World War II. Their teenage years were indeed not without world catastrophes.

Mom became news-oriented during WWII, prompting her to major in history at Sweet Briar College. She liked to brag to my brothers and me that she started reading newspapers at age fifteen, the year Japan attacked Pearl Harbor. Every afternoon around 4:30, when my brothers and I were growing up, she stepped out to fetch *The Ledger Star*, the evening newspaper of *The Virginian-Pilot*, and read away. Then, Mom would ask us to be quiet at 6:30 PM, so she and Dad could watch Walter Cronkite on TV. The last time I visited ninety-four-year-old Mom before she contracted COVID-19, which led to her passing three months later, she sat with the narrower and thinner *The Virginian-Pilot* on her lap and asked in an always stern tone, "Have you read the paper today?" She spent nearly eighty years gluing herself to the newspapers, including *The New York Times*, and her intensity started with the Holocaust reports. Mom was a thinker, a speculator, an observer, and a realist. She knew.

***

Like many other cities across America, Norfolk celebrated the end of World War II on August 16, 1945, with thousands of sailors and citizens piling onto the streets, especially Granby Street. The Nazis had lost in April that year, and Japan surrendered after the bombings of Hiroshima and Nagasaki five months later. The "Buy A Bomber" campaign activated by the General Federation of Women's Clubs had certainly paid off. The Martin Mansion on 524 Fairfax Avenue had graciously provided space for a flurry of voluntary activities to pursue war relief efforts. Women had been a tremendous help during World War II, even off the battlefields, and the "Mother of Women's Clubs," Jane Croly, would have said in her grave, "I told you so."

There was one powerful war story in Norfolk with which others cannot compete even today. Although this story is irrelevant to the book's main subjects, The Woman's Club of

Norfolk and the Martin Mansion, I must include it here. My long-time friend, Bobby Garris, has attended The Woman's Club many times for parties, like almost everyone else in Norfolk. And his late parents, Robert and Travis, must have celebrated at wedding receptions and cocktail parties there as well. Most of all, they were true Norfolkians, and I will tell Bobby's verbal version of his dad's story. It was one of the installments I put in the 2017 history book for our church, The Episcopal Church of the Good Shepherd, during its hundredth anniversary. When I posted this installment on Facebook in February 2017, there were hundreds of likes and dozens of shares, leading to over three thousand views. A beautifully touching story that happened on Christmas Day, 1945...

GOOD SHEPHERD RECEIVED A HUGE SURPRISE DURING ITS CHRISTMAS MORNING SERVICE THAT BROUGHT THE ENTIRE CONGREGATION TO CHEERS AND TEARS: THE HOMECOMING OF A WWII SOLDIER, ROBERT E. GARRIS.

A Norfolk native living on Shirland Avenue just across from Good Shepherd, Robert had to give up UVA law school to join the Navy when World War II first started. He underwent military training at Northwestern University and was promoted to Naval Reserve in January 1942. He served on the destroyer in Europe and then became a skipper of his LST (Landing Ship, Tank) in 1943. That brought Robert to the Philippines. He stayed in the South Pacific until the war ended but had to wait a few more months to bring his ship back to America.

Robert arrived in San Francisco in early December 1945 and learned that the Naval Transportation Office could not send him home for Christmas and would have to wait until January. But Robert was not one to give up. While he devised a Plan B to get home much sooner, Robert enjoyed going out every night with his best childhood friend, Edward W. Wolcott, who was stationed in San Francisco then. Still trying to get home for Christmas, Robert approached Union Pacific Railroad and asked for a ticket but failed. He called his parents, Jack and Margaret Garris, every day to say, "No ticket today." He then had an idea and asked the lady who worked for the railroad to lunch, handing her a bouquet. As luck would have it, on December 23, the lady gave Robert a train ticket. He ran to his quarters, grabbed his duffle bag, and tried to call his parents, but they were not home.

So ... Robert began his journey across the country to Chicago, where everyone parted. Unfortunately, there was no train to Norfolk. Refusing to give up, Robert took a cab to Chicago O'Hare Airport. Still, there was nothing for him; it was 11 p.m. on Christmas Eve. But then Robert heard the intercom: "Special Military Only on one plane to Washington, D.C. First come, first served." He ran fast to the gate and was second in line, and the plane was quickly filling up. Luckily, that same plane took off from D.C. to Norfolk, so Robert no longer had to devise an alternative plan to get home. He landed in his homeland at 8 AM on Christmas Day. Just in time! Robert was going to call his parents, but all the phones at the airport were being used. So, he took a cab to his house on Shirland Avenue.

Robert was excited to surprise his family, but the front

door was locked, and no one was home. He slumped on the doorstep, exhausted and sleepy. He had not shaved, bathed, or even taken off his uniform since he departed from San Francisco two days earlier. But then ... Robert heard the music from Good Shepherd and slowly got up and walked two hundred feet to the church. His two sisters sang in the choir, and his brother was already home from the war.

The Reverend George Purnell Gunn was ready to give a sermon. He was very close to the Garris family since he, his wife, and their two young boys had received room and board at the Garris house for six months after a short stint in Atlanta in 1943. At the time, Good Shepherd was looking to purchase a home for the returning minister. Robert's mother, Margaret, had helped the Rev. Mr. Gunn in many ways, being the pillar of the church. So, when Mr. Gunn stepped up to the pulpit to give the Christmas morning sermon, Robert walked in by the side and quietly sat down on the pew. The Rev. Mr. Gunn looked up, ready to speak, glimpsed Robert in his uniform, and stood paralyzed. He was too stunned to utter a word. It was dead quiet. Of course, the congregation was puzzled by Mr. Gunn's strange behavior and followed his eyes to Robert. They erupted into cheers and tears, especially Robert's entire family. Even the Rev. Mr. Gunn stopped the service because he was too emotional to go on. Margaret, the exuberant mother, invited the whole congregation to her house across the street for an impromptu party. Robert finally achieved his dream of being home for Christmas!

***

While the war was going on, on April 30, 1942, the Woman's Club of Norfolk organized a tea party for two hundred members and guests, honoring Constance DuPont Darden. At the time, "Connie" Darden was the First Lady of Virginia, as her husband, Colgate Whitehead Darden, had been inaugurated as governor four months earlier. Mr. Darden, my great-uncle and my grandmother's brother, was a moderately conservative Democrat who insisted on keeping his inauguration low-key during the beginning phase of World War II. He achieved this by reducing the costs of the ceremony, canceling the traditional military parade and nineteen-gun salute to conserve ammunition, not using the governor's automobile, and walking or taking public transportation whenever possible.

Having served as an ambulance driver and then a fighter pilot twenty-five years earlier in World War I, Uncle Colgate knew that his governorship had to be as modest as possible during another world war. However, he reorganized Virginia's civil defense, reformed Virginia's penal system, and created a pension plan for state employees and teachers. He also eliminated the state debt and created a surplus allocated to vocational schools, colleges, hospitals, and other public services.

Connie Darden, an heiress of the DuPont Company in Wilmington, Delaware, was never flamboyant and treated others just the same, not as if she were married to the governor of Virginia. I remember her as a remarkable lady, a violin player, and a bird-watcher. Therefore, it did not surprise me when I read the article in *The Virginian-Pilot* about her 1942 visit to the Woman's Club as the First Lady of Virginia in a plain long dress, where she gave a talk on several civic topics, notably the Red Cross, and even allowed the club members to practice splinting her arm. In later years, Connie returned to the Martin Mansion many times for our Thanksgiving gatherings with Alvah Martin's descendants. My father-in-law, Kyle Cyrus, once sat next to Connie in her late nineties and chatted at the dining table while the carved wooden dogs on the fireplace mantle watched over them. Kyle had no idea about Connie being a DuPont until we arrived home. He gaped open his mouth and remarked that his seatmate was a lovely, simple lady with no flashiness. She sure was. Connie had an enormous heart for the public—and birds. She taught neighborhood children the thrill of bird-watching, sent many poor people to college, and almost always anonymously donated to local causes. Humble enough to let the Woman's Club members practice applying the splints on her in a long dress!

***

The archives of the Woman's Club of Norfolk reported a fire in the basement on April 7, 1945, without specifying the cause. There is not much information on the fire, which started in the basement, ignited under the front and rear porches, and caused considerable damage to one of the basement rooms. The culprit could have been an old water heater or fuse box. At least the fire department responded fast enough to prevent significant damage, and there was no water or smoke damage on the first floor, which would have devastated the valuable woodwork and landscape mural. Anthony the Butler must have been terrified since he used the basement to prepare for work or take a break. He would have been too smart to cause a careless fire accident, much less smoke in a barely ventilated area. *The Virginian-Pilot* did not report the fire, even though it sent a fire truck to such a well-known historic mansion on Fairfax Avenue. But, at any rate, The Woman's Club still stood firm, and the activities continued.

***

With its inner beauty, the Martin Mansion could never do without Christmas decorations and, therefore, found itself the favorite spot in the neighborhood for holiday parties, even toward the turn of the twenty-first century. Alvah Martin, the original owner of this Georgian Revival mansion, must have thrown parties, given the fortune he spent beautifying the first floor. Since his last child, Dorothy, was seven when they moved into the new mansion, Alvah must have hosted a fancy Christmas party yearly and even hired a Santa Claus impersonator to entertain little Dorothy. Then the Virginia Club, as the next owner of the Martin Mansion for only five years, must have thrown Christmas parties as well, maybe a tad rowdy to enthrall the bourbon-loving men and their champagne-loving lady friends.

The Christmas parties probably toned down a little bit with the arrival of the Woman's Club of Norfolk in 1925. They began hosting an annual Christmas Party for female residents of the Mary Ludlow Home, Lydia Roper Home, and Ballantine Home. All these homes provided for homeless Norfolk women, widowed women, and older women without families. This holiday tradition continued in the 1940s and appeared to lighten the moods of guests during WWII.

The Mary Ludlow Home's history began during the

yellow fever epidemic. Mary Ludlow became a widow after her husband and two of their children perished from yellow fever in 1855. This epidemic hit Norfolk and Portsmouth via the Elizabeth River coastal waterway between those two cities. Yellow fever, brought in by affected mosquitoes on a ship from overseas, killed three thousand people in Norfolk and about a thousand in Portsmouth. Mary Ludlow then married the American-born nephew of the Baron von Zollikofer of Austria-Hungary. During their trip to Europe, Dr. Zollikofer learned he was next in line to inherit the title, and when the old, childless Baron died, he rejected the crown and declared his desire to stay in America. But while they were still in Europe, Dr. Zollikofer unexpectedly passed away, leaving Mary Ludlow to become a new baroness. She never returned to America and enjoyed living a life of royalty until she died in 1907. She left between $100,000 to 150,000 to start a home for older women in Norfolk. The Mary Ludlow Home then accepted homeless women, as did the Lydia Roper Home after it opened in 1921 in honor of Mrs. Roper, dedicated to her service of women widowed by the Civil War. Thomas Ballentine established a home for older adults in memory of his deceased wife in 1896 and insisted in his will that the Mary F. Ballentine Home be considered a "home" rather than an "institution." Mr. Ballentine had a heart for homeless women as well. In fifteen years, he and the city of Norfolk had seen thousands of women who lost their husbands to yellow fever and the Civil War, rendering these women homeless.

The Woman's Club of Norfolk understood the history of

the homes whose residents could use some holiday cheer at the Martin Mansion. So, the club members picked up the party guests from the Mary Ludlow Home on Pembroke Avenue, the Lydia Roper Home on 40th Street, and the Ballentine Home on Park Avenue. And ferried them to 524 Fairfax Avenue for an afternoon of entertainment with Christmas carols and cookies. Anthony the Butler greeted the party guests at the front door, dressed in a brilliant beige butler's suit. He had been at the Martin Mansion for a decade, now in the late 1940s, with no intention of leaving anytime soon. He liked telling people how he ended up at The Woman's Club: "I was hired as a dishwasher on Easter Monday. No one told me not to come back, and I have been here ever since…."

According to a few articles in *The Virginian-Pilot* over the years, the WCN's "annual Yule Party" showcased spectacular holiday decorations throughout the mansion. Unfortunately, there were only descriptions of holiday decor, not their locations inside the mansion, as the newspaper often only used the term "club room." But I can imagine where a "large Christmas tree" was in the West Wing Parlor because it is the only room that has the characteristics of an American living room: No wood trimmings or "coffers" on its ceiling or wall paneling made of dark oak. It has the best sunlight of all the rooms, and the tinsels on the Christmas tree could use some sparkling from the sun's rays. In addition, a stern painting of Miss Virginia Gatewood in the West Wing Parlor could use some holiday cheer from the tree adorned with vintage glass ornaments, crocheted angel ornaments, and maybe a few red Elves on the Shelf. A 1949 article in *The*

Virginian-Pilot gave an interesting description of an upcoming Christmas party at the Martin Mansion:

The program will be centered around a Christmas tree, decorated with old-fashioned, home-made articles and goodies, which will be taken to the Municipal Hospital for distribution among the older Negro patients. ... A part of the decorations will be a crèche with lifelike figures in the club library. The Art Department has arranged this. ... The music and drama divisions of the Fine Arts Department have arranged the club's old-fashioned Christmas celebration. ...

The other rooms at the Martin Mansion must have had holiday decorations, especially in the more manly East Wing Parlor, which probably had green garlands of pine or fir draped over its fireplace and a smaller Christmas tree in the corner. The grand stairway had to have garlands twirled over its handrails and a massive red bow tied around its primary newel post. Poinsettias must have adorned the foyer, where the walls had to be left undecorated because of the landscape mural. And the dining room, with its table taking over most of the space, must have had long candles on the fireplace mantle without obscuring the rare wooden dogs. Finally, the auditorium had to have a Christmas tree on its elevated platform to provide room for party guests to mingle or dance on the open floor.

Whatever the holiday decorations the Martin Mansion had, it had to be glorious. The front door was the first to welcome people inside for the Christmas carols or egg nog punch with its massive green wreath and magnolia garlands. To this day, there is a treasured colored photo of Anthony the Butler in a yellow suit, standing at the half-open door, holding a tray downward at his side; he looks relaxed and welcoming. That picture was taken at Christmastime, given the wreath and garlands on the front door, possibly in the 1960s.

***

I must give an example of a wedding reception at The Woman's Club on January 22, 1949: My good friend Cynthia Smith's parents, Josephine Maffeo and James Wise, celebrating their marriage at Blessed Sacrament. A full-body portrait of Josephine in her wedding gown of white slipper satin was shown on the front page of *The Virginian-Pilot* Society section, along with eight other brides. The newspaper described her attire and wedding in complete detail like a book. Blessed Sacrament Church on Colley Avenue was only a mile and a half from The Woman's Club, so Josephine and James, the newlyweds, enjoyed a few minutes' joy ride in a limo to their celebration where a tiered Italian wedding cake waited on the round table in the East Wing Parlor.

The Woman's Club seemed like a perfect place to celebrate the newlyweds, as there are black-and-white photographs of Josephine and James dancing in the reception hall with a live band. The brunette Josephine and her entire family were Italian. And, of course, her wedding reception was boisterous, with all the Italian relatives enjoying the open bar and hors d'oeuvres. In one photograph, Josephine is seen throwing a bouquet from the stairway toward a small crowd in the foyer, including young girls reaching up to catch it.

This 1949 wedding event was one of the hundreds and hundreds held at The Woman's Club in a hundred-year span, and even today, it is still hectic. Yes, the mansion's interior attracts brides with its elegance and beauty, but the romantic grand stairway and spacious reception hall entice wedding celebrations. And the mansion also can be the site of actual wedding vows. The West Wing Parlor, the East Wing Parlor, and the library have seen their altars, especially in front of the fireplace. In addition, The Woman's Club has been one of Norfolk's favorite settings for wedding bells, champagne toast, and rice (preferably bird feed). These days, I hear from many old friends and even strangers that they got married or had their reception or even both "at The Woman's Club."

Alvah Martin must have had an idea for a bride or a woman in an elegant long gown when he built the mansion in 1910: A grand stairway with a wide landing between the first and second floors and a repeat of the same pattern between the second and third floors. When the first-time visitor sees the stairway from the foyer, that person knows the Martin Mansion makes an excellent wedding venue and imagines a bride descending elegantly down the stairs, her veil trailing behind her. Alvah had the stairway built in a U-shape, beginning with a three-step pattern toward the first small landing against the wall and then a five-foot-wide staircase along the paneled border leading to the wide landing. That landing leads to the second staircase, repeating along the right wall to the next floor. The oak wainscoting rolls along the whole way on the side of each staircase and even slants to go with the steps, again like an accordion.

First, the stairway entrance with the three steps is the most attractive part, with a tall, fluted post on the right standing on two bullnose starting steps that curve around the post bottom. At the foot of the left side of the entry staircase stands a square newel (post) that leads to the first landing by the rail with the second square newel. On top of the tall, fluted post is an opaque light glass sphere with carvings the size of a small cantaloupe. The short Omega-shaped rail runs from the fluted post to the stairway wall, where double upright sconces are mounted at the end of the rail. Most of all, that beginning section of the grand stairway has appeal, especially when both the sphere and sconces are lit simultaneously. Alvah put these light fixtures there, first using gas, and then these fixtures were turned to electricity by the third owner, the Woman's Club of Norfolk.

All the staircases show a spectacular design on their trend sides of steps; the decorative brackets are shaped in swirls like ocean waves. It is a coincidence because those brackets are the same as mine at home. Seeing the swirls of the natural wood color alongside the white staircase brings delight to my husband and me daily. Our Mennonite contractor hired his brother from Georgia to hand-build newels, balusters, and brackets at his shop and brought them to our newly built house in 2015. Alvah Martin must have felt gratified watching his stairway under construction since everything was done delicately by hand, as my husband and I felt the same way at our house. Mennonites are known for their excellent woodwork—and stonework, too. And they work hard without complaining.

At the Martin Mansion, there is something unique about the large room-like landing between the first and second floors that can be seen from the foyer. The landing with wall paneling was built to be a sitting area, possibly for the bride to rest before descending the stairway or ascending to the bridal room on the second floor, as there is a wooden, wall-to-wall, velvet-topped bench of the same wood as in the paneling. The three beveled windows above the bench are decorative; the larger middle one with two sashes has a circle-top shape and usually glows brightly with the morning sun; the two smaller ones in vertical form flank the circle-top window. The three windows' arrangement looks elegant enough for the landing and can be admired by those in the foyer.

That landing was made to be a balcony-like room overlooking the foyer and the front door, and the rail was unique, with an outward curve in the middle. Alvah Martin's purpose was for the bride or guest of honor to stand out for professional photography. Imagine the bride and groom standing on the outward curve kissing in front of the brightly lit circle-top window as the photographer clicks upward from the foyer. The best picture is usually taken from the front door because the entire foyer—with the landscape mural, the wall paneling, a coffered ceiling, and the archway—can be viewed before the stairway and the balcony-like landing. Indeed, the person standing over the rail can be considered the focal point. That entire picture shows the true character of the Martin Mansion, which makes it one of Norfolk's most popular wedding venues.

***

Although he had been deceased for seventy-seven years by June 1947, Charles Dickens had attracted the attention of Mrs. John W. Dickenson of Hampton across the Chesapeake Bay. She was the president of the Sixth District of the Virginia Federation. One afternoon, she spoke at the Woman's Club of Norfolk about how the famed British author had started it all at Delmonico's in New York City. If his event had not occurred, rejected women, or caused Jane Croly to establish Sorosis, which expanded to the General Federation of Women's Clubs, we would not be here today, Mrs. Dickenson told the WCN audience. She explained that the GFWC, with its "Unity in Diversity" motto, had accomplished so much that it now comprised 16,500 clubs with 12,500,000 women, including 50,000 juniors. They all had helped America and her allies win World War II with its "Buy A Bomber" campaign. The GFWC had encouraged the development of state federations, including this Virginia one, as Mrs. Dickenson reported. The Virginia Federation at the time comprised seven districts and 232 clubs with a membership of 15,000 women interested in youth conservation and public welfare.

Again, if Jane Croly had not been rejected at the Dickens dinner, all of this would not have happened, Mrs. Dickenson declared. Women would still be confined to their kitchens, cities across America would still be filthy, college professors would not speak at the club meetings, wool caps would not be sewn for freezing war soldiers, communities would not be enhanced, and World War II would not have been won without the additional 431 planes.

Hence, Mrs. Dickenson gave Charles Dickens a new title: “The Father of Women’s Clubs.”

Tea And Toil at The Woman's Club

Chapter Six

Over 70 million years ago, a plant appeared on Earth somewhere in Asia. This flowering shrub multiplied and deviated into different varieties, throwing a dazzling display of pink, red, purple, and white blossoms over the hills in shady areas. These plants eventually became abundant in China and Japan, where the monks and priests of Buddhist monasteries cultivated them and worshiped them under the emperors. As the FloraQueen website states, the flowering shrub became "a symbol of royals representing their passion and desire for the people and the land." It was so popular in Asia that it became the national flower of Nepal; it dominated Japanese gardens and earned the name "thinking of home bush" by the Chinese. It was extolled upon in flowery Asian poetry, especially in Korea, where Kim So-wol, a world-renowned poet in the early 1900s, published his only collection of poems honoring this shrub.

Having grown countless acres of pink, red, purple, and white blossoms in their vast country, the Chinese were kind enough to share their treasured shrub with the rest of the world, encouraging appreciation of this flower. It was first sent to England from the shores of the Black Sea and then landed in the hand of the noted Swedish botanist Carl Linnaeus in 1735. He named the flower "azalea," which means "dry" in Greek, as this shrub thrives in well-drained or sandy soil. Many people have given the flower's name to their daughters, symbolizing its incredible beauty and temperance. And the Greeks used the azalea as a symbol for animals, expecting it to protect their soil and livestock. British gardeners used this plant to share its language and symbolism in the 19th century. In Britain, the azalea was often presented as a gift to others as a display of public affection as well as personal friendship, romance, or sympathy.

Then, the azalea made its first journey to America from England in the 1830s. Fred Galle, the azalea historian, stated that the shrub was first introduced to the rice plantation Magnolia-on-the-Ashley in Charleston, South Carolina. The new shrub became the signature flower of the South, adopting the name Southern Indica Azalea. Since its landing in America, the azalea has been hybridized into over ten thousand different cultivars. How or when Norfolk, Virginia, received its first azalea is unknown; however, it had to be around the same time South Carolina plantations and Philadelphia greenhouses began nurturing this newcomer plant.

Azaleas belong to the genus *Rhododendron*, which has both evergreen and deciduous species. Evergreen azaleas, more common in Virginia than those losing leaves in the wintertime, generally have five stamens, while rhododendrons have ten or more. Azalea leaves have hairs parallel to the leaf surface, usually along the midrib on the leaf's underside, and tend to be thinner, softer, and more pointed than rhododendron leaves, which look larger and leathery. In addition, azaleas bloom along the sides of the stems and at their tips, while rhododendrons usually bloom only at the tips.

The 1950s were when the entire city of Norfolk discovered the beauty of azaleas. However, it took over a decade for one man to bring these striking plants to public attention. The azalea impressed a young horticulturist, Fred Heutte, who moved to Norfolk from New York in 1937 to begin his job as head of Norfolk Parks, officially named at that time. Born in Paris, Heutte was a leading advocate of urban beautification through horticultural education until he died in 1979. He is credited with initiating Norfolk Botanical Garden, now filled with three of his favorite plants: Azaleas, camellias, and crape myrtles. Heutte so admired the thriving conditions of azaleas in Norfolk that he consulted with the city manager Thomas P. Thompson on establishing an azalea garden to compete with the one in Charleston. After agreeing that Norfolk needed to increase its tourism with such a unique garden, the city provided Heutte and Thompson with a seventy-five-acre section of high, wooded ground and another seventy-five acres of the Little Creek Reservoir to establish a city garden.

The Norfolk Botanical Garden project began when Representative Norman R. Hamilton announced a Works Progress Administration (WPA) grant of $76,278 to hire twenty African-American men and over two hundred African-American women—at twenty-five cents an hour, which would have been three times less than minimum wage today. The economy of Norfolk was destitute before the wartime boom, affecting the black residents the most. Therefore, the WPA workers were willing to work at such a paltry wage so they could put food on their tables. Without hesitation, they began their long, arduous task in the summer of 1938 by clearing dense vegetation, carrying 150 truckloads of dirt by hand, building a levee around the existing lake, and preparing seventy-five acres for planting. These African-American women, often in dresses, labored hard from dawn to dusk along with their male counterparts, enduring the scorching summer heat and freezing temperatures, wading in swampy areas, encountering snakes and mosquitoes, and never taking a vacation—for four years at twenty-five cents an hour.

By March 1939, four thousand azaleas, two thousand rhododendrons, several thousand shrubs and trees, and one hundred bushels of daffodils made a spectacular show in the new garden. But there was still more work ahead for the WPA workers. Five months later, Representative Colgate W. Darden secured an additional $138,553 for the Azalea Garden, and the founding of the Old Dominion Horticultural Society provided volunteer labor to assist the Garden. By 1942, the garden displayed nearly five thousand azaleas and other shrubs on seventy-five acres, encompassing five miles of walking trails. Finally, the WPA workers were sent home for good without so much appreciation and recognition for their hard work.

That didn't change until 2003 when Mr. Matthew Austin attended the board meeting at the Norfolk Botanical Garden (NBG) and shared the story of him and his brother hugging their mother's frozen legs to provide warmth and even lighting a fire while unwrapping her legs at home after she had labored in the garden all day. Mr. Austin said to his shocked and tearful board members, "You really don't know the history of the garden," and explained that the women deserved long-delayed recognition.

Mrs. Elizabeth Ferguson, one of the WPA workers, was

eighty years old in 2004 and had not been back to the garden since the completion of the Azalea Garden in 1942. She called the work "scary." Worse yet, the African-American community was not welcomed in the garden during the segregation era. When Dr. Martha McClenny Williams, the author of *WPA Original Gardeners*, was asked to serve the NBG board in 2003, she began telling her account of women laboring in harsh conditions. All the accounts given by Dr. Williams, Mrs. Ferguson, and Mr. Austin were poignant enough for *The Virginian-Pilot* and Norfolk Botanical Garden to alert the public to the true history of the Azalea Garden. The original WPA gardeners were finally receiving recognition sixty years later. Today, there is a WPA Memorial Garden at NBG honoring these African American gardeners, with a stunning bronze statue of a woman in a dress pushing the shovel into the ground. The larger-than-life statue is called "Breaking Ground," sculpted by Kathleen Farrell from Joliet, Illinois.

By the early 1950s, the entire city of Norfolk was enraptured by the azalea newcomers recently planted in yards, gardens, parks, and even in pots. However, during the peak season, Norfolk Azalea Garden, as it was called before Norfolk Botanical Garden, was the main draw, with bumper-to-bumper traffic two or three miles long. People wanted to see carpets of red, pink, white, and purple flowers. They did not care if airplanes flew dangerously low over their heads as those planes buzzed into the airport next to the Azalea Garden, which was a three-ring circus by the mid-1950s. Fred Heutte, in charge of this floral display, was astounded by such an enormous crowd anxious to visit seventy-five acres of blooming azaleas. One year, he had to develop road improvements around and through the garden to ensure visitors would return every year for the week of lush azalea bloom. Mr. Heutte knew it would be impossible for cars to veer in different directions or block others; therefore, he began directing over three thousand cars one way, from one entrance to another. Turning around was forbidden. And there was no sense in telling visitors not to stop since cameras had taken over moving wheels. However, police were dispatched to different areas to keep the traffic flowing as smoothly as possible since Mr. Heutte could not do this job alone. After that, for one week every April, a massive mob descended on Norfolk Azalea Garden, anxious to see the blooming azaleas. In 1955, the bumper-to-bumper traffic reached seven miles long!

The name "azalea" began popping up across Norfolk and nearby cities and still exists today. Roads, neighborhoods, apartments, restaurants, businesses, churches, schools, and even sports teams took the name. There are Azalea Garden Road, Azalea Acres, Azalea Middle School, Azalea Manor Apartments, Azalea Little League, Azalea Church of God, Azalea Auto Body, Inc., and many more. One of the best restaurants in Norfolk, Azalea Inn, has been still alive and kicking since its establishment in 1957, two miles from Norfolk Botanical Garden. Louis Karangelen, the original Greek owner, made a productive idea of putting Greek and Italian dishes and appetizers on his menu, along with pizza and burgers. Coincidentally, the name "Azalea" was derived from Greek!

***

The azaleas were not only the plant that captivated Fred Heutte and the city of Norfolk; the other plant also hailed from Asia and sailed to America in Charleston, South Carolina, in 1790. It was a medium-sized deciduous tree or shrub with profuse summer flowers, averaging between fifteen to twenty-five feet in height. Classified in the genus *Lagerstroemia*, the crape myrtle was wildly popular in the South because it could tolerate triple-digit temperatures under the scorching sun in most types of soil. And its thick clusters of tiny petals of strangely the same colors as those of azaleas—red, pink, white, and lavender—could last all summer while other trees barely bloomed in the heat. Then, the crape myrtle, with its attractive peeling bark and upright branches, delighted Southerners with its fall color. All these unique characteristics galvanized Fred Heutte into planning to make Norfolk "The Crape Myrtle Capital of the World." He succeeded in planting forty thousand crape myrtles throughout the city, including the Norfolk Azalea Garden. To Heutte and Norfolkians, the crape myrtle was the floral attraction in the summer, as was the azalea in the spring.

The abundance of crape myrtles naturally led to the annual Norfolk Crape Myrtle Festival, established in 1951 with the Woman's Club of Norfolk as one of the sponsors. This popular event eventually transformed into the International Azalea Festival in 1954. What the Woman's Club did with the forerunner, the Crape Myrtle Festival, was to connect its youth program. The WCN had long presented awards and scholarships to high school youths in Norfolk. The General Federation of Woman's Clubs launched its project "Build Freedom with

Youth," which encouraged woman's clubs across America, such as the WCN, to produce their own projects to enhance the youth. The purpose of the GFWC's project was "to get young people between the ages of twelve and twenty-one involved in community improvement through leadership roles. Members of woman's clubs worked with young people in their communities during the planning and completing projects that would result in civic betterment. There were about fifteen thousand woman's clubs in the country in 1951, and all of them could take part in the contest to win one of three cash prizes and acknowledgment by the General Federation of Women's Clubs. The first prize was ten thousand dollars," as the Florida Federation of Women's Clubs pointed out. Inspired by the purpose of the GFWC's "Build Freedom with Youth" project, the Woman's Club of Norfolk prepared to participate in the coronation of the Crape Myrtle Queen – to encourage the youth to develop leadership skills in the community.

This exciting coronation event occurred on the evening of August 10, 1951, at Stone Park on Olney Road, where the west end of The Hague ends before Stockley Gardens and Christ and St. Luke's Episcopal Church. That beautifully designed park, made with off-white stone, had been used as a landing for boaters—and the Cape Henry Pilgrimage celebration annually. *The Virginian-Pilot* went to great lengths to describe the coronation scene, nearly canceled by rain, in which the shores of The Hague were "packed and jammed," and people watched the event from launches, sailboats, and yachts in the creek. Finally, a Navy barge arrived and anchored at the landing of Stone Park, where the sixteen-year-old Lee Dougherty, the first queen of the Crape Myrtle Festival, stepped from the yacht *Emrose* onto the barge. Her nineteen-year-old king escort, Frank Krivas, greeted her amid cheers and claps from the spectators. An apprentice sailor at the naval base, Krivas expressed appreciation for being named king. Then Rear Admiral R. O. Davis placed a gilt crown upon Krivas's head and a crown of crape myrtle blossoms upon Dougherty's head. He pronounced them "King Krivas I and Queen Lee I of the Crape Myrtle Empire" and praised the man behind the whole event, Fred Heutte, who had even knocked on every door on residential streets and encouraged each resident to plant a crape myrtle in their yard. As a result, Norfolk became blush with red, white, pink, and lavender blossoms. And this Crape Myrtle Festival would not have existed if not for Heutte.

However, the festival lasted for only two years, when city business leaders from the Norfolk Chamber of Commerce and other business organizations decided a spring festival would attract more people to the port city than in summer with the hot sun beating down on them. Thus, the Crape Myrtle Festival became the Azalea Festival, moving from hot August to cool April, for the world to enjoy the seventy-five acres of azalea blooms all at once. But then the festival's name changed again in 1954 to the International Azalea Festival in honor of the North Atlantic Treaty Organization (NATO).

A year earlier, NATO had entered Norfolk as its Supreme Allied Commander Transformation headquarters established to the south of the naval base site. This alliance was founded in the aftermath of World War II to secure peace in Europe, promote cooperation among its members, and guard their freedom against the threat of the Soviet Union. Subsequently, Norfolk became the country's offense, defense, and peace leader. Even to this day, Norfolk boasts NATO's only North American post.

So began an annual gala celebration to salute NATO amid the seventy-five acres of blooming azaleas cleared and planted by the original WPA workers. The city of Norfolk and the Hampton Roads Chamber of Commerce hosted the first international festival in 1954, and its rich tradition of friendship began. Now called the Norfolk NATO Festival, each year it "selects one NATO country member as the Most Honored Nation and a young woman from this country is crowned Queen Azalea. Her court comprises princesses from other member NATO nations, with other attendant representatives from local schools and organizations. Their coronation is held in the splendor of the Norfolk Botanical Garden, which is at its peak in spring. In addition, a sampling of the culture of the Most Honored Nation is featured all week in concerts, art exhibits, films, fashions, and cuisine. Since its inception, the International Azalea Festival has developed into a celebration with events that are annually attended by 250,000 people," as stated by the Local Legacies—American Memory website.

Before it became the norm for a woman from the host country to be offered the queen title, the daughters of the U.S. Presidents were crowned at the Azalea Festival. First, Luci Baines, accompanied by her parents Lyndon and Lady Bird Johnson, visited Norfolk as the queen in 1965. Next came Tricia Nixon in 1969. Susan Ford then claimed the queen title in 1976.

During the entire week of the International Azalea Festival, or Norfolk NATO Festival, as it is called today, Norfolk sees itself immersed in sporting and cultural events, an international military tattoo, a grand parade, a gala ball, and dinner, and a breathtaking air show featuring the Blue Angels, a flight demonstration squadron of the United States Navy. It is a time when local citizens, festival participants and organizers, and visitors create new friendships, appreciate cultural exchange, gratify the military's purpose in maintaining world peace, and learn about cultural and scientific development. The festival also brings attention to the city of Norfolk for its unique community and waterways benefiting world trade.

For many years, the Woman's Club of Norfolk sponsored the Queen's Luncheon and Fashion Show, but only after the Golden Triangle Motor Hotel opened in 1961 on a traffic circle between Brambleton Avenue and St. Paul's Boulevard. The Martin Mansion's auditorium did not have sufficient space to hold all the guests. The Golden Triangle, on the other hand, was an enormous 170-foot-high building (it cost seven million dollars to build). One may wonder why it was called a motor hotel: Before automobiles became available, people went to hotels by railroad. But now they could arrive at the hotel by automobile, first unloading their luggage at the front door and then parking at the site. Hence, that was the convenience of a motor hotel, such as The Golden Triangle in Norfolk. That large new hotel garnered admiration for its combination of hotel, motel, office building, and convention center—with an Olympic-size swimming pool in the middle behind the two wings of the V-shaped hotel.

The WCN hosted its annual luncheon and fashion show for the Azalea Queen in, of course, the giant ballroom at the Golden Triangle. The models, some club members, showed off new styles derived from fifteen or more Norfolk stores. According to the 2011 article in *The Virginian-Pilot*, Joseph Sakowski, the hotel's former chief engineer, remembered the old days and said, "During the Azalea Festival, the lobby was nothing but azaleas. Beautiful. Needless to say, the Azalea Queen always stayed there."

In conclusion, the two plants, crape myrtle and azalea, inspired two festivals, the first temporary and the second permanent. The crape myrtles first brought the city community together. Then, the azaleas brought the world community together. It was quite a difference on a global level. But those two plants, hailing from Asia and landing in South Carolina, have a solid connection to Norfolk's history. And to the history of the Woman's Club of Norfolk as well.

***

Since 1951, the Woman's Club of Norfolk had encouraged the French language in its mansion by first inviting Pierre Schmitz, the French consul of William & Mary in Williamsburg, to speak. So many people were interested in learning more about French culture that the WCN agreed to sponsor the French Salon, established by Mr. Schmitz and Miss Cherry Nottingham. The latter was well-known for her remarkable feats as an educator, speaker, translator, and active member of cultural and service organizations in Norfolk. "Miss Cherry," as pupils called her, taught at Maury High School, a mile north of the Martin Mansion, for many years before leaving to teach at the Norfolk Division of William & Mary in 1939. Wherever Miss Cherry taught, she enriched the linguistic skills of her students, mainly in French. She returned to Maury in 1942 to head the modern languages department for over twenty years. Maury was built in 1910, at the same time as the Martin Mansion and Christ and St. Luke's. Miss Cherry must have been proud to teach at this oldest high school in Norfolk that still exists today. Having been educated at several universities, including those in Paris and Madrid, Miss Cherry was president of the American Association of University Women (AAUW) in 1936–38, in which she initiated the scholarship program and encouraged international students into America's colleges and universities. She was also a founder of the Norfolk Forum and a leader in establishing the Norfolk Museum of Arts and Sciences (now the Chrysler Museum). Most of all, Miss Cherry was fluent in French and took credit for bringing this language and its culture into The Woman's Club.

Just then, the French Salon was formed by Miss Cherry and Mr. Schmitz at the Woman's Club of Norfolk. It was now headed by a local painter and art lecturer, Bertha Fanning Taylor. She was also fluent in French, as she had taken painting and art history classes at the École du Louvre in Paris and spoken at its famous museum. As a result of the organizing done by Mr. Schmitz, Miss Cherry, and Miss Taylor, the Martin Mansion saw an influx of club members and the public interested in learning the French language and culture. The students and teachers from Norfolk schools were invited to every French Salon meeting and a social hour afterward to meet the French members.

According to *The Virginian-Pilot* clippings, the French Salon shared a different subject each time it met; one was about "The Religion and Customs of Indo-China," lectured by Lieutenant Commander Paul Raoust, who had served at the Paris Naval Headquarters and spent time in Indochina. And Richard Cobb, the Norfolk Academy teacher, spoke on the French Revolution and showed a short movie. Bertha Fanning Taylor, in charge of the French Salon, once spoke on "The Exciting Life of an Artist During the French Revolution and Empire Period," showing lantern slides (A lantern slide was a glass sheet with an image used to produce a larger image by shining light through it in an early type of projector). Indeed, there was a French school on 524 Fairfax Avenue.

Four French female educators visited Norfolk in August 1955, when the French Salon was a few years old. One was a lawyer from Lyons and founded the French National Association of Women; the second was the director of a girls' school in Strasbourg; the third and fourth were directors of public relations of the National Federation of Women. The Woman's Club of Norfolk invited these French visitors for a tea reception and a tour through its industrial kitchen. According to the WCN's minutes, the visitors were impressed with the comforts provided by a large American kitchen—and delighted in our country's interest in French culture.

The French Salon lasted over a decade in the 1950s, with its regular Sunday meetings and tea receptions entertaining club members, students, teachers, and guests. So, thousands of "Bonjours" and "Au Revoir" were heard and exclaimed more than any other foreign language at the Martin Mansion.

***

As I write this book, I am overwhelmed by how much the Woman's Club of Norfolk has done for itself, the city community, America, and the world. I regret that only a tenth or even a twentieth of their activities and contributions can be mentioned here. If I had described all the WCN's doings from its establishment in 1905, this book would be even longer than Marcel Proust's four-thousand-page *In Search of Lost Time*. And I have relied on Earlye Lee Miller's 2007 history book full of minutes, clippings from *The Virginian-Pilot*, and dusty WCN's scrapbooks—for any exciting article or detail on the club activities or contributions. A few articles about the same topic caught my eye: The Woman's Club of Norfolk cared a great deal about the youth, particularly local needy and delinquent ones who needed help outside their families.

The WCN had regularly used its Public Affairs Forum at the Norfolk Yacht and Country Club five miles north on the Lafayette River. Their knack for hosting speaking events eventually led to the idea of the Norfolk Forum present today. In November 1951, the four distinguished speakers were invited to represent the club life, health, defense, and education of the nation. The WCN chose the theme for its forum, "The Hand that Rocks the Cradle." That forum on November 15, 1951, attended by hundreds, first had Mrs. Hiram Houghton, the GFWC president from Washington, D.C., speak on club life. Then, Miss Catherine Falvey, a Boston lawyer, lectured on defense and shared her experiences as a major in the Women's Army Corps stationed in Germany during World War II. The third speaker was Dr. Albert Chapman, who spoke about his career in the United States Public Health Service, followed by the last speaker, Dr. J.L.B Buck, whose address on "A New Look at Uncle Sam" looked at education in America.

All that said, the Woman's Club of Norfolk had much brilliance in selecting prominent speakers and compelling subjects for its forums. The interesting forum on January 28, 1953, for example, focused on juvenile delinquency and staged a mock trial so the public could learn the preventive, not punitive, methods of keeping young people out of trouble. That was the WCN's goal, and the theme should be again "The Hand that Rocks the Cradle"! The skit, called "Youth on Trial," was to hear the teenagers' side of the problem and help them weave out of delinquency. High school students from Maury, Granby, Norfolk Catholic, and Norfolk Academy volunteered to act as defendants in the mock trial. Adults served as attorneys, witnesses, a judge, and a probation officer.

During the mock trial, former Representative Ralph H. Daughton, acting as a defense attorney, explained that insecurity was the chief cause of juvenile delinquency, traced to broken homes, alcoholic parents, and neglect. And that the "greatest need of a youngster who gets into trouble is love." Then Mrs. Malcolm Stern, acting as a witness, testified that home was the responsibility of upbringing, not the school, church, or social organizations. The following "witness," the Reverend Mr. Fred Lawhon, stressed the lack of a unified religious life and the failure of churches to provide Saturday night entertainment for teenagers were the causes of delinquency.

Imagine the Norfolk Yacht and Country Club becoming a juvenile court with hundreds of club members and guests attending. It was relevant because, in 1952 alone, more than ten thousand children appeared in juvenile courts across the country. In one month, there were sixteen cases in Norfolk in which young people from thirteen to seventeen were arrested for offenses ranging from reckless driving to grand larceny and from store breaking to carrying dangerous weapons. Mrs. Floyd Sumner, one of the WCN members, revealed the spirit behind the mock trial to *The Virginian-Pilot*, quoting, "Norfolk has a new detention center, but we would rather not have it occupied!"

***

The Martin Mansion was also the site of youth enhancement. Beginning in the early 1950s, the WCN threw an annual Christmas party for the "Girl Guards" and "Sunbeams" of the Salvation Army. Those Girl Guards ranged in age from eleven to eighteen, and the Sunbeams comprised younger girls from age six to eleven, which is still the same today. Those two divisions resemble the Brownies and Girl Scouts, learning home and outdoor living skills; however, the Salvation Army girl groups are more focused on Christianity. Their primary purpose is "to save and to serve." According to the Salvation Army Youth website, the goal of both Girl Guards and Sunbeams is "to give girls an opportunity for personal growth spiritually, mentally, physically, and socially, thereby increasing their understanding of life and service. It emphasizes discipleship, evangelism, and the development of life skills. It also offers opportunities for building relationships with the youth members of the program and unique opportunities for presenting the gospel."

Indeed, the Girl Guards and Sunbeams had a grand time at the WCN's Christmas party every year in the 1950s and 1960s. Each time, the WCN members and Anthony the Butler in his smart black suit, greeted the girls at the door. Anthony had a gentle heart for the youngsters at the Martin Mansion, giving them extra sweets throughout his thirty-eight years there. Once they settled in at the Christmas party, the Girl Guards and Sunbeams listened to Christmas readings and music, played games, and enjoyed refreshments. One photograph in one of the WCN scrapbooks stands out today: A large group of Girl Guards, approximately thirty, surrounded the dining table with the background of the East Wing Parlor. They all look blissful, carrying cellophane-wrapped packages, obviously made by the WCN members. The finished plates of refreshments and empty paper cups sit on the table. Finally, it looks like the end of the party, and the girls are ready to go home, sated with hot apple cider and sugar cookies. That eight-by-ten-inch, black-and-white photograph of these happy girls in the scrapbook caught my attention, and it probably represents only one-thousandth of what the Woman's Club of Norfolk has done for the youth, but at least I can include its story in this book.

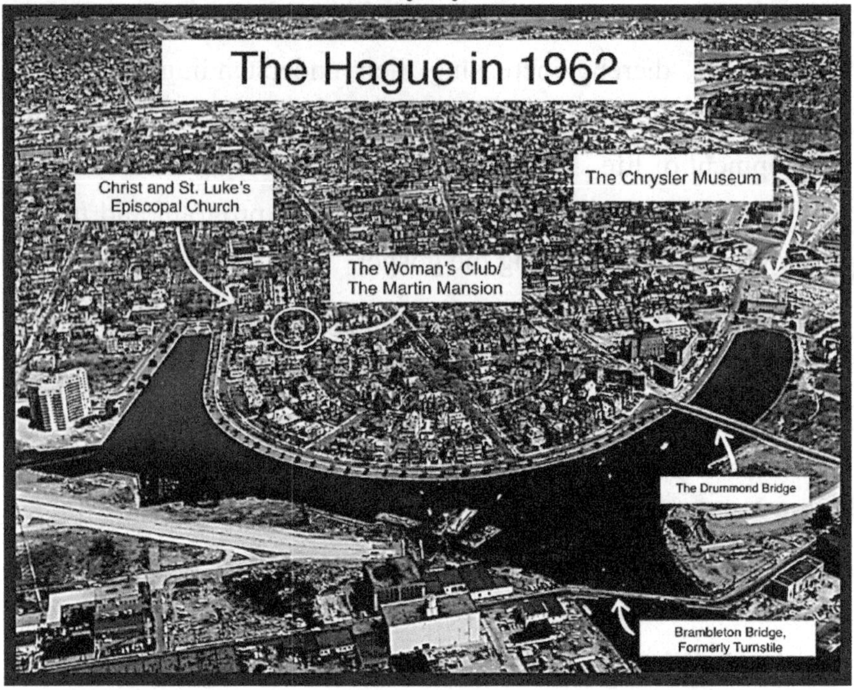

The Hague in 1962

Christ and St. Luke's Episcopal Church

The Chrysler Museum

The Woman's Club/ The Martin Mansion

The Drummond Bridge

Brambleton Bridge, Formerly Turnstile

Courtesy of the author

The Woman's Club in 1925

Courtesy of the Sargeant Memorial Room, Norfolk Public Library

Alvah and Mary Eva "Mamie" Martin

Alvah Martin and his passion for hunting

President William Taft and Alvah H. Martin

All Photos here in Courtesy of "Martin Family History"

Jane Cunningham Croly
Courtesy of General Federation Women's Clubs

Julia Ward Howe in 1908
Derived from National Women's History Museum

Annual Meeting, Board of Directors, General Federation of Women's Clubs,
Washington, D.C., ca. 1926, during the 1924-1928 administration of GFWC President Mary Belle King Sherman (who is standing 7th from left, the only woman without a hat).
The photograph was taken in front of GFWC Headquarters in Washington, D.C.

Virginia Gatewood, Founder of Woman's Club of Norfolk

Lillian "Frantz" Naylor, President of WCN 1920-1931

The Hague with European-style homes on Mowbray Arch, Vintage Postcard, 1907. Courtesy of the author

The Cape Henry Pilgrimage on April 26, 1930: Virginia Governor John Garland Pollard and his wife arriving on The Hague by the Navy barge and ready to receive the Norfolk Mace (seen in the approaching officer's hands)

Courtesy of the Sargeant Memorial Room, Norfolk Public Library

The Christmas Party for the Girl Guards at The Woman's Club in the 1950s

Mortgage Burning Ceremony at the Martin Mansion in 1958
Left to right: Mrs. Harold D. Cole, Mrs. Frantz Naylor, Mrs. Grover Outland

Kinchen Anthony
"Anthony the Butler"

All Photos Courtesy of the Woman's Club of Norfolk

"Saidie Orr Dunbar, elected GFWC president in 1938, is pictured at left as the bookmobile which was made possible by the New Hampshire Federation of Women's Clubs makes a scheduled stop. With Mrs. Dunbar are Frederick B. Preston (center), president of the New Hampshire Federation, and Mrs. LaFell Dickinson, who was serving as the second vice president of the GFWC. The bookmobile was purchased with the proceeds from the sale of a book, *The Folk Tales of New Hampshire*…Revolving bookshelves held more than 600 books." (*From Reaching Out, page 216)*

"A bond campaign called 'Buy A Bomber' was one of several major war efforts mounted by the General Federation during World War II. There was an honor roll for the state federations; planes could be named for a state federation, an individual club, or a group of clubs, and 47 state federations sold enough bonds to buy one or more bombers. Many planes used during the war carried the names of GFWC federations and clubs on their nose." *(From Reaching Out, page 245)*

Former GFWC President Mildred Ahlgren and GFWC member Mildred White Wells handing out CARE packages to children in Hong Kong with the 1959 Round the World tour. *Courtesy of General Federation of Women's Clubs*

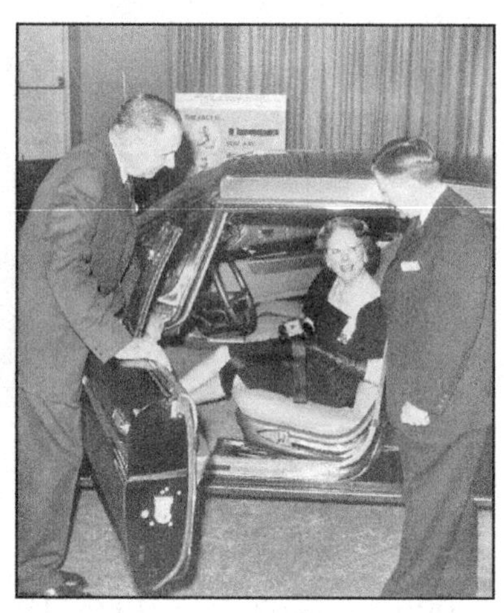

GFWC President Katie Ozbirn (1960-1962) launches the Women's Crusade for Seat Belts campaign with J.B. Wagstaff (left), Chairman of the Auto Industries Highway Safety Committee and Vice President of the Chrysler Corporation, and Alabama Representative Kenneth A. Roberts, 1961. *Courtesy of General Federation of Women's Clubs*

Mary Katherine Barnes Miller, thirtieth international president of the General Federation of Women's Clubs, 1974-1976. During the GFWC President Dorothy Hasebroock's administration (1964-1966), Miller served as chairman of the GFWC Crusade for Light campaign, a division of the GFWC Public Affairs Department. The Crusade for Light campaign promoted adequate public lighting to deter criminals. Miller is shown wearing a large hat decorated with streetlamps, which are lit up (a battery was hidden in her purse). *Photo by Rehman Photo Service.*

International President Mary Katherine Miller with Dr. Dorothy Height, President of the National Council of Negro Women, at the "Hands Up" National Summit Meeting on Crime in Washington, DC, January 1976. Dr. Height served on the Advisory Council for the Summit.

Courtesy of General Federation of Women's Clubs.

"The Woman's Club," a painting by David Robinson which appeared in a 1927 magazine depicting a General Federation of Women's Clubs (GFWC) meeting.

Samuel Leroy Slover
Courtesy of Martin Family History

Frank Batten
Courtesy of The Virginian-Pilot

Paige Rose and Susanne Ott

Polly Jones working on Bylaws

September 2018 Retreat in Outer Banks with my fellow members from the Woman's Club of Norfolk. First Row: Paige Rose and Sarah Petroske. Second Row: Me (Bainy Cyrus), Polly Jones, Wendy Auerbach, Susanne Ott, Ann Cooper, Ashley McOrmond, Ainsley Flynn, Karen Endsley. *Courtesy of the author*

Courtesy of Harvey Bilisoly the artist

Chapter Seven

Fifty years had passed since Virginia Gatewood summoned a group of women to a room at the Atlantic Hotel and started the Woman's Club of Norfolk with five hundred invitations to the local women and two hundred acceptances. Miss Gatewood had exited the earth graciously at age seventy-seven in 1941, followed by a full-column obituary with her portrait in *The Virginian-Pilot.* She was quoted as one who "put Norfolk first."

The WCN celebrated its two anniversaries on November 12, 1955—fifty years at the club and thirty years at the Martin Mansion. Since 1905, fifteen presidents have sculpted the WCN into one of Norfolk's most dynamic women's groups. Ten of the twelve living presidents were present at this fifty-year celebration luncheon. Interesting speeches ensued, beginning with Mrs. James W. Wiltshire, vice president of the Virginia Federation of Women's Clubs. She said, "A club is a fine working organization only as the individuals who compose it are fine, thinking, intelligent, imaginative women. A club is a force in the community and an important segment in the chain in the United States and Alaska, representing some 11,000,000 worldwide, as the individual members and clubs let their voices be heard." Another source stated that in the late 1950s, the General Federation of Women's Clubs had twelve million members in sixty countries.

Next, Mrs. R. R. Schweitzer, president of the Virginia Federation, said she brought fiftieth birthday wishes to the WCN from the state's twenty-five thousand members. A Chicago native and Norfolk transplant, she had been a notorious guest speaker for clubs across Virginia and other states, covering several topics such as the Red Cross, children's hospitals, and even comic books. Concerned about offensive subjects, such as crime, horror, and sex, Mrs. Schweitzer pushed for regulating comic books without affecting the freedom of the press. She pressed that her organization did not desire to endanger press policy but said, "We do feel that censorship of some sort is possible to keep those avaricious publishers from feeding this filthy rot into our newsstands."

There was another notable guest at the anniversary celebration: A former WCN president now seventy-eight years old, far older than the zestful forty-three-year-old when she started her eleven years of service. That guest was Mrs. Frantz Naylor, still looking as glamorous as ever with her striking eyes. Tireless in her eighth decade, Mrs. Naylor had been president of the Order of Cape Henry 1607 for many years, continuing an annual pilgrimage every April 26. And at her persuasion, more azaleas and crape myrtles had been planted along the route from The Hague to Cape Henry. She was even driven enough to send a personal invitation to Princess Elizabeth and Prince Philip to the Cape Henry memorial during their visit to America in 1951. Mrs. Naylor was now planning an opening event at Cape Henry for the Jamestown 350th anniversary celebration in 1957. So, she was destined to be extremely busy in the next two years when celebrating the WCN's fiftieth anniversary at the mansion she helped acquire in 1925.

While all this celebration was going on, Mrs. Naylor must

have been delighted to see an addition to the Martin Mansion she never had a chance to rely on: Anthony the Butler in his black suit and white gloves, passing a silver tray of champagne glasses or petit fours.

***

The city of Norfolk was in severe decline by the early 1950s, and that had been a problem since the sailors left Granby Street after World War II. The waterfront stopped bustling amid decaying piers and warehouses, and the 1800-era city buildings quieted down to the point of neglect. With the wartime boom and revenues gone, Norfolk was no longer respectively observed as a Navy town. Instead, downtown Norfolk had come to a standstill, enveloped by slums without indoor plumbing or access to running water. The slums sagged with rotting wood, surrounded by standing sewage water and not-so-clean laundry on clotheslines. Litter and worn tires abounded on the streets and in the yards. But still, black citizens lived in these slums since they had no other place to go. There was no way they could feel safe standing on the second-floor balconies on the verge of collapsing, staying dry under the porous roofs on rainy days, or keeping warm in houses with broken windows covered with flimsy cloths. The black-and-white photographs show the deplorable conditions of those slums. Life had to be difficult for the blacks, especially when Norfolk reached 95 degrees in the summer and 25 degrees in the winter.

The conditions in downtown Norfolk were so alarming that this city was the first one in the country to receive federal funds to clear out slums and build public housing. The Housing

Act of 1949, signed by President Harry S. Truman, made it possible for Norfolk and other American cities to renew their urban landscapes and improve the quality of life for low-income families. President Truman put in his statement on July 15, 1949:

I have today approved the Housing Act of 1949. This far-reaching measure is of great significance to the welfare of the American people. It opens up the prospect of decent homes in wholesome surroundings for low-income families now living in the squalor of the slums. It equips the Federal Government, for the first time, with effective means for aiding cities in the vital task of clearing slums and rebuilding blighted areas. It authorizes a comprehensive program of housing research aimed at reducing housing costs and raising housing standards. It initiates a program to help farmers obtain better homes.

The demolition of slums began in 1951 after Norfolk received twenty-five million dollars to clear acres and build three thousand units of public housing. Most of the clearing project centered on the areas around Brambleton Avenue and along St. Paul's Boulevard. In the following decade, during the extensive mid-century makeover, public housing developed farther east toward downtown, mostly between Monticello Street and Church Street. Elongated, single-story, red-brick buildings appeared, one of which would be named Calvert Square. Low-income families moved in and possibly had indoor plumbing for the first time. However, the public housing project was not an entire solution for black families since Norfolk was still racially divided. It was still difficult for black people to find employment and earn enough money to pay even low rent in public housing. Many black families had moved to East Ghent, less than a mile from The Hague, after World War II and settled in their homes, where they felt comfortable until the unfortunate and unreasonable gentrification in the late 1970s.

As the 1950s proceeded, city leaders in Norfolk "fell in love with the bulldozer," as NYC journalist Alex Marshall wrote in his 1999 article, "Urban Renewal in Norfolk." It might be true that since the Housing Act of 1949 provided 80 percent of funding for its urban renewal, Norfolk was overzealous, tearing down almost everything. It destroyed hundreds of buildings, some of which were historically valuable. Unfortunately, Norfolk could have resembled Charleston if it had retained many of those brick and stone buildings. If future tourism had come to mind, perhaps the buildings in such poor condition would have been restored. But it was in the 1950s when everyone wanted everything new. The streets were ripped out, some of which had cobblestones. Only Freemason Street and a few others nearby were spared. Only a few eighteenth-century buildings were left on this vast, cleared land. As luck would have it, the bulldozer did not reach one of the oldest buildings in Norfolk: St. Paul's Episcopal Church downtown. Built in 1739, this red-brick church was the only structure that survived the British destruction of the city in 1776. The cannonball, fired from the British ship *Liverpool*, remains lodged in one of the brick walls of St. Paul's today. And it was where my husband Steve and I were married in 1994.

The razing continued in the "Atlantic City," once a thriving seafood and lumber industry and once a serene neighborhood despite run-down dwellings. But no more. Families moved out, and homes crumbled to the ground. Atlantic City, close to Fort Norfolk on the water, would become a medical community in the following decade, which, of course, was not included in the twenty-five million dollars given by the government.

In 1953, Norfolk was given another round of federal funding with the help of its organization, Norfolk Redevelopment and Housing Authority (NRHA). More demolition was mapped out, and more building plans were pulled out. As Alex Marshall wrote in his article, the bulldozer continued trampling all over Norfolk, knocking out more buildings. Then, the hammers took over, building civic buildings and more low-income apartments. A new eleven-story city hall of modern architecture replaced the two previous city halls. The first was a two-story stuccoed-and-granite one built in 1847, which was thankfully saved. It would later be gutted inside while its beautiful exterior with a portico, large columns, and cupola remained intact—to become the MacArthur Memorial, one of the city's main attractions today. The next previous three-story city hall of Neo-Palladium Revival style in stone-and-yellow brick was spared, too, and is now the Slover Library. At least Norfolk still has a few historical treasures saved from the ravenous bulldozer.

The urban renewal craze also prompted Norfolk to build new highways, one of which would permanently close boat access to The Hague. The Brambleton Bridge replaced the turnstile one, so frolicking and picnicking on sailboats and yachts at The Hague was over. There would be no more Navy barges heading to the Stone Park landing for special events. The Hague was now super calm, like ice without a ripple or wake. Some people may not have liked the sudden quietness, while others may not have liked the lack of excitement in the water. Still, the semi-circle street called Mowbray Arch continued to inspire residents, locals, and visitors to stroll, bike, jog, lay down a blanket on the grassy area for a picnic, sit on a bench, and enjoy the view of the water formerly called Smith's Creek.

***

Aside from the sweeping urban renewal, Norfolk faced a turbulent situation that amassed national attention: School segregation, which changed to integration. It all started when Senator Harry Flood Byrd, the former Virginia governor who participated in the Cape Henry pilgrimage and visited the Martin Mansion in 1930, promoted the "Southern Manifesto," opposing integrated schools. He reacted to the landmark decision of the U.S. Supreme Court's *Brown vs. Board of Education*, which ruled that the state laws establishing racial segregation in public schools were unconstitutional. However, Norfolk and other counties were about to integrate its schools, so Senator Byrd called for "Massive Resistance" on February 25, 1956; this was a group of laws intended to prevent integration or desegregation.

Governor Thomas B. Stanley was still reeling from the *Brown vs. Board of Education* decision. He created the Stanley Plan, which threatened to stop funding for schools that planned to integrate. But District Court Judge Walter E. Hoffman declared it unjustified, ordered all-white schools to admit black students, and overturned Norfolk's long-time concept of "separate but equal."

Since 1910, Norfolk had adhered to its "dividing lines" in which white and black students did not attend schools together, and residential areas had "white blocks" and "black blocks." Judge Hoffman objected to the concept that Norfolk was not guilty of keeping blacks within its population but still separated them from whites.

The year 1958 was tumultuous, making Norfolk the focus of the segregation era in America. Along with over a hundred Southern congress members' petitions, Senator Byrd was supported by the newly elected Virginia governor J. Lindsay Almond and Norfolk mayor Kevin Duckworth in threatening to close schools rather than see them desegregated. In the meantime, the Norfolk School Board conducted exhaustive interviews with 151 black students who applied to white schools. At first, all these students were rejected. But under court pressure, the school board relented and agreed to admit seventeen black students considered fit. These courageous students would become known as the Norfolk 17, attending six middle and high schools, including Maury High and Blair Junior High.

However, officials delayed the reopening of schools in the fall of 1958 as Norfolk 17 prepared to start their first school year in white schools. Several weeks passed, and the schools finally opened. But not those six schools admitting the Norfolk 17 who came to find the doors padlocked shut. Hence, nearly ten thousand white students were shut out as well. They became known as the "Lost Class of 1959" and spent five months stuck at home, some privately tutored and others joining the YMCA to beat boredom. Finally, one parent of a white student became fed up and brought attention to the state supreme court, which declared the closures illegal. Those six schools finally reopened in February 1959.

There was one brave man in the city council, Roy Martin, who would later become mayor of Norfolk from 1962 to 1974. He and his wife, Louise, were dear friends of my parents. In early 1959, during the Massive Resistance movement, Roy did not like when the schools closed in Norfolk to prevent racial integration. The city council then held a vote to additionally shut down all-black schools. Roy was the only dissenting vote. He voted to keep the schools open.

The Norfolk 17 arrived to integrate Norfolk's schools and unsurprisingly faced mistreatment by white schoolmates and teachers; they were jeered, spat on, knocked off the stairs, and thrown things. Authorities were hired to protect Norfolk 17 only from those throwing tree branches, rocks, or heavy objects but did nothing when they threw small sticks. Louis Cousins was the only student of the Norfolk 17 attending one school that did not bother to remove a black effigy hanging in a tree on its campus. Yet, despite all the hostility inflicted by white students, teachers, and even parents, the Norfolk 17 did not miss a day of school and endured the torment every day to ensure that desegregation would happen.

***

The Norfolk 17 must be the most courageous people amid turmoil and abuse; however, one other brave person, who grew up in the red-brick home next to the Martin Mansion, pushed on despite bomb threats to his office building, only to see his business flourish. It was Frank Batten, the publisher of *The Virginian-Pilot*. He began his newspaper career at age thirteen as a copyboy and then as a reporter and advertising salesman during the summer. His Uncle Sam "The Colonel" Slover, who raised Frank after moving him and his newly widowed mother Dorothy into his house, owned *The Virginian-Pilot* and *The Ledger-Dispatch* (later renamed *The Ledger Star*) for years. When Frank was twenty-seven, having graduated from the University of Virginia and then Harvard Business School, his uncle took a risk placing him in charge of the newspapers after the publisher unexpectedly died. The Colonel knew Frank would perform extraordinarily well, even after a mischievous, undisciplined childhood with poor grades and school suspensions. Later, Frank credited Culver Military Academy for setting him straight.

As the new publisher of *The Virginian-Pilot*, Frank was surrounded by long-time employees, twenty-five or thirty years older than him. Now, he had the enormous responsibility of improving the newspapers' content and staffing more experienced and educated people. "Gradually, I built a team of energetic younger managers who wanted to change things," Frank later said.

Then Frank did something no other publisher would dare to: He organized a full-page ad of local businesspeople in unison to oppose the Massive Resistance movement. And he hired more people of color, even though he expected outrage among segregationists. "The only way to discharge this obligation is to make up our minds that it is going to be done and that the obstacles are going to be overcome," Frank said several years later. "It will take courage. It will cost some money, and there will be risks. But the alternatives are unacceptable."

Even hate letters, bomb threats, and racist graffiti on the newspaper building did not sway Frank. Better yet, under his leadership, *The Virginian-Pilot* won the 1960 Pulitzer Prize for a series of editorials condemning this state's decision to close public schools rather than desegregate them. Frank championed the integration of schools and encouraged civic involvement from his employees and the Norfolk community.

Over the following years, Frank bought or began ten daily newspapers, over one hundred non-daily newspapers, magazines, and many cable television and radio stations. And he became chairman of Landmark Communications, which grew even more extensive with a cable company, TeleCable. In 1982, Frank took his riskiest venture—to start The Weather Channel, much to everyone's skepticism. Who cares about the weather 24/7? They derided. This network developed so slowly that Frank almost closed it but gave it a few more months. Voilà, The Weather Channel became one of the most successful TV channels. Jim Cantore, the hurricane reporter who has nearly gotten blown off many times, must thank Frank for his million viewers annually!

Frank credited his Uncle Sam Slover for instilling his love for news and newspapering. He said decades later, "He was the biggest influence on my life. It was not so much his style but his values that influenced me. He had a lot of simple but very strong values—about truthfulness, the way you deal with people, being straightforward." He also learned from Slover, a contributor to many local causes and a one-time mayor, that community enrichment can encourage one to return the favor with their time and talent.

Interestingly, something had passed from the Martin Mansion to the Slover home on Fairfax Avenue: The genes of humility, versatility, perseverance, diligence, courage, and success from grandfather to grandson. Although those two never met due to nine years between the former's death and the latter's birth, Alvah Howard Martin and Frank Batten were eerily similar in many ways. Alvah may not have influenced Frank as much as the non-blood Sam Slover did, but it is apparent that grandfather and grandson shared strikingly similar attributes. Both were tall and slender, with athletic and outdoor abilities. These passionate sportsmen owned boats and hunted ducks on the Back Bay. They worked diligently to bring their businesses to top-level prosperity without relying on inheritance. And grandfather and grandson were highly meticulous with articulation and credibility; the former was repeatedly elected as the deputy clerk for thirty-eight years, and the latter insisted all editorials and reports in his newspapers be free of blunder or fabrication. Alvah and Frank prospered on versatility; the former founded a bank, owned coal lands, and organized a global expedition. The latter was a college rector, founded a scholarship foundation, and established a relocation department in a friend's real estate company. Above all, grandfather and grandson advocated for white and black people to work together in all aspects; the former led the Fusionists, a combination of black Republicans and white leaders, during Jim Crow days, and the latter led a mixed-race newspaper business during the segregation era.

Alvah and Frank each shook hands, conversed, consulted, collaborated, and even chuckled with U.S. presidents. They both had the rarity of working in person with America's top leader of the time, not by happenstance but by their perseverance in making the world more productive. Alvah pushed for the port entry in Norfolk for state, national, and global trades when meeting with President Taft in 1911. Frank, as the chairman of Associated Press, likely pushed for improved transmission and credibility of news when meeting with President Reagan in 1984 and then with the Emperor of Japan in the same year.

So much for the power of genes from the Martin Mansion to the Slover home.

***

In the summer of 1957, the former president of WCN, Mrs. Grover C. Outland, announced at a Finance Committee meeting that there was $3,200 left in the Martin Mansion's coffers. When the purchase occurred in 1925 at the price of forty-five thousand dollars, the club used twelve thousand dollars as equity in their previous residence on Westover Avenue and made a cash payment of three thousand dollars. That brought the home debt down to thirty thousand dollars. Hence, for thirty-three years, the WCN had been paying a monthly mortgage of $500.45 through 1958. Unfortunately, several newspaper clippings or the WCN minutes did not specify how the latest monthly mortgage ended up nearly seven times higher toward the end. But we all know a mortgage typically consists of four components: Principal, taxes, interest, and insurance. It is assumed that the unfinished auditorium at the time of the purchase added more to the mortgage.

At that meeting of the Finance Committee, Mrs. Outland suggested that the balance of $3,200 remaining on the home debt be "paid in full through a concerted effort in obtaining subscriptions from the members," as Earlye Lee Miller's history book states. Unsurprisingly, the Woman's Club of Norfolk installed another of its countless departments: The Building Fund Department.

Once the last mortgage payment of $500.45, along with the rest of the balance, was made on February 28, 1958, the Woman's Club of Norfolk, like always, wanted to celebrate such a milestone. For this reason, they held a mortgage-burning and dedication ceremony at the Martin Mansion on March 24. This accomplishment was so admirable that *The Virginian-Pilot* published an article a few days before the ceremony, remarking the WCN could make a down payment of only three thousand dollars for a forty-five-thousand-dollar home in 1925. It is not known why these women were able to reach such a deal or if it was because they were women. But they did put down a full, complete down payment upon request. Further, the article stated the club members bought a new home "on a substantial shoestring" and "some magic can work by time and a shoestring if the shoestring belongs to a woman."

The mortgage-burning ceremony occurred on a Monday

afternoon, attended by the club members and guests. Mrs. Frantz Naylor assisted Mrs. Grover Outland and the current WCN president, Mrs. H. D. Cole, with the mortgage burning. First, those three ladies posed for a photograph as Mrs. Naylor stood between Mrs. Cole—and Mrs. Outland, who, with a flashy grin, held up a piece of paper, with her other hand lighting up with a match. There had to be loud applause and cheering inside the entire Martin Mansion. Then, the Reverend John McKenry of Ghent Methodist Church and Dr. Walter C. Gum, the pastor of Park Place Methodist Church, performed the dedication to the Martin Mansion. Tea, cookies, and the famous wassail punch accompanied the friendship hour. The Woman's Club of Norfolk was known for its best non-alcoholic libation, the wassail punch that contained a mixture of apple cider, orange juice, lemon juice, whole cloves, cinnamon sticks, ground ginger, and nutmeg.

The Virginian-Pilot posted a short, powerful article the day after the ceremony with an eye-catching headline:

Debt-Free Home

The mortgage-burning and dedication ceremonies conducted yesterday at the Norfolk Woman's Club building on Fairfax Avenue marked the attainment of an important goal in the life of this organization while giving the community at large another occasion to reflect on the valuable role the club has played here for 53 years.

When the old Alvah H. Martin family residence—which for the immediately preceding years had been owned by the Virginia Club—was purchased by the Woman's Club in 1925, it *became the fourth home the organization had occupied since its founding in 1905. And the $45,000 purchase price, which would be a formidable sum even in today's shrunken dollars, must have seemed astronomical, even after the $3,000 down payment.*

The successful amortization of this debt in the intervening 33 years— including a full-scale depression and two wars—provides its own testimony to these women's determination, dedication, and fiscal skill. And this home from which they have conducted their affairs during that time, to the considerable benefit of the whole civic body, now stands as an appropriate—and lien-free—memorial to more than half a century of community service.

***

With the home debt paid off, the Woman's Club of Norfolk surprised everyone by announcing there may be a *new* mortgage for them to pay. It would be for the girls' camp at a site they had not yet found with the city's approval. That project had been in the members' minds long before the mortgage burning. They found a suitable lot for their dream: A new city property near the beach. And even hired an architect to design a camp building, collected private donations for the project, ordered building materials, and arranged carpools to take children to and from the camp. The WCN had cleared fifteen hundred dollars for the project.

But all that crashed when the city considered the WCN's potential too valuable for just a small recreation building and camping site. So, the club had to go back to the drawing board.

They were now searching for the right place—at a reasonably low cost. The club historian, Mrs. Ralph W. Eberly, told *The Norfolk Ledger-Dispatch*, "Now we want to do something bigger and better, something to improve Norfolk's future. This project of a summer day camp for the girls of the Girls Club of Norfolk is something that should be dear to the heart of every Norfolk citizen."

The Woman's Club of Norfolk, devoid of a camp lot, wasted no time in setting up the Girls Camp Fund and sponsoring fashion shows with its Junior Club to raise money for the camp. *The Virginian-Pilot* began placing the WCN ads for the presentation of the "Ten Best-Dressed Women of Tidewater," inciting excitement for the change in the fashion trend in the 1950s. I would not be surprised if poodle skirts, swing dresses, or bobby socks were a hit! One show occurred at the Norfolk Municipal Auditorium and another at Nicholson and Marks, a famous dress shop in Norfolk. In addition, the Junior Woman's Club of Norfolk organized their fashion shows, presenting one show at Sears, Roebuck, and Company. These junior members did not only raise money but also participated in the day program with the camp girls. In 1959, the WCN raised enough money to send thirty girls to Camp Owaissa, a Christian camp on Chesapeake Beach, and two girls to the Iron Rail Camp in Bedford, Connecticut.

So, the Ten Best Dressed Women of Tidewater made it possible for the young girls, primarily underprivileged ones aged eight to fifteen, to frolic on the grass or the beach in their skimpy summer clothes, not giving one hoot about their fashion looks.

***

Not one to let a single minute pass without productivity, the WCN members redecorated and renovated the Martin Mansion, using their hands and muscles to clean the entire interior. It was a great way to save money; at least they would not spend dollars destined for the Girls Camp Fund. Those Rosie the Riveters even painted some rooms, upgraded bathrooms, freed the kitchen of molds and spills, braved the dank basement, straightened up the eight bedrooms for new tenants, and did everything they could do to spruce up an aging mansion. And they had draperies cleaned, new shades ordered, and parlor furniture re-upholstered. Some club members even donated paintings to enliven the walls, furniture to enhance the parlors, and kitchen appliances to replace old ones.

In their fifty-five years, the Woman's Club of Norfolk members never wasted a second, much less waiting for anything. Instead, they just forged ahead, always with hope and optimism. A rejected lot for their girls' camp dream did not slow them down. The Martin Mansion emerged shinier than ever, and even Alvah Martin's crystal chandeliers sparkled more.

Chapter Eight

The view from the curved, handblown window in the West Wing Parlor at the Martin Mansion began taking in new buildings in the distance behind The Hague. That area was formerly Atlantic City, where seafood, lumber, and cotton warehousing dominated the industry landscape until the crazed bulldozer of the 1950s flattened them. Now, in the 1960s, Atlantic City had become a Medical City. As Peggy Haile McPhillips, retired city historian, wrote: "When the village of Atlantic City was annexed to Norfolk in 1890, it was a thriving community, with lumber and oyster industries and the Norfolk Knitting and Cotton Manufacturing Company to employ its residents. Adjacent to Fort Norfolk, Atlantic City was roughly bounded by the present Front Street, Raleigh Avenue, Elizabeth River, and Colley Avenue. … [In the early 1950s] the project targeted 135 acres in Atlantic City for the extension of Brambleton Avenue and establishment of a medical center complex: Expansion of Norfolk General Hospital and construction of the Medical Arts Tower, Municipal Public Health Center, and Children's Hospital of the Kings Daughters."

Anyone from the Martin Mansion could walk no more than four blocks to get stitches or even a baby delivered. Anthony the Butler once injured his arm at work, walked to the hospital, and checked out with a bill of two dollars. Due to its close proximity, the Woman's Club of Norfolk began a lasting connection to the medical community, often sending its members to volunteer at a children's hospital and raising money for medical causes.

As it is called Sentara today, Norfolk General Hospital's history began in 1888 when a small twenty-five-bed retreat for the sick opened in downtown Norfolk, but then there was no room for expansion. Hence, the hospital moved over a mile away in 1903 to Raleigh Street and was renamed Norfolk Protestant Hospital, which accommodated twenty-two private and fifty-five ward patients. Around the same time, another hospital opened nearby: Sarah Leigh Hospital on The Hague. Sure enough, the Martin Mansion stood almost halfway between two hospitals for sixty-six years until Sarah Leigh moved to Kempsville, several miles away. I have heard that many residents of The Hague and Ghent, some deceased and others still living, were born at either one of those two hospitals only a half mile from each other. What a choice a laboring mother had to make!

In 1906, a fire destroyed Norfolk Protestant Hospital, but fortunately, no one perished. According to *Sentara Healthcare Historical Timeline, 1888–2007*: "Fashionably gowned women of the Ghent section, among the first on the scene, braved death to rescue patients." They also opened their houses to the rescued patients for shelter and protection, as *The Virginian-Pilot* stated. The city wasted no time rebuilding the hospital at the speed of light, making it even bigger and better with more advanced equipment. The community opened their wallets and purses to contribute to rebuilding the hospital. When the new hospital was completed the following year or so, it charged an overnight stay of only $2.75, including three meals. As time passed, Norfolk Protestant Hospital increased its health safety by requiring gauze face masks and rubber gloves in the operating room. It also welcomed new inventions that would increase medical knowledge for safety; they were a chart of human blood types, a blood pressure cuff, and an electrocardiogram. In 1916, the hospital's president was notified of a mysterious patient who checked in every night and disappeared in the morning. The patient was confronted and admitted he was not ill, saying, "Where else in town can I get a bed and three meals for $2.75?"

The X-ray machines appeared at hospitals across America in the early 1920s, although the first came out in 1895 in Germany. Norfolk Protestant Hospital got one, with funding from various community groups, including the Woman's Club of Norfolk, which had long been heavily involved in contributing to the Red Cross and the healthcare world. The WCN also sponsored cancer drives, as it still does today. Then, the respirator made its first show at the Norfolk Protestant Hospital in 1932. After that, it just kept getting better and better at the hospitals as more and more inventions piled in.

By the late 1950s, Norfolk General Hospital, renamed in 1936, was on its own, developing a new wing and increasing its capacity to 475 beds. Thus, more floors were added, now seen at a distance from the West Wing Parlor's curved handblown window. In the meantime, Sarah Leigh Hospital was renamed Leigh Memorial and added a nursing school, enriching the neighborhood of The Hague. Being motivated by a medical community within proximity, the Woman's Club of Norfolk was the first of the Virginia Federation of the Women's Clubs in 1960 to contribute to the purchase of the two-million-volt X-ray machine for the Medical College of Virginia in Richmond. That machine, at the cost of $160,000, would be used to treat various forms of cancer.

***

The WCN not only contributed to Norfolk General Hospital. Since 1922, it has raised funding for the King's Daughters Union, later known as the Norfolk City Union of the King's Daughters. In 1896, a group of Christian women formed the King's Daughters to provide medical care for needy mothers and their children, owing the name to Psalms 45:13: "The king's daughter is all glorious within her clothing is of wrought gold." Edith Nason was the first nurse hired by the King's Daughters to care for the sick in the city's poorest neighborhoods. After tirelessly pursuing over seventeen hundred house calls on foot during her first year, Miss Nason was given a bicycle that she would soon wear out. She pedaled all over the city to care for the sick, often free to families unable to afford her services. Consequently, the King's Daughters earned a reputation for its charitable care, which increased funding from the community, as it still does today, with the help of circles, philanthropists, businesses, organizations, and residents.

Five years after its establishment, the King's Daughters opened its first clinic at 304 Charlotte Street. Miss Nason, possibly the fittest of all Norfolkians with powerful biking legs, was one of seven visiting nurses who braved tending to children with contagious illnesses like typhoid, malaria, pneumonia, dysentery, and tuberculosis. In 1916, the King's Daughters purchased a more significant residence at 300 W. York Street for their headquarters, naming it the King's Daughters Children's Clinic. In addition, maternity services became available with a doctor and nurse attending the homes of women in labor.

In 1919, a prominent Norfolk businessman came home with his card game prize of five hundred dollars, and his wife declared she would take the money to the King's Daughters. The result was the first car for the visiting nurses, who must have been thrilled to give their legs a break. Money continued to flow in from local groups, including the Kiwanis Club, the Lions Club, *The Norfolk Ledger-Dispatch*, the Anti-Tuberculosis League, the Norfolk Health Department, the Red Cross, and many others—to improve the lives of poor local families. However, money was still tight since the King's Daughters carried no more than a hundred dollars in its bank balance. Every penny went to the children. The clinic on York Street had only a lab and twenty-six beds; it could use a good expansion, but not on its tight space. At least the visiting nurses continued to care outside the clinic, tending to patients at homes where their own beds provided comfort. The King's Daughters began seeing additions of the first specialty services in the 1930s: Ophthalmology, ENT, and Orthopedics. It was one busy clinic in dire need of space.

Finally, in 1954, the King's Daughters eyed a site in the former Atlantic City for a full-service children's hospital. Funding requests spread over the city, and the King's Daughters got their wish a few years later: Nearly one million dollars was raised enough to break ground for its new eighty-eight-bed hospital in 1959. Dedicated on April 23, 1961, the new hospital showed off its ultra-modern architecture with a white square canopy over the red-brick entrance and a stainless-steel Maltese cross on its right, followed by two lines of protruding, thin, silver letters reading KINGS DAUGHTERS CHILDREN HOSPITAL. The one-story access extended to the three-story white-and-black building behind it. The entire hospital housed the King's Daughters' headquarters, inpatient wards, an outpatient clinic, and a visiting nurse station. The second floor connected the children's hospital to Norfolk General by an enclosed bridge in case critical care equipment was needed for the young patients. Over the next year, ninety employees of the King's Daughters helped care for over 3,395 children, 48 percent of whom were "service" patients who could not pay.

The medical complex cost over eleven million dollars to take over Atlantic City, and surrounding old and new apartments began taking in nurses and medical staff. Now, there was an expanded Norfolk General Hospital, a brand-new children's hospital, a nurse dormitory, a municipal health center, and a medical tower. The last building brings nostalgia to me because my dad, an internist, began renting his office at the Medical Tower as soon as it was erected in 1960. The ten-story, ultra-modern square building with large windows was the tallest on the campus, with a splendid view of the Elizabeth River and the glorious sunset. The 360-degree view showed the panoramic scene of the city to the east and beyond, toward the Oceanfront twenty miles away. Toward the west, the Elizabeth River merged with the James River northward and the Chesapeake Bay eastward. Finally, new medical buildings and a heavily developed area with numerous neighborhoods slightly obstructed the view northward toward the naval base. Still, the Medical Tower on 400 Gresham Drive was the beacon of Norfolk before taller buildings went up in later years.

If I recall correctly, my dad, Dr. Frank Nash Bilisoly III, had his internal medicine practice on the fourth floor of the Medical Tower for nearly twenty years before relocating to the new Norfolk Diagnostic Center in Kempsville, which he helped establish.

There was one object my dad carried everywhere in his hand, even to our house in the evenings and maybe next to his bed, as most doctors did these days: A small, elongated, black doctor's bag that contained a stethoscope, a reflex hammer, an ear scope, and whatever else was needed in an emergency. My oldest brother, named after his dad, Frank "Nash," was so enthralled with how our dad rushed out of the house with the doctor's bag in his hand that he drew a picture of Dad sprinting under the sky with clouds. His legs in black pants appeared in a giant stride; his arms in a white shirt spread out, one holding the doctor's bag, which seemed to be the focal point of an awkward drawing done by a seven-year-old. Over that bag, he scrawled "Dr. Bilisoly / My Daddy" in two lines.

The drawing won a part of *The Virginian-Pilot*'s Sunday cover for the Home and Family section on June 18, 1961, which was Father's Day. On that full-page special section titled "My Daddy," Nash and Dad had the first of seven other drawings done by sons of professionals. A paragraph about my dad next to his smiling portrait and under the drawing rang true: *Purposeful stride, white coat, and doctor's bag indicate a dramatic emergency call for Dr. Frank Bilisoly in this rendering by son Nash, 7.* I will never forget the doctor's bag, aging over the years with softening cracked black leather, that I occasionally played with as a little girl.

***

At the same time that the medical community was developing, the Midtown Tunnel opened, once again connecting Norfolk and Portsmouth across the Elizabeth River. What I mean by once again connecting was that a tunnel between those two cities, called the Downtown Tunnel, had opened a decade earlier, in 1952, over two miles away. The Midtown Tunnel, only half a mile from The Hague neighborhood, would become one of the most traveled tunnels in Virginia, with tractor-trailers coming from Portsmouth Marine Terminal or Norfolk International Terminals, often clogging the six-mile-long Hampton Boulevard from the naval base to the tunnel.

With all the new highways and the new Brambleton Bridge, the southern part of Norfolk became the hot spot for bumper-to-bumper traffic during rush hour. And that new bridge would not draw or turn for boat access to The Hague. If the turnstile bridge still existed today, the creek scene would have been vastly different from the past. The Hague, only a quarter mile long and a couple of hundred feet wide, would have to face heavy boat traffic or even become a marina. We know the number of boats has drastically increased these days. The worst-case scenario, if the turnstile bridge still managed today, would be an undesirable Fourth-of-July flotilla crammed into The Hague's tiny body of water. So, we must thank the Brambleton Bridge for keeping the boat traffic at bay!

Even today, the Martin Mansion remains serene in its neighborhood despite being a few minutes away from traffic jams. Mowbray Arch stays quiet with slow-moving cars, cyclists, pedestrians, dog walkers, and roller skaters – far enough from the noise of tractor-trailers on Hampton Boulevard.

***

There must be streetlights on every street, including Mowbray Arch, thanks to the persuasion of the General Federation of Women's Clubs in 1960 and beyond. The GFWC launched a "Brighten the Night" campaign for streetlights to prevent accidents and crime, and that name eventually changed to a more serious tone, "Crusade for Light." Several newspapers across the country published the campaign article through the United Press International (UPI), beginning with the same sentence: "Darkness is the criminal's best friend; light his deterrent." Working with the Street and Highway Safety Lighting Bureau and the nation's police chiefs, the GFWC found that, on average, 75 percent of all crimes, more than 85 percent of rape attacks, two-thirds of auto thefts, and 95 percent of burglaries occurred after dark. Worse yet, most police chiefs stated that 30 to 90 percent of their communities' streets were poorly lit.

That prompted the GFWC to send representatives across America to crusade for lighting on streets, schoolyards, playgrounds, public places, city parks, and even residential front porches. The federation ran a contest for club affiliates, encouraging them to increase lighting in their cities—with a deadline. According to a July 1962 article in the *Richmond News Leader,* entitled "Club Sheds Light on Shadows," the Monument Heights Woman's Club in Richmond, Virginia, initiated its project in the hopes of a cash award from the GFWC. Those club members, called the light brigade, "charged" to their neighbors' doorsteps armed with copies of a mimeographed petition for the city council.

But that petition was beaten by a mere phone call to the chief city electrical engineer, who immediately had the blocks in Richmond between Broad and Monument from Chantilly Street to Staples Mill Road all lit up. Additional light posts went up, and old-fashioned overhead lights were replaced. The city of Richmond was now safer, minus shadows. The reward for Monument Heights Woman's Club was not cash but a well-deserved citation for their community improvement from the General Federation of Women's Clubs.

One GFWC representative, Mrs. Mary Katherine Barnes Miller of Missoula, Montana, toured the country in 1965 to explain the light crusade to the officials—wearing her trademark headgear: A large cartwheel hat topped by ten miniature streetlamps, lit by batteries concealed in her purse. The UPI article reads: "The hat causes many a double take and masculine comment to the effect, 'Wait 'til I tell my wife. No, I won't. She'd never believe it.'"

Street lighting was not the only thing the GFWC crusaded

for; it also advocated for seat belts in all cars. In 1961, Mrs. E. Lee Ozbirn, the GFWC's president, called for a redoubling of efforts in the "Women's Crusade for Seat Belts" created in conjunction with the Automotive Safety Foundation. The program promoted the importance of installing seat belts in cars and helped to educate consumers on the proper use of seat belts. The GFWC had a goal for its crusade: "A million and one in '61." Mrs. Ozbirn stated that fifteen thousand lives could be saved if all cars were equipped with seat belts; however, it would be more challenging to convince drivers to click them on. You could take a driver to the steering wheel, but you could not make him pick up and swipe the seat belt over his lap. Complacency was even more work than the installation of seat belts. However, at the time, the GFWC had sixteen thousand clubs and 5.5 million members, and Mrs. Ozbirn figured that all the supporting groups could help encourage the public to wear seat belts voluntarily.

Luckily, automobile agencies cooperated in the seat belt crusade by advertising the GFWC's program on flyers, posters, and road signs. For instance, a 1963 Chevrolet Impala ad showed a shiny car on the lawn with an inset picture of father and son in the front seat with large, noticeable seat belts over their laps. The wording over the car read: "Custom feature accessories for added SAFETY." And there was a 1962 Chevron ad offering a free installment of a $5.95 seat belt in any vehicle, stating, "Why are we making this non-profit offer? Because seat belts save lives." Undoubtedly, the GFWC and club members took time and effort to pass around the seat belt posters across the country, reminding the public that 75 percent of all accidents took place within twenty-five miles of the homes of those involved and that seat belts were a necessity.

More interestingly, the auto industry considered women the appropriate leaders in a safety program because women drivers appeared to be more safety-conscious than men. According to the National Safety Council's figures for 1959, women accounted for 38.2 percent of all licensed drivers. They were involved in only 20 percent of the total accidents and only 12 percent of fatal accidents. Of course, the number of fatalities could reduce drastically with women more complacent with their seat belts. The auto industry understood that women could exert their safety influence in securing the installation of seat belts in vehicles used by their families, particularly to prevent their minor children from bouncing around or playfully climbing over seats during travel, putting them at greater risk in the case of an accident.

Thanks to the GFWC crusade, over one million seatbelts were installed in American cars in 1961 alone. It is unknown if the Woman's Club of Norfolk ever did anything about the seat belt since there is no mention of it in the minutes or *The Virginian-Pilot*. However, the WCN members likely discussed the seat belt crusade at their regular meetings since any action from the GFWC could not be ignored. The federation was and still is the boss of all woman's clubs.

On September 25, 1961, Wisconsin became the first state to require seat belts to be installed in the front seats of cars in all models built in and after 1962. However, this law only required cars to *have* seat belts. There was no such rule that passengers had to *wear* them. Therefore, the GFWC was not done with its crusade even after its goal of "A million and one in '61" had been achieved. People were still not wearing seat belts. According to YourAAAToday.com, as recently as the 1980s, only 10 percent of Americans wore seat belts when riding in a car. It took twenty-three years for the seat belt law to become effective in 1984. The GFWC finally had its dream come true.

When I was attending Virginia Tech in 1984, the year the seat belt law finally came into effect, there was a display on the campus drill field of a smashed-up sedan with a banner warning us to wear seat belts. That rustless car looked frightening, obviously, a recent victim of a highway accident over 25 MPH, as its windshield had been cracked from the inside, and one front corner was partly caved in. Someone had to get hurt, I thought, trying to brush the death scene off my mind. The placard next to the "Wear Your Seat Belt" banner explained that the windshield would not have been smashed if the driver had worn his seat belt. I turned to my sorority sister, Sue, and we both vowed to wear seat belts. While the news of the seat belt law was circulating, my cousin Kate Moring said, "You should wear it even when you go to 7-Eleven," pointing to the convenience store only a half mile away on the beach road. Her words had a profound effect on me as a sometimes careless twenty-two-year-old. I have heard of a few accidents causing serious injuries when people unbuckled before entering their driveways. The General Federation of Woman's Clubs had a good reason to push the crusade as early as 1961, only to have the law put into effort a bit late. Very late.

The seat belt was not the only safety measure the GFWC lobbied for; a prior instance occurred in 1924 when a California GFWC woman, Dr. June McCarroll, came up with the idea of painting a white line down the center of highways as a safety measure. However, that idea has existed since 1918 in the United Kingdom and has taken effect. Still, Dr. McCarroll convinced the California Highway Commission with her story of being nearly run off the highway by a large truck that carelessly took half of her lane. Finally, the commission agreed to paint 3,500 miles of road as a trial. The entire country followed suit. Dr. McCarroll said, "I do know that the Federation of Women's Clubs has given time and strong influence to make the line a reality."

***

The General Federation of Women's Clubs earned a spot on the top right corner of every envelope thrown into mailboxes across the country and then mailed to towns, states, Canada, South America, and over the Atlantic and Pacific Oceans. The United States Post Office awarded the GFWC a stamp in honor of its seventy-fifth anniversary in 1966. The off-white rectangle stamp showed the organization's full name running across the top; a large blue oblong banner reading "75 Years of Service for Freedom and Growth" across three lines; two ladies standing abreast the banner: One in an 1800-style dress and another in a 1960-style dress; and the five-cent symbol in the bottom right corner. So, for all its hard work in improving the world, the GFWC deserved the delicate licking and pasting of its commemorative stamps on millions of envelopes for one year and possibly more if people saved those stamps!

***

There is no such house that can pass fifty years without needing repairs. The Martin Mansion would not be livable in 1960 if it failed to upgrade, replace aging appliances, or put in a fresh coat of paint. A heavily occupied one with club members and tenants must have some refurbishment, as often as replacing old flowers in a vase with fresh ones. Indeed, at The Woman's Club, hundreds of meetings, parties, dances, weddings, and fashion shows used electricity, plumbing, and gas fitting, all of which needed constant upgrading over the years. The Martin Mansion had to be the most serviced house on the block, given the number of repair trucks coming in and out like party guests. Even a brand-new auditorium had to have its hardwood floor refinished after a dance at $92.75, only one year after the WCN purchased the mansion (close to $1,500 today). So, it would not be a surprise that each time the club received revenues from membership dues and events, they had to set aside a large amount for house repairs.

Unfortunately, in 1963, the budget exceeded by a large margin the amount the club could afford to keep a 53-year-old mansion in mint condition. They did not have the $33,500 required to do all the necessary repairs and improvements, and that amount accounted for a third of the home's value. Therefore, the Woman's Club of Norfolk had to come up with a painful decision: Put the property up for sale. *The Virginian-Pilot* announced the club's decision, explaining the budget situation and another time posted a photograph of the Martin Mansion, calling it "The Clubwomen's Landmark." The paper must have been asked by the WCN to publish for the second time.

The club members changed their minds when an independent appraiser set a price of $16,500 on the Martin Mansion property. The two bids to buy the property were ridiculously low, one for $16,000, including the furniture, and the other for $16,050. It would be like giving away what Alvah Martin had meticulously built with its unique interior woodwork. Therefore, the club members agreed not to sell the property, at least temporarily, and made plans to address the most significant issues, including the unsafe aging furnace. And since the auditorium was the primary source of club revenues with its events, its badly leaking roof was a priority, followed by floor repairs.

With its clever way of raising money, the Woman's Club of Norfolk vowed to host more events. The Junior Woman's Club of Norfolk would help with the funding received from their popular fashion shows. And thanks to *The Virginian-Pilot*'s announcement of the WCN's intention to sell the property, it would not be surprising if prominent locals sent in money to keep one of their favorite party venues aloft.

***

So, all went back to normal at the Martin Mansion with the WCN bronze placard still tacked to the right side of the front door. A few things had been replaced; the sale sign was pulled off; the chatter of well-dressed hatted ladies persisted; and the committee meetings continued. But there was one thing still firmly poised on the oriental rug at The Woman's Club, delicately moving from one rug to the next. Irreplaceable, treasured, and multifaceted. Anthony the Butler was not going anywhere after twenty-five-some years of waiting on ladies and keeping the mansion in top-notch shape. He had aged to venerability with thinning gray hair, a beefier physique, thick spectacles, and a persistent broad grin. He was not as youthful as when he was first thrust into the kitchen to wash dishes at the last minute without any idea of his future at The Woman's Club. Now, Anthony's feet must have endured hundreds of miles of trekking from room to room instead of being glued in front of the kitchen sink. And he wore the same kind of outfit every day instead of a kitchen apron. Sometimes, Anthony came in a pitch-black suit, other times in mustard yellow, cranberry maroon, or pearl white. His suits changed in color, but his black bowtie, white shirt, and black trousers always remained the same. Because of the heavy walking he did, Anthony had to be wise enough to choose the most comfortable black shoes he could ever find. His boss ladies had no say in this.

Anthony was serious about dressing correctly for himself and the guests he encountered at parties and events, particularly men. He did not have to worry about the ladies who embraced fashion and knew not to let their threads hang loose. But men were a different story, Anthony told a journalist years later. It annoyed him to see local wealthy and prominent men dress as if "they didn't have a dime." His pet peeve was seeing one corner of the shirt untucked, a cockeyed tie, or even a shoelace dragging on the floor.

When he was not working at The Woman's Club,

Anthony bartended for party hosts at their homes while his wife, Mabel Rose, catered her famous appetizers at these same parties. He once sat the poorly dressed male host down, saying, “You are a perfect mess,” and polished his shoes before the guests arrived. Anthony was not afraid to do whatever he wanted to fix without being asked because he was regarded by the many he served as a family member. And for himself, he had a basement at The Woman’s Club to briefly go down and tuck in his shirt, wipe a fresh morsel off his suit, or peel a crushed piece of paper off the bottom of his shoe. Nevertheless, Anthony would never permit himself to dress shabbily—or male guests or hosts, for that matter.

Anthony was excellent at bartending, remembering every frequent guest’s favorite drink. One prominent local lady told Lawrence Maddry of *The Virginian-Pilot*, “First, you get Anthony, then you order the bourbon.” Anthony had a story about the drinker he admired the most, as the 1973 article read: “He was a gentleman from New York who happened to be at a party where I did the bartending. He was a small, disabled man who had flown his private plane to Norfolk,” Anthony recalled. The party started at 6 PM, and the frail New Yorker seated himself in a comfortable chair and motioned to Anthony. “Anthony,” he said, “Now it’s 6:15 in the evening, and I will give you $2 for every drink you pour into this glass. Let me know when you get tired.” About once every half-hour, Anthony left the bar when he saw the stranger’s hand raise the empty glass above the chairback. Each time, the glass was filled with bourbon and water. The stranger was still sitting in the chair with his glass raised at 7 AM the following day. Finally, Anthony gave up but walked home with a bulging wallet. "Now there," Anthony recalled with admiration, "was a drinker."

***

The Woman's Club of Norfolk's connection with the College of William & Mary went a long way back to 1920. The club first cooperated with William & Mary in Williamsburg, about fifty miles north, to sponsor a series of lectures on citizenship. The WCN, under the presidency of Mrs. Frantz Naylor, invited professors from William & Mary to speak to the club members and guests on several subjects, such as Shakespeare and the US Government. The Dramatic Club of William & Mary presented plays at the Martin Mansion. It was not the only gold coins the WCN paid to the college for its lectures and plays; the club also donated part of its revenues to William & Mary out of respect since this college, founded in 1693, is the second oldest institution of higher education in America and the ninth oldest in the English-speaking world. The Woman's Club of Norfolk and William & Mary had a long, professional relationship that benefited them financially.

Most of that relationship occurred after William & Mary expanded its territorial range by establishing a branch in Norfolk in 1930 in conjunction with Virginia Polytechnic Institute (VPI). That new branch, located midway between the naval base and downtown Norfolk, was named the Norfolk Division of the College of William & Mary and Virginia Polytechnic Institute. The name was quite a mouthful, but the signs on the campus read:

The College of William & Mary and VPI, Norfolk. This extension would eventually become the independent state-supported institution known as Old Dominion University today. From 1930 to 1962, students could take their first two years of coursework at the Norfolk Division and then transfer to VPI, now Virginia Tech, for their final two years. My alma mater, five hours away in mountainous Blacksburg, is not as old as William & Mary, but still, its 1872 establishment brings a rich history to the orange and maroon spirit!

Beginning in 1930, the Woman's Club of Norfolk enjoyed working with the new two-year Norfolk Division, only three miles away instead of fifty miles. Their relationship intensified with more lectures from the professors at The Woman's Club, often packing the auditorium. In addition, the WCN donated funds to the Norfolk Division, as did the city community, other organizations, and philanthropists.

Then, in 1962, the Norfolk Division rapidly developed into a four-year institution, gaining independence from William & Mary and VPI. On February 16 of that year, the William & Mary system was dissolved under General Assembly legislation signed by Governor Albertis S. Harrison. Hence, the Norfolk Division was renamed Old Dominion College. Dr. Lewis W. Webb served as the first president of Old Dominion College from 1962 to 1969. Known as the "Father of Old Dominion," Dr. Webb was involved in pushing for the Norfolk Division's independence and found his dream come true after a long time. After his presidency, he went on to teach physics on campus and lived long enough to see his beloved school move up to university status in 1969.

The boy who grew up next door to the Martin Mansion would find himself to be the first rector of Old Dominion College on May 27, 1962. It was the versatile Frank Batten who had succeeded in his newspaper business since 1954. His long relationship with Old Dominion began in 1955 when he served as a member of the advisory board to the Norfolk Division of the College of William & Mary and VPI. Like Dr. Webb, Frank lobbied for the Norfolk Division to become an independent college. When he became the rector with the dominating role in academics, Frank was appointed by the governor to the Board of Visitors, which had the power to control and expand Old Dominion College's funds, make all rules and regulations, and appoint the president of the college. So, aside from newspapering, Frank had two prominent roles at Old Dominion: Managing academics and finance.

My maternal grandmother, Katherine Lindsay, was simultaneously on the Board of Visitors with Frank from 1962 to 1970. She was no novice to chairing several groups and advocating for education and conservation. "Donnie," as her large brood of grandchildren called her, was once chairman of the women's division of the Norfolk Community Fund, served several times as chairman of fund drives for the Children's Home Society, and was the president of the Norfolk Historical Society, the Garden Club of Norfolk, and the Associated Garden Clubs of Virginia for Roadside Development. She was also on the board of directors of the Garden Club of America.

Besides serving on the Board of Visitors for Old Dominion College, Donnie had her most significant achievement:

She led garden clubs in persuading the General Assembly to adopt a bill regulating billboards on interstate highways. Her success in that long battle resulted in her appointment in 1965 to a state commission to study the beautification of Virginia's roads. Next, she worked for that cause on a national commission. During the 1960s, she was among those who fought to keep Seashore State Park in Virginia Beach intact when the state was considering multiple uses for that park, which had been closed during court battles over racial desegregation of parks. That park is next to the Cape Henry Memorial, where the granite cross stands over the first landing of British settlers in 1607. And to which Mrs. Frantz Naylor, the long-time president of the WCN and the founder of Cape Henry Pilgrimage, invited President Truman while sitting with him at the White House in 1950.

One might wonder if my grandmother was a member of the Woman's Club of Norfolk. No, she was not. She must have had no time to join another club while chairing a community fund, presiding over a garden club, sitting on a college board, saving a state park, and fighting to keep a billboard off the highway. Donnie had done enough besides tending to her family and her cancer-stricken husband, Harvey Lindsay, Sr., who passed away at age seventy-four in 1969.

***

On April 23, 1963, a lone male bystander stood in the lobby of the Golden Triangle, a gigantic two-year-old hotel in downtown Norfolk, and was startled by a crowd of hatted, well-dressed, chatty women filing in and even fighting for the spot in front of the registration desk. Surrounded by such a chaotic mob, the bystander exclaimed to the spectating reporter, "Washington in wartime!" The check-in time was at 3 PM; therefore, there was a bottleneck of over five hundred club women and 250 junior club women acting as delegates trying to get their rooms. Suitcases and hat boxes piled up on the first floor like an over-occupied train. So, it was for the three-day convention of the Virginia Federation of Women's Clubs, expecting around thirteen hundred members, right here at the Golden Triangle, barely in its juvenility.

I must reveal I need clarification on the age range of junior club women; now I realize these clubs did not consist of only teenagers or college-age women as they used to. The junior clubs across America eventually became older, graduating at twenty-five, then at thirty, and finally thirty-five. The Woman's Club of Norfolk had a junior division since 1928 and invited mostly daughters and granddaughters of club members between ten and twenty years of age, which I had assumed. But by 1963, junior clubs now consisted of young women under thirty-five, the maximum age limit.

At the time of the Virginia Federation convention, there were 423 Woman's Clubs and 83 Junior Woman's Clubs in that state alone. In total, there were 23,700 members, including 4,000 juniors. Most junior clubs wanted a change in the age limit; therefore, the rules committee expected a hot debate at this convention. Knowing women could be talkative, that committee enforced a rule mandating no one could speak for more than two minutes during the debate unless there was a unanimous vote.

One newcomer to the convention complained to *The Virginian-Pilot* reporter about those strict regulations. As she checked into the Golden Triangle, the newcomer muttered, "These rules are going to be hard for me to live up to. Whoever heard of talking just for two minutes?"

The federation bylaws had long required that junior clubs comprise "young women" and defined as "under thirty-five." But, at the time of the convention, most junior clubs wanted to move the age limit to forty for several reasons. First, five more years of training would help the juniors gain enough experience, dedication to the club, and community service before they moved to the more experienced Woman's Club of Norfolk. And the WCN was affiliated with the GFWC, but its junior club was not.

Second, the junior and woman's clubs had a graduation "dropout" issue in which members disappeared after training or reaching the age limit. Understandably, the junior clubs wanted to eradicate that problem and keep members active until the new age limit of forty. Last, raising the age to forty would help bridge the gap between general federation clubs and junior clubs. As many sources pointed out, the junior clubs did not mind being called "junior" but wanted five more years of membership to be a part of "general" federation clubs.

That must be why the rules committee prepared for such an intensive debate at the Golden Triangle, enforcing the two-minute limit for talking during discussions. The conference was for Virginia club members, including those of Portsmouth Woman's Club and Suffolk Woman's Club (to my surprise, many woman's clubs within a thirty-mile radius were established immediately after Miss Virginia Gatewood founded the WCN in 1905). Those conference attendees needed to hear different opinions from other states on whether to raise the age limit for junior clubs, even if they were in for a heated discussion. Take one idea outside of Virginia: The Florida Federation opposed raising the age limit to forty and pointed out that some states could solve the dilemma by saying, "A junior club shall be a junior club until it is five years old, then it automatically comes under the general federation."

Mrs. Donald Pollie of Virginia Beach Princess Anne Woman's Club supported raising the junior age limit. She declared, "Junior clubs are not playgrounds, but groups whose projects have become more sophisticated and equal to senior projects. Most of all, we do not want to feel intimidated, nor want our right to be heard abridged in our own organization." She also explained that in her area, families were increasing rapidly in population; junior club members were young mothers themselves and would contribute more to the community if they had five more years in their clubs.

However, not all the conference attendees supported it since the revisions committee comprised four senior members and the junior director, Mrs. Watson, who admitted she did not favor the raising. With clarity, she told *The Virginian-Pilot* reporter, "I want to leave the club while they still call me 'Betty' and before they start saying 'Yes, ma'am!'"

The revisions committee of the Virginia Federation of

Women's Clubs did not make any change at this three-day conference, and junior clubs stayed "young at thirty-five." So, the Golden Triangle saw quite an emotional, animated conference under its V-shaped roof, and the male bystander was right in exclaiming, "Washington in wartime!"

***

Everything in Norfolk stopped around 1:30 in the afternoon on a Friday. Shoppers at Sears, Roebuck, and Co. loosened their grips on their shopping bags, and others slowly abandoned their carts. Silence engulfed that popular department store on 21st Street, except for the running demo TVs to which shoppers walked toward in a daze and began listening. The same occurred at other department stores. Schools across the city halted their classroom lectures and allowed the students to slump over their desks and listen to the radio. Even cars pulled over on the curb and just sat idle. Radios and televisions were the only noise amid the stunned silence of the entire city population. The staff at Norfolk Naval Base also discontinued their duties briefly, their minds flashing back to a recently publicized visitor who changed the military landscape of their employment. It was not only Norfolk that stopped cold on that sunny afternoon; it was the whole of America.

My brother Harvey, a seven-year-old student at Norfolk Academy, noticed the eerie silence on the campus and just learned that school had been dismissed early because of the horrible news affecting the nation. He walked to the empty school bus and saw the driver slump over the steering wheel. Harvey did not know what to make of it as he stood motionless at the bus door. Finally, the bus driver, tears running down his cheeks, turned to Harvey and said, "President Kennedy was shot."

Several months earlier, on April 13, 1962, President Kennedy visited Norfolk Naval Base to meet the team he had established for covert operations against enemies: Navy SEALs. Eleven months before his visit, Kennedy instructed the secretary of defense to officially establish what is known today as the "Sea, Air, and Land Teams." Thus, the two teams were formed in January 1962, and Kennedy met one of them here in Norfolk. After landing at the airbase Oceana in Virginia Beach, President Kennedy spent three hours touring the Norfolk Naval Base and chatting with members of the Navy SEAL Team 2. That team was based at the Naval Amphibious Base Little Creek, now known as Joint Expeditionary Base Little Creek, ten miles east toward Fort Story in Virginia Beach. (The other Navy SEAL Team, known as Team 1, was stationed at Naval Amphibious Base Coronado in San Diego, California.) During his visit to the Norfolk Naval Base, Kennedy boarded the USS *Thomas A. Edison* submarine, peeked through the periscope, and watched the sea exercises from Northampton's command ship. After a two-day military visit along the coast, President Kennedy was impressed with the Norfolk Naval Base, Oceana, and Camp Lejeune in North Carolina. He called the Atlantic Fleet's elaborate demonstration of sea-power versatility a source of "confidence and hope" for the cause of freedom and peace.

After the death of John F. Kennedy, the Naval Air Station was given a significant role in his vision that he announced in his

1962 Rice University speech before forty thousand cheering spectators: "We choose to go to the moon." Fighting in competition with the Soviet Union, Kennedy vowed to put a man on the moon before 1970. And he sure got his wish posthumously. In 1968, the Norfolk Naval Air Station became Recovery Control Center Atlantic, which provided command, control, and communications for the ships and aircraft that participated in the recovery operations of Apollo 7. That project was the testing of the Apollo program in low earth orbit and was a significant step toward NASA's goal of landing astronauts on the Moon. Hence, the slightly battered space capsule of Apollo 7, after its splashdown into the Atlantic Ocean with three men inside, arrived in Norfolk on the aircraft carrier USS *Essex*. The thirteen-thousand-pound capsule, partly corroded from the flammable reentry into the earth's atmosphere, was carried to the hanger, where it was inspected and cleaned. Then, the Air Force flew the capsule to Los Angeles for transportation to the California headquarters of the spacecraft manufacturer.

Referring to Kennedy, Norfolk first saw the national hero meeting with the newly formed Navy SEALs, dealt with his devastating loss, and finally encountered a piece of his space dream. In such a tumultuous decade, John F. Kennedy put a unique stamp on Norfolk's history.

***

The Vietnam War, vastly unsuccessful on all fronts and unpopular with the American people, caused an anti-war movement in which students began protesting on college campuses, including Old

Dominion University. TV and news media brought disturbing images of war atrocities and napalm victims, especially a naked Vietnamese girl running and screaming in pain. Those images increased the intensity of war protests, which were sometimes violent, as in the case of Kent State shootings in 1970 in which the Ohio National Guard killed four students. In addition, teens and young men burned their draft cards and waved Viet Cong flags, threatening support for the war.

Although the Vietnam War posed problems for law enforcement and residents, it also caused something peaceful. The Counterculture Movement consisted mainly of hippies who promoted peace over war and embraced rebellion against mainstream American culture. Hippies promoted their distinctive brand of defiance: Long hair, beards, colorful thrift-shop clothing, psychedelic drugs, love of rock music, and eco-conscious lifestyle. Most of them were only teens and twenty-somethings, advocating nonviolence and love. They used the phrase "Make love, not war" and were sometimes called "flower children" since they wore clothing with embroidered flowers and vibrant colors. They also pinned flowers to their hair and distributed the petals to the public. Those hippies mostly came from middle-class and dysfunctional families. Jenny, the character in the Academy Award–winning movie *Forrest Gump,* is one example; she escaped her abusive father by joining a Volkswagen van in front of her nearly dilapidated family home and being cheered on by her hippie friends before taking off on a road trip, away from restrictions and, unfortunately, to drug abuse. That powerful scene resonated with most hippies across America over twenty-five years before *Forrest Gump* was filmed. Hippies were peaceful and joined the civil rights and gay movements to advocate for freedom and peace. However, many sources pointed out that those hippies were more participants than protestors. They only watched the protest, walked along with the protestors, and stayed quiet amid the chants.

But many cities across the country complained about "Long Hairs" who had no money since they did not want to work. Panhandling was one big problem for merchants, motel guests, and residents in cities across the country, and the Oceanfront in Virginia Beach didn't escape the onslaught. Indeed, hippies flocked to the beach for openness and a lot of space for napping, frolicking, and listening to the Beatles and Bob Dylan on their portable radios. Concentrated between 17th and 25th Streets, hippies with their bedrolls were observed sleeping on the Boardwalk, beachfront lawns, and motel lounge chairs, much to the merchants' and motel guests' annoyance. Police were notified and asked the hippies to "move on," but the latter stopped after a few feet and lay back down on the grass to take a nap. That way, they responded by staying just inside the law, making the "failure to move on" ordinance ineffective. As *The Virginian-Pilot* stated in its July 20, 1970, article headlined "Long Hairs Worry Beach," the increasing numbers of "idle young nomads" were to blame for the cancelation of city-sponsored shows in the Civic Center aimed for family-type tourists. And their presence, often involving panhandling and vulgarity, was hurting businesses. One hippie defended his lack of employment to the reporter, saying he was fired from his last job because of his long hair, but insisted that hippies should be allowed to "live our lives and not be put down because of long hairs." Finally, at the end of the article, the city manager admitted that the revenues of the Oceanfront were still adequate thanks to nine new hotels that catered to a beach packed with families.

Norfolk, too, was beset with hippies sleeping on benches and in public spaces. With his huge heart, Anthony the Butler got into trouble with the ladies of the Woman's Club of Norfolk. As he was usually the last to leave at night, Anthony let hippies sleep on the porch of the Martin Mansion. Still, somehow, hippies climbed into the arch openings under the mansion and slept on the spacious dry dirt between the exterior part and the brick foundation. One started an accidental fire that was put down quickly. Alvah Martin, in his grave, must have gasped in horror at the sight of long-haired, unkempt young men with funny-looking colorful clothes sleeping on and under his fancy front porch, whose ceiling had been delicately painted sky blue to fool birds out of nesting in the corners. The incident never happened again after the ladies chided Anthony but understood his heart. Those hippies stayed within the law and moved on not a few feet but far enough from the Martin Mansion.

Chapter Nine

"A community united by the ideals of compassion and creativity has incredible power. Art of all kinds—music, literature, traditional arts, visual arts—can lift a community."

That quote by former Maryland governor from 2007 to 2015, Martin O'Malley, proves true for the Woman's Club of Norfolk, The Hague, and the city of Norfolk for the past century. In the 1970s, art flourished at the Martin Mansion, with a nationally acclaimed painter and art teacher giving art lessons to the club members and guests. It was Bertha Fanning Taylor who headed the French Salon there in the 1950s, and I would like to explain more about this amazing painter. She had done quite a bit for the art community in Norfolk, entirely different from what she did with the French Salon. And Mrs. Taylor minimally led the Chrysler Museum to where it is today. Art was the reason she moved to Norfolk in 1945 from her birthplace, New York City. Mrs. Taylor had some interesting background; she competed for the United States in the painting event for the 1936 Summer Olympics, submitting her "Horse Race at Saint Cloud," which was a venue for the polo tournament near Paris. It is not known if Mrs. Taylor ever won a gold medal!

In her early sixties, Mrs. Taylor was asked to move to Norfolk and work as curator of the Sloane Collection at the Hermitage Foundation Museum, which has quite a rich history in the art world. The Hermitage, located on the Lafayette River in the Lochhaven neighborhood five miles north of the Martin Mansion, was built in 1908 by William and Florence Sloane, wealthy New Yorkers. They had come to Norfolk fifteen years earlier to operate textile mills outside the city and named their new arts-and-crafts style home "Hermitage," a tiny summer home near North Shore Road that became their permanent residence. The Hermitage was expanded from its little hideaway of five rooms to a good-size Tudor-style house of forty-two rooms by 1936. Most of these rooms today hold a worldwide art collection and contemporary exhibition galleries, as the Sloanes were educated collectors and brought their art passion to the Norfolk community. They also helped found the Museum of Arts and Sciences in 1933 (now the Chrysler Museum). Then, they established the non-profit Hermitage Foundation in 1937, donating the furnished house, gardens, and outbuildings to the organization. They allowed the public to visit the Hermitage Museum beginning in 1942.

Mrs. Taylor was then asked by Florence Sloane to give a series of lectures called "The Art of Living" at the Hermitage. She must have referred to "art" as skill and "living" as a manner of life since she painted mostly outdoor scenes exhibiting serenity and happiness. Mrs. Sloane, who continued to live at the Hermitage after her husband's death, wanted the public to learn the background of each art collection she and her husband had brought from abroad. So, Mrs. Taylor provided her speaking and teaching skills and offered art classes at the Hermitage.

Between 1948 and 1951, Mrs. Taylor taught art appreciation, art history, painting, and drawing at the Norfolk Division of the College of William & Mary (now Old Dominion University). During this period, Mrs. Taylor taught classes in painting and drawing at the Norfolk Museum of Arts and Sciences and the YWCA until 1960. An active member of the WCN from 1968 until 1977, the widowed Mrs. Taylor continued teaching art students personally, so it is believed she resided on the second floor of the Martin Mansion toward the end of her life. Upon her death in 1980 at ninety-six, her long-time friend, Mr. Benjamin F. Clymer of the Reference Department at Old Dominion University, called Mrs. Taylor "Blue Blood, Blue Stocking, and True Blue with the brilliance of gold and the warmth of red."

It was good Mrs. Taylor lived long enough to see one of her teaching posts change its name to the Chrysler Museum in 1971. She was eighty-seven at the time.

Miraculously, one of the former WCN presidents brought in the Chrysler name without intention. Mrs. Grover Outland, who burned the mortgage of the Martin Mansion in 1958, saw her daughter Jean marry Walter P. Chrysler, Jr., an heir of New York's powerful Chrysler family of car-company fame. Jeff Harrison, curator emeritus, wrote an interesting lengthy article on Jean for the Chrysler Museum website:

Yet one woman stands apart in her singular commitment to, and extraordinary influence on, the Museum and the region's broader cultural life. Jean Outland Chrysler played a critical—indeed decisive—role in one of the most significant moments in the modern history of American museums in 1970–71 when the Norfolk Museum of Arts and Sciences received an enormous, epoch-changing gift of art. In August 1970, after careful courting by the Norfolk town fathers, Jean's husband—Walter P. Chrysler, Jr. of New York and Provincetown, Massachusetts—officially agreed to donate nearly 8,000 works of art from his nationally known collection to the Norfolk Museum. The gift was a veritable treasure trove of European and American paintings, sculptures, glass, silver, and furniture. Overnight, it transformed a small, local museum known mainly for its natural history displays and modest period rooms into one of the nation's foremost art institutions. The Norfolk Museum was renamed the Chrysler Museum of Art to honor its newfound patron. Chrysler's patronage would extend another eighteen years until he died in 1988. Throughout that period, he gave hundreds of additional works—a torrent of paintings, sculptures, and decorative arts objects—that dramatically expanded upon his initial donation and cemented the Chrysler Museum's role as the chief cultural resource of Virginia's Hampton Roads region and one of the premier fine arts museums in the southeastern United States. As Walter's devoted, art-loving wife, Jean labored alongside him for decades to build the collection and was vital in choosing its ultimate home. Without her, Norfolk might never have had a Chrysler Museum of Art.

The trail to the Chrysler Museum began as far back as 1914 when Anna Wood established the Irene Leache Art Association to promote artistic skills and opened the first museum in Norfolk, honoring her deceased friend, Miss Leache. Next, Bertha Fanning Taylor brought her art expertise from New York City to Norfolk, enriched the Hermitage Museum, and inspired the community to learn to paint. Next, Florence Sloane, who hired

Taylor to curate and teach at her beloved Hermitage, was pivotal in founding the Norfolk Museum of Arts and Sciences in 1933. Finally, it was Jean Outland Chrysler, along with her husband Walter, who brought over ten thousand pieces of art to a small, humble museum on the east side of The Hague, turning it into "one any museum in the world would kill for," as described by *The New York Times*. Now, the Chrysler Museum comprises over thirty thousand objects spanning over five thousand years of world history.

That fascinating group of women unquestionably instilled a love for art in the Norfolk community and the motivation to "lift a community."

***

In 1933, a school arrived on the corner of Colonial and Fairfax Avenues that would develop a close relationship with the Woman's Club of Norfolk for decades to come. Before that relocation, Virginia Garrison Williams and her husband, John, founded in 1927 a non-sectarian private school for boys and girls from kindergarten to eighth grade in a home on Boissevain Avenue. She remained the headmaster until her daughter Joan Graham took over in 1969. The Garrison-Williams School, occupying a charming, tan brick home with an arched front door, had small classes and a large recess yard; however, it did not have an auditorium. Therefore, The Woman's Club, only 425 feet away, rented theirs to Garrison-Williams about every week for assemblies, school plays, Christmas caroling practices, and even science fairs. Today, this school is just called The Williams

School.

I attended the school for four years in the mid-seventies and visited the Martin Mansion hundreds of times. However, we rarely had access to the fancy part of the mansion. Instead, we walked in single or double file on Fairfax Avenue after crossing the street from the front of the school on Colonial Avenue. We passed seven tall, narrow homes on Fairfax and climbed up the steps toward The Woman's Club. Then we turned right on its vast porch, waited at the side door at the right end of the porch, and finally entered the auditorium through the small, narrow hall—without ever touching the front door. I would not blame the club members for preventing preadolescents from barreling into the foyer and possibly knocking down a vase. We exited the auditorium the same way through the porch, not even seeing the wooden dogs on the mantle in the dining room or the grandfather clock in the foyer.

As I remember, a gray silk curtain ran across the back of the auditorium with a grand piano at the far right, and we did not even know about the four windows behind the curtain. Maybe earlier club members found the morning sun too blinding, so they covered the windows. Nevertheless, the curtain helped our school play as an easily visible stage. I was Thomas Jefferson, in powdered hair, my mom's navy-blue cardigan, and a makeshift white ruffle collar, in our fifth-grade play called "The American Revolution." Luckily, I did not have to say a single word, but my only role, a very important one, was to pass a significant piece of paper to another student whose acting role I cannot remember. Maybe it was Benjamin Franklin taking my Declaration of

Independence, and that student had to wear glasses. Some of my classmates were entertaining with their soldier costumes, as one wore a torn white headband with a smeared red mark. She was "wounded" in the Woman's Club of Norfolk auditorium.

Every holiday season, my classmates and I practiced Christmas caroling in the WCN auditorium and then at Christ and St. Luke's Episcopal Church at only two turns and six hundred feet away from the mansion, first up to Mowbray Arch and then right toward West Olney Road. Finally, after several weeks of rehearsal, we put on red or green hooded robes, held battery-operated candles, and marched over to Christ and St. Luke's for a formal choir attended by hundreds of spectators. It was always on a late Friday afternoon, the last day before our two-week holiday break. If I recall correctly, we went to The Woman's Club afterward for a reception in the auditorium. I believe so because Garrison-Williams School did not have a party room. My mom came each time and congratulated me, although she knew I did not do a single squat during the choir but only blended into a sea of red and green carolers—silently.

To be honest, I never sang. I only moved my lips to fit into the Christmas caroling choir. Most everyone, especially my classmates and teachers, knew my inability to sing along with them, and they took in stride with their only silent caroler. I was born profoundly deaf due to my mother contracting German measles during pregnancy. I was not officially diagnosed as having bilateral nerve deafness until I was three in 1964. At that time, many parents of deaf children decided on oralism (learning to speak and lipread) - unlike today, when there are more options, along with sign language. So, my parents took me to a well-known oral residential school in Massachusetts, and it was agonizingly painful for them to leave a clueless five-year-old six hundred miles away. However, I adapted well at Clarke School for the Deaf for seven years, bonding with my deaf friends, many of whom I still contact, especially on Facebook and rare visits.

My life changed in March 1973 when I came home to attend regular school for the first time. It was not easy after seven years at a deaf school where I had a strong sense of belonging. Now, I had to face the challenges in the hearing world, and it took two years for me to adapt even halfway, both academically and socially. However, to this day, I am grateful to Garrison-Williams School and Joan Graham, the headmaster (and a personal acquaintance of my mom's), for agreeing to take their first deaf student ever and making my transition smoother with its small classrooms like Clarke. I still maintain tremendous friendships with my hearing classmates after fifty years. We call ourselves the "GWS Girls" whenever we meet for lunch or an annual holiday party.

Because of the time-consuming oral education at Clarke, my English language development was severely delayed; therefore, my writing skills were at the kindergarten level with limited vocabulary. It is no longer the case with today's deaf children, who are much more advanced with better education and technology. The ability to hear is the ability to read and write. One picks up new words and entire, complete sentences in daily conversation, missing no small word—and then writes what they hear. Deaf children today work around the English language obstacle by relying on sign language to pick up sufficient details. Unfortunately, my deaf friends and I did not have that advantage, given our school's ban on sign language in the 1960s. For example, we had to learn to pronounce "George Washington" repeatedly, but who was he? We could have known that by sign language. Babies, even hearing ones, can learn – and show signs – before learning to speak. It is now understood that sign language has numerous benefits for language development and increased access to information and communication. For example, you show several pictures of George Washington to a deaf child and explain in sign language about him presiding over America and even cutting down a cherry tree. Then, use fingerspelling so that the child can learn to pronounce "George Washington" with motivation. Sign language can also help explain how to pronounce a letter or word. My deaf friends and I never had that chance to learn anything quickly. Therefore, I was several years behind in the English language and was put in regular third grade at almost twelve in March 1973. And, of course, I was the tallest one in my new class—and the only one with budding bumps on my chest. Then, the Garrison-Williams staff had me skip fourth grade to be closer to my peers, although I would stay two years behind in college.

I discovered my passion for writing at age thirty and realized I could improve my English skills by reading word by word and focusing on complete sentences. First, I kept pecking away at my Corona typewriter and then a MacIntosh. To further increase my appetite for writing, I took private lessons with a sweet Jewish lady named Anne Kramer and then attended creative writing classes at Old Dominion University. So, I am gluing myself to the keyboard after thirty years.

The Woman's Club also rented the auditorium for our annual science fair, only for students over sixth grade. We each brought our cardboard table, propped up our folding pegboard, and presented whatever selected subject to three judges. Some of us won ribbons. I have been trying to remember every topic I chose for four years, but I did present bees and honey in fifth grade, handing a small piece of wax honey on the napkin to one of the judges who politely put it in his suit pocket. As I watched in astonishment, I visualized him coming home with a sticky mess and a scolding from his wife.

And then, in eighth grade, unfortunately, I do remember what I presented. To this day, I am appalled at myself for even thinking of this subject for my science project. People would cringe when hearing of a topic haphazardly selected by a fifteen-year-old who had no idea that it was the most painful thing ever mentioned on anyone's lips: Headaches. But my doctor's dad took it with enthusiasm by creating a pulsing blood vessel with an elongated red balloon wrapped around with a white string. He squeezed it into multiple red puffs, turned to me with expectant eyes, and proudly said, "That's a headache." I cannot believe my mother even let him put that extraordinarily dreadful topic into my science project since she was prone to migraines, which I also experienced in my twenties and thirties. I tried to speak clearly to the science fair judges and explained a headache's symptoms and treatments (if any). Unsurprisingly, the judges refrained from recoiling at the sight of my blood vessel balloon as I squeezed it into imaginable pain. I should have returned to bees and honey, even if it was a fifth-grade repeat.

***

Norfolk was revitalized in 1971 with the addition of a multipurpose complex comprising an eleven-thousand-person arena named Scope, a 2,500-person theater known as Chrysler Hall, and a six-hundred-car parking garage. Located at the northern perimeter of downtown Norfolk, the arena was designed by the Italian architect Pier Luigi Nervi in conjunction with the (now defunct) local firm Williams and Tazewell, which designed the entire complex. Nervi's design for the arena's reinforced concrete dome looked like a UFO next to the normal-looking building of Chrysler Hall. The unique architecture of Scope brought thousands of gawkers to sports games, concerts, comedy shows, circuses, and many other loud and exciting events. At the same time, Chrysler Hall attracted ballet, opera, and symphony lovers. When Scope opened formally on November 12, 1971, the structure was the second-largest public complex in Virginia, behind only the Pentagon.

My parents' close friend, Anne Addington, was kind enough to take me to the basketball games at Scope every week in Spring 1973, immediately after I came home for good from the deaf school. I had few friends to play with in the afternoon since I was still new in Norfolk after seven years away. Residing in The Hague neighborhood, Anne was a die-hard fan of the Virginia Squires, a basketball team based in Norfolk, which played in several other Virginia cities. They were members of the American

Basketball Association from 1970 to 1976. We were amazed by the six-foot-seven Julius "Dr. J" Erving dunking at the net.

To this day, I am profoundly grateful to the late Anne Addington for bringing me out of loneliness during the most challenging phase of my life, transitioning from the deaf world to the hearing world. At least Anne brought me to the excitement of the sports world as I played basketball for Garrison-Williams.

***

My experiences with The Woman's Club continued into high school. We, as teenagers, often attended Young Life night gatherings at someone's house, a church reception hall, and even The Woman's Club. I remember a large crowd of us cheering on and clapping in the WCN auditorium. In case some of you do not know what Young Life is, It is a Christian ministry that reaches out to middle school, high school, and college students in all fifty of the United States and in more than one hundred countries around the world. Its mission is to introduce adolescents to Jesus Christ and help them grow in their faith. So, The Woman's Club heard informal guitar bands with tempo and gospel songs, comedy skits, silly contests, and a brief gospel sermon. And, of course, the front door was sealed shut, and we all piled into and out of the side door at the right end of the porch, never noticing the crystal chandeliers inside the mansion. If we had refreshments, the swing door from the kitchen to the back of the auditorium would deliver popcorn, grocery store cookies, or ginger ale. And leftovers and trash went out that way, too, without so much as going through the fancy dining room with the wooden dogs on the mantel.

The Woman's Club, with its grand architecture on Fairfax Avenue, drew the curiosity of children living on the block. The three Miller girls from the enormous Bruce house catty-corner from The Woman's Club were always delighted to watch food and rental trucks arriving at the mansion, so they knew a party, with fancy finger foods, was about to take place. Cory, Carter, and Meredith all attended Garrison-Williams, as I did. Cory was the oldest, around twelve, with wavy, light brown hair; Carter was ten, with straight brown hair to her shoulders; and Meredith was seven, with curly blond hair. Their stylish mother, Carolyn, dressed them in identical dresses for an occasional formal portrait and ensured they were well-mannered. However, she allowed her girls to play outside and only sometimes knew what they were up to when the Woman's Club of Norfolk had a garden party. Carolyn later said, "They all had a mind of their own." So, Cory and Carter, sometimes followed by their baby sister Meredith, briskly walked over to the Wards' house on the right of the Martin Mansion and scaled the six-foot-tall brick wall to watch the WCN garden party—and wait for it to end. I wonder what the WCN ladies thought of those little heads bobbing up and down over the top of the brick wall. I am sure they knew the Miller sisters wanted their sugar-laced cookies.

When the garden party finally ended, the girls caught the attention of Anthony the Butler who never hesitated to pass leftover cookies and finger sandwiches over the brick wall. Carter, years later, called him "a super kind man," and Cory instantly recognized him in his picture at the front door fifty years later. Meredith was too young to remember everything, but she was fascinated with the stylish dresses the WCN members wore. So was Cory, who told me that it was "such an elegant, mysterious fête, and I wanted to see the beautiful outfits and imagine what it would be like to attend." When I asked Carter if she was interested in fashion at the garden party, she replied no and called herself a tomboy, more interested in cookies handed by Anthony. The girls also sneaked onto the porch at the Martin Mansion when no one was inside and peeked into the curved front windows out of curiosity. Meredith reminisced that, like everyone else, she "parked in the windows when it was empty" and loved seeing the ladies "all dressed up."

Another girl, Kristen Pucher, lived at the Slover house next to The Woman's Club. She, too, attended Garrison-Williams and was around the same age as the Miller sisters and me. Her family bought the brick house from the estate of Sam and Fay Slover through their adopted son, Frank Batten, in 1968. And they kept the Slover House for twenty-six years, so Kristen saw quite a bit from her fancy next-door neighbor, The Woman's Club. She stated in her email to me on February 22, 2023:

"During the nice weather, I can remember seeing several ladies sitting in rocking chairs on the massive front porch. They would say hello and wave to my mom when she would stroll my brothers down the block. Ah, but Saturdays were special because that is when the wedding receptions happened. The brides in their beautiful long white dresses were like princesses to me, and as a little girl, I would eagerly wait for them to descend the front stairs and sometimes even participate in the rice throwing. During this

time, there was a lovely African-American gentleman named Anthony, who was a caretaker and handyman for the residents of the Woman's Club. He also was the resident bartender for several of the events and weddings. In fact, he was so well known in the bartending field that my parents and several other neighbors hired Anthony to bartend at their own cocktail parties and dinners. Anthony was so docile and sweet. At the end of every wedding reception, he would bring over slices of leftover wedding cake for my brothers and me to feast on."

Indeed, Kristen and the Miller sisters developed a sweet tooth from Anthony, who was not only the butler but everything to the residents of the Martin Mansion and the entire 500 block of Fairfax Avenue.

It was during this 1970s decade that Anthony hung up his butler suit for good after thirty-eight years. The WCN minutes gave different stories of his exit from the Martin Mansion, stating that he was ill with undisclosed health issues but kept working. And the club members, appreciative of his long-time loyalty, gave him a salary after years of paying him by the hour to help with his sick days. One meeting minutes quoted, "After he died …," but I could not find any death report or obituary during 1975 or so when he left. Strangely, Anthony may have lived until 1994 at age eighty-six. I found an obituary dated April 26 of that year, and it gave sufficient evidence of "Kinchen Anthony," his legal name, which did not seem as ordinary as "Anthony Kinchen." It stated he was born in 1907 in Tarboro, North Carolina, exactly where Anthony the Butler hailed from. And he was thirty at the start of his job at The Woman's Club in 1937. Then, a 1973 newspaper article on him in *The Virginian-Pilot*, written with humor by Lawrence Maddry, put Anthony's age at sixty-six. So, yes, that had to be him leaving the earth at age eighty-six in 1994.

I tried reaching out to one of his grandchildren for confirmation to no avail. At least, Anthony must have enjoyed his lengthy retirement, or he must have continued bartending at other homes—and making sure that male hosts dressed appropriately before the guests arrived.

***

Ever since it originated in 1928, the Junior Woman's Club of Norfolk, still young, under thirty-five, had sponsored numerous fashion shows at the Martin Mansion and other city places, while the General Woman's Club of Norfolk, thirty-five and up, were more focused on educational lectures, public issues, prayer groups, and bridge games. However, the most impressive feat the Junior Club members ever did was initiate a layout plan for the ten-thousand-dollar children's playground for Norfolk's Tidewater Rehabilitation Institute (TRI). That institute, located not too far from The Hague on Brambleton Avenue, offered a broad rehabilitative program for 125 disabled children, shaping them up for regular school. (As a former job coach for the disabled, I am avoiding the term handicapped, as suggested by the Americans with Disabilities Act. However, *The Virginian-Pilot* did use that outdated term in the 1970s, when the Junior Woman's Club was given recognition for their playground idea.) The institute needed a playground for their patients from ages three to thirteen. The Junior Woman's Club of Norfolk knew it had to be a special one accessible to the physical needs of these disabled children, so they did a layout with the advice of the TRI director, Thaddeus Gaber.

However, the Junior Club could not complete the playground project alone with sufficient funding, so they invited other women's organizations to help finance it. Their request was accepted handsomely, as several groups jumped in to make the playground feasible. They were the Suburban Junior's Woman Club, Chesapeake Beach Woman's Club, American Association of University Women, the former Tidewater Association for Retarded Children (Yes, that R-word is outdated and unacceptable), and several other organizations.

And, of course, like always, the Woman's Club of Norfolk financially helped with their young ones' playground project. Those two clubs under the same roof of the Martin Mansion had assisted one another for decades, although they had their own bylaws and regulations. Age was the difference. But still, they were highly similar in one aspect: Dedication to the community and volunteerism.

As of 1972, there were over four thousand members in the Junior and Woman's Clubs of the Hampton Roads area; that is, in seven cities, including Norfolk, surrounded by the Atlantic Ocean, Chesapeake Bay, James River, and multiple other rivers. A 1973 article in *The Virginian-Pilot* with the headline "Woman's Clubs Sum Up '72" showcases the outstanding contributions of all these woman's clubs:

The Tidewater District of the Virginia Federation of

Woman's Clubs held its 51st annual meeting Tuesday at the Lake Wright Motel.

The 4,150 Tidewater Junior and General Woman's Club members donated $60,775 to projects during 1972 in education, mental health, child abuse, and conservation.

The clubs sponsored defensive driving courses, first aid classes, art shows, choral concerts, and tutoring sessions as educational activities. The Portsmouth Junior Woman's Club was awarded the Denbigh Humanitarian Award for establishing an Individualized Learning Center for children with learning disabilities.

District clubs donated $6,200 to the Virginia Mental Health Foundation. Clubs collected glass bottles, newspapers, and phone books for recycling and wrote and distributed a handbook called "Ecology and You."

The Hampton Junior Woman's Club was awarded a certificate for establishing a child abuse action group composed of a pediatrician, two social workers, and club members.

The [Tidewater] federation's 19 junior clubs donated $2,250, a truckload of linen, and a portable refrigerator to Camp Easter Seal.

The following clubs received awards at the junior luncheon: Junior Woman's Club of Phoebus and Junior Woman's Club of Hampton for "The Neglected and Abused Children"; Junior Woman's Club of Cradock for "Camp Easter Seal"; Junior Woman's Club of Portsmouth for "Cradle to College";

and Junior Woman's Club of Bayside for attendance.

Mrs. Timothy O. Kenny of the Virginia Beach-Princess Anne Junior Woman's Club was named the Outstanding Junior of 1973.

Imagine all those similar accomplishments across the country and in sixty countries. It started in 1890 with the establishment of the General Federation of Women's Clubs, first with sixty-three clubs. Then, the community contribution and volunteer service spread across the globe at lightning speed. As did women's rights. Rejection might be a good thing since it can make one fight harder and even win on a much broader scale. If … Jane Cunningham Croly had not been forbidden to listen to Charles Dickens at Delmonico's, the Woman's Clubs might not be here …

***

During the decade, the GFWC became the first women's organization in the world to undertake a relief program for food-deficient nations of the world, particularly in Africa. The organization had initiated "Signs of Crisis" with CARE as its partner. CARE started in 1945 as an international relief agency to funnel food packages from Americans to loved ones affected by World War II in Europe, so it stands for Cooperative for American Remittances to Europe. While the world was smoldering from the World War II ruins, Arthur Ringland and Dr. Lincoln Clark asked twenty-two American charities to propose a non-profit corporation to send food, and it was agreed by all these charities to incorporate with CARE—and send food rations known as CARE Packages, as that symbol still exists today.

The GFWC became involved with CARE in 1950 during the invasion of the Republic of Korea since the organization's sisters in Korea appeared to be in danger. President Dorothy Houghton expressed concern on American radio: "Our deepest sympathy goes to the citizens of this free republic and especially to the women, many of whom are affiliated with the General Federation."

The GFWC then partnered with CARE and "solicited funds from schools and businesses, held food and rummage sales, and garnered positive local publicity for the Care-for-Korea campaign, which raised over $325,000 for CARE packages during the Thanksgiving season." That was an impressive amount of money from the hearts of GFWC women and American citizens then, as it would have been close to four million dollars today.

Since then, the GFWC has incorporated with CARE, as did the Woman's Club of Norfolk, which raised funds with its "Count Your Blessings" Thanksgiving program to help twelve countries in 1959. Then, the WCN contributed funds to the building of schools in Mexico. In 1972, the club participated in the GFWC–CARE program "Challenge for Change," focusing on African women and children. Two years later, the WCN helped the GFWC raise funds for the "America Cares" campaign, concentrating on community development and food production in Ecuador, Guatemala, Nicaragua, Peru, and Honduras after a devastating hurricane in September 1974.

Indeed, the GFWC generated compassion for underdeveloped, food-deficient, war-afflicted, and weather-damaged nations worldwide. All it took to raise funds was to garner sentiment for the food packages and basic needs to be sent to countries. But the GFWC's next project, possibly the most extensive and most strenuous one in its lifetime, would require actual hands and brains from the club members and American citizens, not just digging into their pocketbooks, to save America from being infested with crime.

***

The 1970s saw a spike in crime nationwide, and I can see the unfortunate facts on the "Virginia Crime Rates 1960 to 2019" spreadsheet on the Disaster Center website. There were noticeable and significant crime increases between the 1960s and 1970s, although the state population remained in the four million digits (increasing to five million after 1976). Several crimes, such as burglary, robbery, and larceny, skyrocketed, while violence, rape, aggravated assault, and murder steadily increased. For instance, the crime index for Virginia in 1965 was over 98,000, whereas in 1975, it was nearly 226,000. Robbery, the most common of all criminal actions, spiked from 1,780 instances in 1965 to 6,878 in 1975. Virginia was not the only state with a major crime problem in the 1970s; it was happening nationwide.

So, we see a spike in crime during that tumultuous decade but a slow increase in the 1980s. There appears to be a reason for that gentle break: The "Hands Up," a citizen-based grassroots program launched by the General Federation for Women's Clubs in 1975. President Gerald R. Ford applauded the program as a "valuable public service" and invited the GFWC leaders to the White House to discuss crime prevention. As almost everyone in the federal government agreed, the GFWC decided citizen involvement was essential to reduce crime and should not be left to the criminal justice agencies alone. Hence, the GFWC received a grant of $380,476 from the Law Enforcement Assistance Administration (LEAA) to study possibilities and organize programs involving citizens in reducing crime. By then, the GFWC had 13,067 affiliated clubs and around six hundred thousand members, and this umbrella organization had all the clubs involved in the Hands Up program. (Yes, the number of club members in the GFWC had diminished by half because they no longer had to fight for women's rights, such as voting and working. And it was becoming more difficult for suburban working women to find time to volunteer.)

The 13,067 woman's clubs across the nation jumped in to assist with crime prevention on the local level. Each club was asked to perform a community-wide inquiry of citizens and agencies and then collate the survey reports for the state chairman, who would turn the results into a national crime "summit" meeting in Washington, D.C. The primary purpose of the inquiry was to provide an overview of the work done by local private social agencies like United Way and the Legal Aid Society. The other goal was to assess citizens' attitudes toward crime issues. The GFWC members could also include perspectives and suggestions in the inquiry. For example, most citizens and club members agreed that the criminal justice system could do more to prevent crime and juvenile delinquency by not resisting community-based programs for offenders in the neighborhoods since prisons seemed to fail to rehabilitate prisoners. Finally, a delegate from each GFWC-affiliated club would attend the national conference on crime prevention, listen to experts from the Justice Department and other organizations, and return home to assist local agencies with developing workable plans to reduce crime in their communities. Overall, the primary goals of the GFWC's Hands Up program were to raise awareness for the crime problem and establish community coalitions to develop realistic crime reduction programs and projects.

The Texas Federation of Women's Clubs did an excellent job with the Hands Up program; it was possibly the most creative of all the clubs involved. Citizens in Texas were given minimal training for acting as cops and walking patrols in their neighborhoods; a Goodyear blimp flew with Hands Up ads and 7,500 electronically controlled lamps on its sides and bottom flashing anti-crime slogans; and policemen visited a camping site occupied by more than two hundred Girl Scouts, age six to eleven, and used an education presentation to warn them to stay away from "Dangerous Stranger." The Texas Federation of Women's Clubs also made realistic suggestions: A "Fuzz Festival" to bring youth and police officers together under friendly circumstances with exhibits, shows, you-name-it—and a puppet show at each elementary school to begin early training against crime for small children.

The Woman's Club of Norfolk did not get much publicity

on the Hands Up program but did participate in the juvenile aid program to prevent the rise of crime. It cooperated with the Virginia State Crime Commission and the Division of Youth Services. The WCN also sponsored a one-day seminar, "Aid to Juveniles: How Can We Help?" at the Martin Mansion on January 12, 1975, and over two hundred people, mostly from local organizations, attended by invitation. Local and state experts lectured and answered questions about volunteer assistance in juvenile programs, child and family relations, education, and mental health. Like the majority of the Hands Up participants, the WCN knew prison was not the place for rehabilitation; therefore, it was pivotal to reorient juvenile offenders to the community after these youths received adequate help.

After all this, crime slowed down nationwide toward the better-behaved 1980s. The General Federation of Women's Clubs takes colossal credit for stopping such a sudden massive rise in crime that might have spiraled out of control and made every American citizen feel unsafe to open the front door and walk to their car.

***

As expected of a sixty-five-year-old mansion with chipping paint, worn hardwood floors, and outdated appliances, the Martin Mansion desperately needed a significant do-over— which could only be achieved in phases, money-wise. Therefore, a house chairperson was appointed at the Woman's Club of Norfolk, in charge of dealing with home and fire inspectors and then sharing a list of needed repairs at the club meetings. If voted yes by the members, then the work began. But again, it was never done all at once because of money.

The house chairperson always had a new list to present at every monthly meeting. It would be nice if the WCN won a million dollars in the lottery, hired several contractors to do everything from foundation to roof, and then sat back without a worry. However, the club members took their beloved Martin Mansion in stride and even rolled up their sleeves to do some of the manual work. Mrs. James White, the house chairperson in the 1970s, painted rooms with the help of her husband, furnished a room on the second floor, purchased new rugs, made drapes, and replaced equipment in the kitchen.

Then, the feisty Mrs. Edna Schweitzer took over as the house chairperson in 1976 and did various work around the mansion. One night in January 1977, during one of Norfolk's rare deep freezes, the pipes froze and burst. Fortunately, members and neighbors brought their tap water in gallons to the tenants on the second floor. Mrs. Schweitzer could not thank them enough and continued renovating as much as possible. She had the powder room painted and even installed another toilet to meet the ladies' needs, while the men's bathroom stayed in the basement but did get a fresh coat of paint. New wallpaper went up. The house's exterior was painted for $2,092, which had to be quite exorbitant (over ten thousand dollars today) due to the extensive size. Better yet, Mrs. Schweitzer remembered Anthony the Butler's mistake of allowing hippies to sleep under the porch, so she installed new grills vertically over the opening arches.

Then, she would have to ask the club members at the next meeting for approval in paying $1,200 to repair the chimneys. If the club considered that amount too much, then Mrs. Schweitzer would call for another estimate. The house chairperson, regardless of who she was, never attended a monthly meeting without a list of needed repairs, appliances, rugs, or whatever the Martin Mansion needed. Paige Rose, dealing with the declining but salvageable mansion in 2014, called the constant need for repairs a "whack-a-mole."

The best way to raise money for the house upkeep, the WCN realized, was to host bazaars. The club members were encouraged to collect as many goods as they could, occasionally with the help of relatives and friends. A Christmas bazaar would bring in a reasonable amount of money to afford the mansion's most urgent repairs. The WCN once teamed with a country store, a bakery, and a Christmas shop to host a large bazaar. It would not be surprising if several members of the WCN used their talents to paint flowerpots, dress up dolls, decorate Christmas wreaths, or even make home décor for the bazaar.

One item was a hit at all the bazaars—at churches, schools, festivals, and other markets in Norfolk: A quart of Brunswick stew. Round plastic containers appeared everywhere, frozen, refrigerated, or freshly cooked. Doubtlessly, the WCN members began making Brunswick stew alone at home or together in that industrial kitchen of the Martin Mansion, throwing corn, okra, lima beans, potato cubes, onion, and shredded or cut chicken into a gigantic pot of canned tomato stew. And they, like everyone else in town, sold those quarts like hotcakes. My mom made Brunswick stew for charity at the Episcopal Church of Good Shepherd, often with her friends Cutie Park and Babe Simpson. Those chatty ladies must have had a ball in their church's industrial kitchen since they all loved to laugh while tossing ingredients into the boiling pot. Much to her family's delight, Mom brought home a few quarts of Brunswick stew for our dinner. And she was the ultimate joker, as I remember when Cutie's daughter Mary came by to exchange Christmas presents with me in 1977. Mom beamed and asked Mary to wait. She reappeared with a frozen quart of Brunswick stew topped with a red bow and a note that read, "Merry Christmas, Cutie! Enjoy this soup. Love, Indie."

The history of Brunswick stew is sketchy, and its specific origin has yet to be discovered. Brunswick stew is a tomato-based soup consisting of lima beans, corn, potato cubes, and cut or shredded chicken. Onion, okra, and even sherry can be added as well. The states of Virginia, North Carolina, and Georgia all claim its birth, with Brunswick County in Virginia and the city of Brunswick in Georgia claiming it was developed there. However, it may have originated earlier in northern Germany. Regardless of where the Brunswick stew originated, it is still a damn good soup.

***

By the late 1970s, The Hague remained the same after nearly a century, although the two high-rise luxury apartments had recently appeared along the waterway across from Mowbray Arch. The Hague Towers and the Pembroke Towers stood about a quarter mile apart. The former was on the right side of the historic

Unitarian Church of Norfolk from the Mowbray Arch view. It is interesting how those two buildings contrasted in architecture. The Hague Towers exhibited a contemporary look, and the Unitarian Church, built in 1902 for the Second Presbyterian Church, showed the Gothic Revival style. Then, the Hague Medical Building, with three floors, came up next to the twenty-story Hague Towers in 1976. Since then, there has been no further development along The Hague.

It turned out that by the end of the 1970s, the Martin Mansion stood on two historic districts on the national and state levels. Nine years earlier, the Mowbray Arch area with stylish homes was listed as a state historic district in Virginia. Later, The Hague neighborhood was considered a part of the national historic district; that is, the Ghent Historic District.

Then in 1979, a drastic change occurred in East Ghent, less than a mile from The Hague. It was a ninety-acre area northeast of The Hague bordered by Olney Road, 21st Street, Colonial Avenue, and Granby Street. Deteriorating due to neglect and lack of city maintenance since World War II, East Ghent had mostly black families who moved in the 1940s and '50s – when many white people fled to the suburbs, known as the white flight. Several black families adapted well to their neighborhood in East Ghent, often looking out for each other. Then, as time went on, the homes and streets went into decline, despite the black owners repeatedly notifying the city, only to be ignored. However, the blacks had nowhere else to settle in another neighborhood; they just stayed in East Ghent and did the best they could.

Then, it all changed when Norfolk brought in its bulldozers to raze the entire community of East Ghent. The city had begun its gentrification and renovation project, which was disastrous for black families who had to move elsewhere. Unfortunately, it looks like the city seized their homes through eminent domain and replaced them with new expensive houses, condominiums, and townhouses in the same area now called Ghent Square. The original black residents were then priced out of their own neighborhoods. For those who worked in the area, if they didn't have a car, they also had to leave their jobs and find new work closer to their new home. Some found secure neighborhoods with improved living conditions miles away, while others never recovered and struggled with drugs and crime.

Michael Daniels, a former resident of East Ghent, told the WHRO media on July 22, 2020, that "the social implications of displacement are staggering. When you disperse people and put them in different neighborhoods, and you move them away from their culture, and from that background, it does have a psychological effect on people."

The story of East Ghent is not one to be forgotten because that area is now a part of the Ghent Historic District, as is The Hague. The first four blocks of Colonial Avenue leading from Olney Road *are* historic due to the beautiful First Presbyterian Church in Perpendicular Gothic style, Victorian homes, and brick apartment buildings, most of which were built in the early part of the twentieth century. However, I would not consider the area of the former East Ghent historic since its background story is not a pretty one. As it had occurred a few times since the 1950s, the black population in Norfolk has been forced to leave their homes and move elsewhere, as in many other cities across America. East Ghent then lost its name to such a harsh, abrupt gentrification in Norfolk. As of today, several sources have stated that Norfolk has learned its past—and history—of gentrification and is now aiming to prevent such unreasonably excessive actions in the future.

Chapter Ten

Five and a half blocks from the Martin Mansion, something miraculous happened at 7:46 a.m. on December 28, 1981, that would immediately garner worldwide attention. Nearly nine months earlier, the conception of a unique kind occurred in a test tube for the first time at the Eastern Virginia Medical School, performed by a husband-and-wife team. The following months brought hope and anguish for everyone involved. A married couple from Massachusetts resided temporarily in a condominium close to the hospital and lay low, keeping their identity private from the curious public at the doctors' advice.

Then, the long-awaited miracle finally happened, bringing joy and relief amid loud cheers, clapping, and tears. Imaginable confetti rained down on Norfolk. Elizabeth Jordan Carr was born as the first test-tube baby in America and the fifteenth in the world. Dr. Mason Andrews had the most successful delivery of his long obstetrics career. Drs. Howard and Georgeanna Jones, pioneers in reproductive medicine, had finally succeeded in their long-time complicated and worrisome in-vitro fertilization treatment. Those two doctors finally made possible the first test-tube baby in America. And Judy and Roger Carr, after several unsuccessful pregnancies and heartbreaks, became parents of America's new star.

Three years earlier, on July 25, 1978, the world's first test tube baby, Louise Brown, was born in England and appeared on the cover of every magazine across the globe. Therefore, the public had known about in-vitro fertilization, a process in which doctors fertilize an egg outside of a woman's body and implant the developing embryo in the womb. So, women with damaged or missing Fallopian tubes carrying fertilized eggs from the ovaries to the uterus can become pregnant. But the public did not expect Norfolk to be the site of America's first test tube baby until Dr. Howard Jones entered a conference room at Norfolk General Hospital and announced, "It's a girl." Elizabeth Carr, weighing five pounds and twelve ounces, was indeed a healthy baby.

This in-vitro fertilization (IVF) milestone touches me profoundly because my only niece, Anica, was born as a test-tube baby on February 10, 1989. By then, more than five hundred babies had been conceived through IVF at the Jones Institute for Reproductive Medicine at Eastern Virginia Medical School. Drs. Howard and Georgeanna Jones had maintained their spot as the country's most successful IVF doctors. They deserve gratitude for beginning my niece and goddaughter's life prematurely in a test tube—actually, a Petri dish. I will never forget the tearful scene at the hospital when my overjoyed brother Nash waved at me and my other brothers in a crowded lobby several yards away through the hall window. He was holding the fifteen-minute-old Anica in his arms and caught my attention. I bolted with my brothers Lindsay, Harvey, and their wives following me. We all cried at the sight of red-faced Anica looking at us with wide, intelligent eyes. Nash handed me his newborn daughter in a blanket, and I held her in my arms for a long moment. Anica, in a white cap, looked at all of us in curiosity, apparently wondering what the teary fuss was about. This was a test-tube baby finally achieved after Nash and Vickie's four long years of trying to have children.

Three months after Anica's miraculous entry into the world, Drs. Howard and Georgeanna Jones threw a Mother's Day party for the families of 175 children conceived at their IVF clinic. The Associated Press News covered the event and stated that these families were among the lucky few; about 20 percent of the couples who underwent the IVF program emerged with a baby. Nash and Vickie were included in that article, so here is what the AP News wrote:

Nash Bilisoly, a Norfolk lawyer, cradled one of the youngest partygoers, 3-month-old Anica Bilisoly. After four years of trying to have a baby, Bilisoly and his wife, Vickie Bowdoin, succeeded in their first attempt at in-vitro fertilization. "I don't know if we would have done it again. It's expensive," Ms. Bowdoin said. The couple just paid the institute's $6,000 bill, none of it covered by insurance. "You just have to cross your fingers and hope for the best," Ms. Bowdoin said. "I really think it's a roll of the dice." Like other in-vitro parents, Bilisoly and Ms. Bowdoin said they plan to tell their daughter that she was conceived in a laboratory. "I think I'll have her first formal portrait taken holding her petri dish," Ms. Bowdoin said.

Then another miracle happened to Nash and Vickie a year and a half later: Their son Frank was conceived naturally and born as a healthy, bouncy baby. And his first formal portrait did not include a Petri dish, of course. And, once a test-tube baby, our beloved Anica is now in her mid-thirties, accomplishing in the education field, climbing mountains worldwide, running marathons, and living in San Diego with her husband, Nicholas Roberts.

Born and raised in Baltimore, Howard and Georgeanna Jones were respectively seventy-one and sixty-nine years old when they achieved their first in-vitro fertilization milestone in Norfolk. They could have retired, as most physicians across the country had to put away their white coats by the time they turned sixty-five. However, as the pioneer couple prepared to go fishing full-time after a long career in obstetrics at Johns Hopkins, they received a call from an old friend, Mason Andrews, at the fledgling Eastern Virginia Medical School in Norfolk, asking them to help get the in-vitro dream started. Howard and Georgeanna wholeheartedly agreed. They had worked with English scientist Robert Edwards, who produced the world's first test-tube baby in Oldham in northwest England. The baby was named Louise Brown. Howard and Georgeanna saw potential in Norfolk as a place to produce America's first test-tube baby.

As strange as it might sound, Howard and Georgeanna moved to Norfolk on the day Louise Brown was born across the Atlantic. They began working with the local doctors in preparation and opened the IVF clinic in March 1980. A year later, Judy and Roger Carr were the perfect candidates. They conceived in a test tube and struck gold eight and a half months later. As it turned out, Howard and Georgeanna stayed in Norfolk for almost thirty years— as a working couple of *far-advanced* retirement age. They cared too much for desperate couples trying to have children to relinquish their careers to fishing poles. Georgeanna kept on working until her diagnosis of Alzheimer's disease in the 1990s, and Howard continued working at the clinic named after him and his wife, training new IVF doctors and writing books. She died in 2005 at ninety-two, and he died ten years later at 104. Married for sixty years, Howard and Georgeanna were a phenomenal couple devoted to an in-vitro fertilization career that added over three thousand pairs of baby footprints scrambling over Norfolk and onto their homes across the country.

***

Eastern Virginia Medical School (EVMS) was expanding in the 1980s after opening its doors to the first twenty-three students in 1973. But its history goes back to 1964 when the Virginia legislature realized that Norfolk and the Hampton Roads region comprised the nation's largest metropolitan area without a medical school; it also needed more physicians to accommodate the growing population. So, the General Assembly created the Norfolk Area Medical Center Authority, appointing Dr. Mason Andrews as its chair—and the driving force behind EVMS.

Henry Clay Hofheimer II, a prominent businessman and philanthropist who dedicated much of his life to improving Norfolk, led a group of supporters to establish the Eastern Virginia Medical School Foundation in 1969. Often seen walking his Doberman in his Ghent neighborhood, the tall and slender Mr. Hofheimer had also helped arrange for the movement of Walter Chrysler's art collection to Norfolk in 1971, and he was a true civic leader with numerous distinguished awards. Thanks to the hard work of Mr. Hofheimer and Dr. Andrews, sufficient funding helped open EVMS, which today "holds an honored position in American history as one of the only schools of medicine and health professions in the nation to be founded by a grassroots effort," according to the EVMS website.

In the following years, some EVMS students—if they wanted a quiet space during times of intense studying—found themselves in a perfect one-bedroom apartment within a few minutes' walk to the medical campus: One of the rooms on the second or third floor at The Woman's Club.

***

The EVMS students were not the only ones to pitch a tent at The Woman's Club. Returning from college for a late spring break in 1985, I was aghast to learn that my brother Harvey Bilisoly was now living at The Woman's Club after moving back from Washington, D.C. A footloose and fancy-free bachelor with a head of curly black hair living at *The Woman's Club*? I did not know the WCN rented rooms upstairs then and had never been on the second floor, so I was curious to see Harvey's new place. I rang the doorbell at the enormous front door with house number 524 above it, peeked through the beveled side window, and saw my brother running down the grand stairway. I shook my head in utter disbelief that my brother was residing at this house known to cater for decades to classy WCN ladies over wassail punch. Mrs. Frantz Naylor, who died after a full life in 1960, would have looked in astonishment at a young bachelor in shorts barreling through the fancy foyer of the Martin Mansion she had acquired for her club in 1925.

Harvey let me in, proudly sweeping his arm toward the stairway. I looked him up and down; he wore a sea blue polo shirt, running shorts, striped tube socks, and sneakers. Because of my deafness, I usually have an excellent visual memory, even decades later. Harvey did look like he was selling surfboards. And he was no medical student in a white lab coat. His was not the attire I expected at this mansion where I had seen cocktail dresses and coat-and-ties for years on the first floor. Anthony the Butler would have chastened Harvey to dress more appropriately, but my brother lived there and might as well wear pajamas.

Harvey showed me his "apartment" on the second floor, the one in the corner with the front windows overlooking Fairfax Avenue. His place was not as big as an eighteen-wheeler cargo, but still, he was satisfied. A few chairs, a small sofa, Dad's handmade table, and a large drawing board occupied the room. Harvey was rarely a clutterer, which was a good thing. Only the drawing board with his pencil drawings took up most of the room view. Later, Harvey moved to a bigger room across the suite, exited by the previous tenant, and then an even bigger one on the same floor when another tenant moved out. So, he lived in all three rooms at the WCN, hauling his two-by-three-foot drawing board from dwelling to dwelling.

Harvey, being highly social, spent two exciting years bringing in friends and showing off, using his quote, "my house, so to speak," with all the elegant woodwork and landscape mural. But Harvey was forbidden to throw wild parties, as he was known to do that quite frequently at our parents' house, sometimes with their permission and other times without. But not here in this precious Martin Mansion, Mrs. Edna Schweitzer, the landlord, stamped her foot for clarity. She did not have to worry about the quiet, studious EVMS tenants, but my brother, yes. However, Harvey respected her wishes and continued to get along well with her. However, he later reminisced that Mrs. Schweitzer was a "fireball," keeping her beloved mansion free of a mishap. She was the WCN president for two years, from 1967 to 1969, and miraculously again twenty years later for one year. Mrs. Schweitzer was strongly attached to the mansion she had renovated many times.

***

A humongous birthday cake made a debut on the grassy area under the blue-and-white tent at the naval base. Initially created on the spot, the vanilla cake with blue icing, about eleven feet high and twelve feet wide, was held together with two-by-fours—enough to feed eight thousand to ten thousand people. The bold white icing letters in four lines on the front of the towering cake read HAPPY 300TH BIRTHDAY NORFOLK, while the three twenty-four-inch-tall battery-operated candles stood on top of the cake. With an estimated crowd of 125,000 people in attendance, not everyone could have a piece of that cake, but there were plenty of food concessions at the naval base's party hall and on the parade ground. Skydivers floated down; singing bands reverberated the atmosphere; Navy ships welcomed the tours; and fireworks burst in the nighttime sky. The six thousand pounds of two ice sculptures shaped like tall ships melted in the summer temperatures; however, the joyful attendees expected that anyway. And stepladders were used to cut the giant birthday cake.

Indeed, 1982 was an endless celebration for Norfolk,

established on August 16, 1682. It was two years after Army officers Lieutenant Colonel Anthony Lawson and Captain William Robinson followed the British decree that every Virginia county purchase fifty acres and lay out a town to encourage "trade and manufacture." So, those two officers paid a carpenter, Nicholas Wise, ten thousand pounds of tobacco in 1680 for his fifty acres on the Elizabeth River, the site of today's downtown. Then, the townsite was laid out, and hence, Norfolk was born as a coastal city, thanks to abundant tobacco in the fertile lands of Southeastern Virginia.

Earlier that summer of 1982, Norfolk celebrated its three-hundredth birthday by hosting its sixth annual Harborfest downtown, attracting half a million people. This three-day festival honoring Norfolk and Hampton Roads as a historical and naval community, dating back almost half a century, is America's most extensive, longest-running, free maritime celebration.

The annual parade of tall ships rolls by the townsite on the Elizabeth River, surrounded by hundreds of personal yachts, sailboats, and motorboats. On Town Point Park, live music occurs on the center stage; Navy exhibits and demonstrations engage people; interactive games and activities entertain families and children; and vendors sell turkey legs, funnel cakes, t-shirts, artisans, and much more. Norfolk is one big, wild party once a year, obviously with more beer than tobacco.

Harborfest in 1982, which I attended, was a huge celebration for Norfolk's upcoming three-hundredth birthday with majestic fireworks on a Saturday night. My brother Nash and our cousin's husband, Chris Moring, began designing the annual Harborfest poster in 1980, and the first one was a flop—its neon-colored drawing looked too youthful. The following year, a better poster emerged with an impressive waterfront painting by Charles Sibley. The twenty-four-inch white tubes selling for ten dollars each disappeared right off the booth counter during the festival, and better yet, people were so fascinated with Harborfest that they bought the unsuccessful 1980 version available on the counter as well. Nash and Chris continued selling Harborfest posters for six years, using a different artist for each year.

The origin of Harborfest in 1976 is interesting: First, it was OpSail '76 that brought an international gathering of tall ships to New York City for the bicentennial celebration. I was there on that day with my mom and my grandmother, Donnie. My first cousin Jamie Kabler worked as the White House protocol under Gerald Ford and put us on the USS *Forrestal* ship in New York Harbor surrounded by the OpSail tall ships and thousands of boats. President Ford and his daughter Susan flew down from Philadelphia to the flight deck by helicopter, where Betty met them. My mom, Donnie, and I did not get close to the First Family but did see them waving from the deck. We were enraptured by the majestic view around us on the Hudson River beneath the midday sun. It was a colossal bicentennial celebration. We were indeed grateful to Jamie for giving us a rare opportunity to be in New York City and watch the parade of OpSail from the ship with the thirty-eighth U.S. President in 1976.

Operation Sail or "OpSail" did not start in 1976, to be

precise. It began in 1961 when maritime historians Frank Braynard and Nils Hansell of IBM wanted to foster global goodwill by inviting the world's remaining sailing ships to visit New York City. Being an ardent sailor, President John F. Kennedy endorsed this non-profit organization in 1963. OpSail grew bigger annually, with more foreign tall ships joining. It still runs today, as does Harborfest – simultaneously. Both events actually began in Norfolk with one lost ship…

The year before the 1976 bicentennial celebration, a single tall ship that was a part of OpSail unexpectedly tied up in downtown Norfolk. The Norwegian three-mast ship *Christian Radich* was so unique on such a rat-infested, muddy waterfront that it drew thirteen thousand visitors. Norfolk, therefore, asked several tall ships to stop by on the way to or from New York City's OpSail. A few did stop by in 1976, and that started Harborfest with fifty thousand visitors. "It would be almost unthinkable," said Mills Godwin Jr., Virginia's governor at the time, "for these great ships not to make Hampton Roads one of their ports of call." Since then, a fleet of tall ships has stopped by during Harborfest, and locals have taken delight in communicating with Russian, French, and other foreign sailors.

Then, in 1983, Norfolk celebrated Harborfest with the opening of a festival marketplace and a riverfront park downtown. The seventy-five-thousand-square-foot Waterside with 122 stores, restaurants, and gift shops kicked off with the urban planner James Rouse and the Norfolk mayor Vincent Thomas cutting the red ribbon. People packed into the seven-acre Town Point Park, where bands performed on the center stage, and enjoyed

Harborfest with beer, turkey legs, and funnel cakes. Downtown Norfolk got a tremendous facelift, no longer dirty with outdated warehouses, decaying piers, muddy banks, or rats.

All the credit went to James Rouse, a pioneering American real estate developer, urban planner, civic activist, and free enterprise-based philanthropist. He had initiated the idea of a festival marketplace to redevelop the declining downtown area and bring revenues to the city. Originally from Easton, Maryland, Jim Rouse developed several marketplaces across the country: Faneuil Hall in Boston, South Street Seaport in New York City, Harborplace in Baltimore, Riverwalk Marketplace in New Orleans, Pioneer Place in Portland, Oregon, etc. The Rouse Company was so successful in revitalizing old cities that Jim earned the August 1981 cover of *Time* magazine with his bespectacled smiling face over the words "Master Planner, James Rouse" and under the larger text "Cities Are Fun!" I will never forget my surprise when those magazines arrived at the drugstore where I was working as a cashier and stocker. I phoned Mom to exclaim, "Jim Rouse is on the cover of *Time* magazine!" She, too, was surprised and replied that Jim did not tell her when they socialized the weekend before.

Jim Rouse was my parents' dear, humble friend since he married Mom's friend Patty Traugott Rixey in 1974 and stayed at our house several times. A devout Democrat and the grandfather of actor Edward Norton, Jim once told me he had passed a twenty-dollar bill to people in Baltimore and Columbia, Maryland, where he was residing. He knew people would use his twenty dollars for refreshments, not drugs. Jim taught me the value of contributing to the city community with his giving stories. After forty years at the Rouse Company, he and Patty founded the Enterprise Community Partners, a not-for-profit foundation dedicated to increasing housing supply, advancing racial equity, building resilience and upward mobility, and associating social services with low-income neighborhoods. Jim cared about people with disabilities and made a touching toast about my deafness the night before my wedding in 1994. All so appreciated Jim for his hard work revamping cities and enlivening communities. In 1995, he received the Presidential Medal of Freedom, the highest civilian award, for his lifetime achievements.

Like Alvah H. Martin seventy years earlier, Jim Rouse changed the vision of Norfolk in the 1980s. Alvah made Norfolk a port city, and Jim made Norfolk a fun town.

***

The headquarters of the General Federation of Women's Clubs has been on N Street NW in Washington, D.C., since 1922. Known as the Miles Mansion, built in 1875, the GFWC headquarters consists of five stories built out of ashlar stone in a Renaissance Revival style. The most interesting part of its front is a splayed glass and iron marquee above the low-level entrance. All the windows are elongated, topped by transoms and keystone lintels. Extraordinarily beautiful on the inside, the Miles Mansion was declared a national historic landmark in 1991 for its association with such a powerful women's organization that has changed the world in many productive ways.

Shown in this book, an iconic black-and-white photo taken in 1926 is much admired; twenty-seven middle-aged and older women in dark coats and cloche hats pose in front of their newly acquired mansion in which the glass and iron marquee is the focal point. Four ladies sit in chairs while the rest of the group stands behind them. And no one smiles openly. However, these women knew it was not destined to be a party photo; they wanted to look serious about their organization—which promoted not only women's rights but also community improvement, eight-hour-a-day employment, the National Park Service, military warplanes, seatbelt safety, street lighting, crime prevention, and countless more important issues.

Since the organization's establishment in 1890, GFWC members have considered history the best teacher for everyone, including themselves. They understand that history puts us where we are today; as the world-renowned American writer in the twentieth century, William Faulkner, said, "History is not was, it is." In 1953, the GFWC cared enough about the education of American history to campaign and donate more than two hundred thousand dollars to the National Park Service for the restoration of Independence Hall in Philadelphia. That is the root of our Declaration of Independence, which fostered America's birth. The GFWC wanted themselves, new members, and the public to understand the importance of its historic mission to improve communities through volunteer service.

So, on May 1, 1984, the organization opened the Women's History and Resource Center (WHRC) inside its headquarters. As the GFWC website states, the WHRC strives to "educate and inspire GFWC members and potential members, the research community, and the public to explore the rich, historical role of women volunteers through GFWC's expansive collections. ... And it offers readily available reference services and an online research catalog."

The WHRC is an extensive archive, even given its medium-sized room at the GFWC headquarters (whereas the Woman's Club of Norfolk has its library in a tiny closet on the third floor at the Martin Mansion). However, dedication to volunteer service is the same between the general federation and its affiliated club. Documents, newspaper clippings, photos, online catalogs, scrapbooks, and related books stay in one place, regardless of their size, to educate all in improving the world.

***

The GFWC kept itself busy with Phyllis Roberts, the thirty-sixth president, who resided at the headquarters. A North Carolina native and an energetic lady with curly red hair, Mrs. Roberts had served over fifty years in the organization at the local, district, state, regional, and international levels. Now, she had reached the highest position of the GFWC as president for the 1986–1988 term, traveling to all fifty states and to fifty-six countries on six continents (eliminating Antarctica, of course). Mrs. Roberts met with national and world leaders and her favorite, Mother Teresa, with whom she worked on education, medical, and social issues in India. She cared deeply about the blight of impoverished people worldwide, people with AIDS, and smokers, for which her administration raised awareness and advocacy for improvement.

Mrs. Roberts was also concerned about the environment and endangered species. It disturbed her to see that the Endangered Species Act had not done enough to prevent whales and turtles from ingesting plastic discarded in the ocean or acid rain from killing trees and polluting drinking water for animals, so she urged over five hundred thousand GFWC members in the country and a million more abroad to act, not just study issues. A fan of networking, Mrs. Roberts urged club members to approach those in the animal field such as park rangers, law enforcement authorities, and even grocery store managers—and push for further protection of animals. One of my favorite sayings when urging for action is, "Don't go through paralysis by analysis. Get moving." That is what Mrs. Phyllis Roberts, as one vigorous GFWC president, projected to her club members and to the public.

As of October 1986, the U.S. Fish and Wildlife Service had named four thousand species as endangered, and the House of Representatives had approved an endangered species act. However, the Senate had yet to reauthorize the needed bill since four senators were holding it up. Mrs. Roberts encouraged the Woman's Club members to write to their members of Congress, urging them to act. She said, "When animals and man come into conflict, most often animals lose." She also stated that conservationists could not just protest and that "they must offer an alternative plan, something cheaper, and at the same time environmentally helpful. We are working to see what we can do." Being an ultra-activist for endangered species and animals in general, Mrs. Roberts established a nature preserve in Utah (name unknown), worked with the environmentalists Jane Goodall and Jack Hanna, advocated against fur traps, opposed the use of wildlife as pets, campaigned against Greyhound racing, and involved law authorities in dog fighting prevention. She did all she could do to fight for paws, claws, fins, wings, antennas, tendrils, and backbones on our fragile Earth.

***

Around the same time as its campaign to protect endangered species, the General Federation of Women's Clubs encouraged grocery store cashiers and baggers nationwide to say a critical question to a customer: "Paper or plastic?" It all began in 1987 when Jeanne Bakelar, a thirty-nine-year-old New Jersey woman, wrote a letter of gratitude to her grocer for making biodegradable paper bags available to those who did not want plastic. However, she was dismayed to learn that plastic bags had taken over the "unsung, all-American grocery paper bag" and wanted to give people a choice between those two different bags. Mrs. Bakelar said, "We want the public to know they have a right to tell store clerks they want the brown paper bags. It's the age of consumer awareness. The environment can't handle any more plastic." She then had her Woman's Club members approach their grocers and request paper bags to give customers a choice.

Sure enough, the General Federation of Women's Clubs heard about Jeanne Bakelar's paper bag campaign and started their two-year project. Mrs. Phyllis Roberts, who herself protested the use of plastic bags in grocery stores but acknowledged that people had a right to choose, assigned Mrs. Bakelar to represent the GFWC campaign. Moreover, the federation asked Mrs. Bakelar to help launch "a more extensive 'environmental packaging' campaign for using paper coffee cups, paper egg cartons, paper meat trays and other items that won't simply overflow the nation's landfills as indestructible plastic does." (And styrofoam, unfortunately.)

Interestingly, there was a difference between urban and suburban customers when choosing paper or plastic. "You could say it's an urban vs. suburban split," said William J. Vitulli, vice president of community relations for A & P, whose company policy gave customers a choice between paper and plastic bags. "Paper bags seem to stand up better in the trunk of a car," he said. "But people in the city don't drive. Plastic bags with handles are better for carrying groceries a few blocks."

Agnes Nemeth of Manhattan told *The New York Times* in November 1984 that she preferred plastic bags. "I use them for my garbage," she said, pushing her shopping cart home from the Fairway market on Broadway near 74th Street. "The paper ones break, they leak, they make a mess. These are prettier, and when I get them home, I can use them to line the garbage can."

Jeanne Bakelar, on the other hand, told *The New York Times* that she was a suburbanite who preferred paper bags. The plastic ones "scrunch the English muffins and the canned vegetables and the eggs together."

The third person interviewed by *The New York Times* was Heather Dembert, a Columbia University law student who felt that paper and plastic were beneficial for preventing leaking and slipping over. "I go to places that put one inside the other," she said. "I like my paper in my plastic."

That was before people increasingly relinquished the controversy of paper and plastic bags and instead brought to the stores their own tote or insulated bags.

Now state conservation chairman of the Junior Woman's Clubs of New Jersey, Jeanne Bakelar was pleased to see many of her thirty thousand members writing letters to grocery stores, thanking them for using paper bags, and passing out bumper stickers that read "Have you hugged your paper bag today?" and "Paper bags have sacks appeal." Mrs. Bakelar had amassed so much attention for her travels across the country to advocate fiercely for the all-American paper bag that she was called "The Bag Lady."

***

Several members of the Woman's Club of Norfolk hopped on a bus to Roanoke on August 14, 1987, for the annual conference of the Virginia Federation of Women's Clubs (VFWC). That conference ran for two days, attended by six hundred leaders and members of the Women's Clubs statewide. They fell in love with the two stars of the event: A twenty-eight-year-old Karen Drummond and her young German Shepherd named Odell. The whole thing started when, fourteen months earlier, the General Federation of Women's Clubs selected two home life department projects: The Arthritis Foundation and the Support Dogs for the Handicapped. Jean Burcher became chairman of that department, and immediately, she wanted to produce a team of an arthritic person and a support dog to "kill two birds with one stone."

The GFWC members applauded Mrs. Burcher's idea, although they expected it to be challenging. Six months passed without finding a disabled person with arthritis, though the search for a support dog was more hopeful. The Support Dogs for the Handicapped in Ohio had prospective dogs in training, one of which could be of tremendous help to an arthritic person. Just then, a miracle happened with one phone call from a vulnerable lady in Chesapeake, Virginia, to an overjoyed lady in Columbus, Ohio.

Karen Drummond, of a perfectly normal, intelligent mind, developed juvenile rheumatoid arthritis at age five. That disease had significantly damaged her hands and joints by the time she turned seven. Now Karen was a tiny, attractive woman with misshapen hands and only one hip joint. She had to end her employment as a telephone operator after eight-and-half years when her condition worsened with a broken leg, and she was rendered disabled. However, her profoundly religious attitude kept her strong and hopeful about the future.

One day at a doctor's office, Karen picked up a magazine about dogs and read an article about support dogs for arthritic people. She asked her doctor, who then encouraged her to call The Support Dogs for the Handicapped in Ohio. Jean Burcher of the GFWC finally achieved her dream of finding a disabled person with arthritis, and her organization paid four thousand dollars for Karen to travel to Ohio and train with her new dog for two weeks. The Arthritis Foundation chipped in a thousand dollars for the training fee, while the Communication Workers of America labor union, Telephone Pioneers of America, and her former employer AT&T covered additional expenses.

Karen met her service dog Odell, a flop-eared, long-haired German Shepherd, at the Support Dogs for the Handicapped in Columbus, which has since merged with Canine Companions for Independence, strongly supported by the GFWC. Those two, woman and dog, endured strenuous training sessions, sometimes exhausting, for two long weeks but finally passed the test for companionship.

Karen and Odell surely made a hit at the VFWC conference, where six hundred club members from across the state fawned over them. She shared with the audience how her life had improved. Odell could switch on lights, open doors, pick up things off the floor, help Karen get up from her bed, and even snarl at suspicious-looking people. Better yet, Karen's social life turned from nonexistent to lively—her companion dog enticed people to speak to her and ask questions, especially at her apartment's swimming pool.

It has been decades since the touching story of the woman-dog pair unfolded, and I have tried searching Karen online without luck, despite living only three cities apart. I sure hope she has obtained more Odells in sequence. However, the most crucial part of her story is that the Virginia Federation was the first in the nation to finance the four thousand dollars to train a support dog as a GFWC project, encouraged by Jean Burcher's kill-two-birds-with-one-stone fabulous idea.

***

The twenty-six alumni of Norfolk State College's first class attended the fiftieth-anniversary celebration on May 18, 1985; they all were in their seventies, graying and well-accomplished with higher education or more. Samuel F. Scott, the college's first director, referred to those twenty-six members of the 1939 class, saying, "They wanted an education, and they couldn't go away to school. We made the tradition. They believed in it."

Long inhibited in education, the African-Americans finally had their dream come true on September 18, 1935, when Norfolk State College opened its door to eighty-five students, providing "a setting in which the youth of the region could give expression to their hopes and aspirations." Those first classes took place in an old YMCA building downtown, but still, it was of higher education. Even during the Depression, many of the eighty-five students saw how the education provided by this new school would help increase their employment opportunities. At that time, Norfolk State College was a branch of Richmond's Virginia Union University, and graduates were awarded a two-year certificate.

Norfolk State College was able to pursue an expanded mission with even greater emphasis in 1956 when an Act of the Legislature enabled the institution to offer its first bachelor's degree. The school separated itself from Virginia State College and became fully independent in 1969, similar to when Old Dominion College broke away from the College of William & Mary in 1962. In that same year, 1969, Norfolk State College received accreditation from the Southern Association of Colleges and Schools—and had an enrollment of 5,400 students, making it one of the more prominent historically black colleges and universities (HBCUs) in the nation. Finally, in 1979, Norfolk State College received university status by granting graduate degrees. And it now had an entire, attractive campus just a mile and a half from downtown Norfolk.

No wonder the Reverend St. Paul Epps, one of the first eighty-five students at Norfolk State College, was ecstatic to be at the fiftieth-anniversary reunion in 1985. He graduated from Booker T. Washington High School with honors in 1935 and became the first enrolled at the new college only a few blocks from his home. St. Paul, as he was called, was so impressed with Norfolk State College that he personally recruited others to join him. Upon his college graduation in 1939, St. Paul did not stop pursuing further education; he graduated from Knoxville College in Tennessee and later became the only African American in his graduating class when he received his Master of Divinity from Pittsburgh-Xenia Theological Seminary in 1942. After doing missionary work, marrying a schoolteacher, and raising a family for several years, St. Paul received an honorary doctorate in 1955 from Sterling College in Kansas and later received additional postgraduate training at the University of Southern California. Most of all, his wealth of education began the day he entered the new college in the midst of the Great Depression. He told *The Virginian-Pilot* during the 1985 reunion, "I welcomed the opportunity when the Norfolk school came along. I would never have been able to leave town for an education if I hadn't got a start there. I never dreamed in those days that Norfolk State would emerge as a great university."

Ms. Woodard was at the reunion and agreed with St. Paul but warned there was still work to do to bring African-Americans into higher education. She had recently led a drive to raise five thousand dollars in contributions from the first class of Norfolk State, stating the money would be used for scholarships for students from low-income families. "There are still many of them out there who can't afford to pay for college," she said.

That quote must have led the boy who grew up in the Slover home next to the Martin Mansion to do something about it. It was Frank Batten, the founder of The Weather Channel. From his experience of serving as the first rector of Old Dominion College in the 1960s, Frank was a fierce supporter of education. He would not let anyone miss the chance to achieve their college dream as promising as the glorious sunrise over the glistening ocean infinite for a vast opportunity.

***

It all started in 1988 with an article in *The New York Times* that prompted Frank Batten and his friend Joshua Darden to work together on increasing college attainment for those who could not afford it. So, the idea for the ACCESS College Foundation was born. Reading the article, Frank and Josh admired the educational approach by New York businessman Eugene Lang, who adopted a sixth-grade class in Harlem and promised to pay for their college education if they graduated from high school and were admitted into college. Six years later, over 90 percent of the students graduated, and over half went to college. It was a significant achievement considering the high school's 75 percent dropout projection.

It was Josh's father, Pretlow Darden, who pushed for desegregation in Norfolk's public schools in the 1950s when he was mayor, as did Frank when he was the new publisher of *The Virginian-Pilot*. Pretlow, my grandmother's younger brother, also committed to educational opportunities for black Virginians and helped find a new site for Norfolk State College, where he was a member of the board of visitors for five years. Frank, in the meantime, did the same for Old Dominion College. Advocacy for desegregation and education placed Frank and Josh's father in the same element, and then, after the latter died in 1986, Frank and Pretlow's son Josh made a compatible duo team, founding the ACCESS College Foundation. Ironically, this shows the transition from the friend-and-father team for the desegregation of public schools to the friend-and-son team for higher education for the disadvantaged.

But before launching ACCESS, Frank and Josh had to consider the extensive cost of a college tuition promise for the graduating students or even the entire school system. They researched similar programs and learned that, unfortunately, hundreds of thousands of dollars in federal, state, and local institutional grants and scholarships for colleges were unclaimed by qualified low-income students. In most cases, the students and parents were unaware that the money existed, and they often needed to learn how to apply for the funds.

The Norfolk superintendent, Dr. Gene Carter, helped Frank and Josh with this tricky problem. As they had heard about the scholarship program there, Dr. Carter and a few school board members visited the Cleveland Public Schools and learned how kids had achieved higher education with assistance. Upon his return to Norfolk, Dr. Carter explained to Frank and Josh about the Cleveland model, which worked with middle and high school students in schools and community-based settings, and the advisors created a "college-going" culture in the schools by engaging students and their families individually and in group sessions. A group of interested professionals joined Frank, Josh, and Dr. Carter in establishing ACCESS in 1988; they were Anne Shumadine, Clifford Cutchins, Dr. Lucy Wilson, and John O. Wynne. They all began attaining their goal of eliminating barriers to postsecondary education and increasing college attainment for underrepresented and low-income students. Since then, ACCESS "has helped more than 77,000 students from low-to-moderate-income families enroll in a certification or degree program while leveraging $780 million in financial aid and scholarships. Additionally, ACCESS has awarded more than $14 million in ACCESS 'Last-Dollar' Scholarships to students, helping to make their educational paths possible," as stated on the ACCESS website. That is impressive, indeed.

Frank Batten was also involved with another university on the border between Norfolk and Virginia Beach. Virginia Wesleyan, rooted in the Methodist heritage, is a liberal arts institution with approximately sixteen hundred students. It was chartered in 1961, graduated its first class in 1970, and received university status in 2017. But it is Frank's wife, Jane, who has molded Virginia Wesleyan into the reputable school it is today. She joined the Board of Trustees in 1981 and began her impressive list of roles at this school for decades before receiving an honorary Doctor of Law degree. Such a driving force behind the development and revitalization of Virginia Wesleyan, Jane Batten is credited enough to have several campus buildings named after her.

Norfolk is now surrounded by institutions of higher education: Old Dominion University, Virginia Wesleyan University, Norfolk State University, and Tidewater Community College, with four campuses (one in Norfolk, the second in Portsmouth, the third in Chesapeake, and the fourth in Virginia Beach), and Eastern Virginia Medical School. Back in 1920, there was no college or university in Norfolk, and the closest one was William & Mary College, fifty miles north. However, there was a "university" on 524 Fairfax Avenue, beginning in 1925 when the education-driven Woman's Club purchased the home. The professors of William & Mary were invited and paid with gold coins to educate the club members and the public with their lectures. The foreign professors joined as well to educate about the culture, history, and government of their countries. It was not only professors and professional speakers who brought education to the Woman's Club of Norfolk. The club members brought it on themselves with an incredible array of departments, readings, and presentations. When I found a 1908 newspaper clipping about these women in the current events department discussing the Aldrich Act, which a first-year college student would find complicated and tedious, I realized the WCN was a true champion of education, like other clubs nationwide and worldwide. Thus began The Woman's Club University on Fairfax Avenue. Jane Croly, the founder of Sorosis and the GFWC, had her wish: Women had enriched themselves with education outside their kitchens.

***

The Woman's Club and The Hague saw an increase of festivity a block away or two in the 1980s, with the advantage of belonging to the Ghent Historic District, Norfolk's most popular area. The garden clubs organized walking tours on Mowbray Arch and along thirteen blocks of The Hague, where mostly ladies in bright-colored outfits admired rows of European-style homes and gardens, especially those in a semi-circle pattern facing the calm creek sans boats. The Stockley Gardens hosted an annual Mother's Day art festival that bore its name, and people filled this shady park, admiring artwork done by local, state, and national artists, each in a booth under the tent. The bands played in the park's first section on West Olney Road. The Stockley Gardens Art Festival grew so popular that it added another annual event in the fall. This bi-annual art festival still exists today.

The seven blocks of Colley Avenue from Maury Avenue to 21st Street became the Greenwich Village of Norfolk, a vibrant street named for a well-known shipbuilder of the early to mid-19th century, John G. Colley. Doubtlessly, this part of Norfolk is in the Ghent Historic District. If he had been alive, Mr. Colley would have been pleased to hear that his name was often mentioned throughout the city, referring to a business district street that runs three miles from the Elizabeth River north to the Lafayette River. There are Colley Printing, Colley Executive Offices, Colley Cantina, and Colleywood. That street began its revival in the late 1970s with new restaurants and gift shops. At the same time, the old 1936 Naro Theatre on Colley Avenue was upgraded with new ownership and a selection of classic, foreign, art, and independent films. Diversity on that popular street increased tremendously with small store owners, chefs, artists, yuppies, bachelors, bachelorettes, and gay people. The 80's fashion and hairstyles brightened the atmosphere with neon colors and spiky trends, so those seven blocks of Colley Avenue were indeed the entertainment center of Ghent. And still are.

My brother Lindsay Bilisoly, who regularly worked as a leasing agent for our Uncle Harvey's commercial real estate company, admired Ghent so much that he bought a tiny 1952 restaurant on Colley Avenue named Do-Nut Dinette in 1985. The size of a small school bus, that aluminum-plated place had its thin-lettered name at the top, vintage Coca-Cola signs, two large windows in the front, and a windowed entrance in the middle. Strictly counter service, Do-Nut Dinette resembled the 1942 Edward Hopper painting "Nighthawks" since dock workers would stumble into the harshly lit, empty space at four in the morning, when it opened, to prepare their day with eggs, bacon, and its famous greasy, sweet donuts. Lindsay was the proud owner of Do-Nut Dinette for two years before selling it to Sheila, the long-time waiter.

Possibly born an innovator, my brother still could not get

enough of Colley Avenue, so he rented an abandoned small storefront building three blocks from Do-Nut Dinette and remodeled it into a seafood café named Raw Bar Bay with the help of his wife, Koggie. People flocked there for its famous steamed shrimp and broccoli with Hollandaise sauce, followed by a delicious Key lime pie. Lindsay juggled working at Harvey Lindsay Commercial Real Estate during the day and managing his restaurant at night. A music zealot, he drove a few miles to Kings Head Inn, where the guest bands, some notable, were playing, and invited them to come and eat at Raw Bar Bay at his expense. They always accepted. Chris Isaak came to enjoy beer, possibly with steamed shrimp. And in another time, a member of the prominent band asked Lindsay if he had a Raw Bar Bay T-shirt. Since the restaurant was still new, Lindsay regretted he did not have one. The band member said, "Well, I was hoping to wear it tomorrow night on the David Letterman Show." Within a week or so, the Raw Bar Bay T-shirts arrived. A few years later, Lindsay sold the restaurant to someone who turned it into a Mexican restaurant named Colley Cantina.

So, that shows the come-and-go of restaurants and stores on Colley Avenue. Only the Naro Theatre, the Laundry Land Laundromat, and Hall's Shoe Repair have stayed all these years in the busy part of Colley Avenue. Sadly, the Colley Discount Pharmacy recently closed its doors permanently after several decades, and it was where I worked as a cashier and stocker in the summer of 1981 under the highly respected pharmacist David Halla. The Ghent Historic District does change with stores and restaurants, but the iconic European-style homes, three-story brick apartments, contemporary condominiums, churches and synagogues, parks, and the Martin Mansion remain the same. Most of all, Ghent brings together a diverse community of different professions, lifestyles, cultures, and numerous dogs.

***

The Ghent Historic District's wealth of religious buildings, including Christ and St. Luke's, Ohef Sholom, and Ghent Methodist, drew couples there to get married. The Hague seems the most romantic spot for exchanging vows, within a few feet of the Venetian-like canal minus gondolas. Then, the Martin Mansion became the site of marriage vows as well. Of the entire Mowbray Arch neighborhood, it was the only wedding venue—until September 23, 1989, when the newly renovated and expanded Chrysler Museum, after four years of work and $13.5 million, held its first wedding reception in an enclosed, Italian Renaissance-style, magnificently spacious, skylit court that dropped jaws and still does.

That wedding reception happened to belong to one of my best friends, Elizabeth Forsberg, who had married David Wadman at St. Paul's Episcopal Church in downtown Norfolk. When the Chrysler Museum announced that wedding receptions could be held in the new enclosed court at the entrance, Bruce and Fred Forsberg immediately joined a growing list of interested people. And they were delighted to hear that their daughter Elizabeth would be the first bride ever to celebrate at the Chrysler Museum. I felt honored to be her bridesmaid, along with our high school friend, Helen Roberts, whose father worked for years as a chief executive of TeleCable which was founded by Frank Batten in 1964. Richard "Dick" Roberts and his wife Shirley were heavily involved with the Chrysler Museum and made generous contributions to this new wedding venue. I was floored by the beauty of Elizabeth and Dave's wedding reception under the two-story-high skylight, surrounded by smaller galleries and white walls with Roman arches and facing a monumental limestone staircase leading to the second floor and more galleries. Since that first reception in 1989, the Chrysler Museum has hosted hundreds of weddings, cocktail parties, charity drives, and even New Year's celebrations. Elizabeth was one lucky bride to grab that first slot, and I was fortunate to be there!

Chapter Eleven

Jane Cunningham Croly was making news again one hundred years after founding Sorosis and the General Federation of Women's Clubs. Newspaper articles put out one or two similar brief paragraphs about her history dating back to 1868. Jane was gaining notoriety in 1990, even eighty-nine years after her death. It was because the GFWC had reached its centennial anniversary, although this organization now had a smaller umbrella to handle all the woman's club chicks. It was not as extensive as back in the 1960s, down from 12,000,000 members and over 16,500 clubs.

The significant decrease in the GFWC membership was caused by more opportunities for women outside the woman's clubs, and women could now enter the workforce, join book clubs, and attend extra-curricular activities with their children. And younger working women barely had time for leisure or involvement in any club. Therefore, GFWC, on its one-hundredth anniversary on April 24, 1990, had four hundred thousand members in fifty states, plus Washington, D.C., and Puerto Rico. On top of that, there were hundreds of thousands more members in forty-six countries. At least the woman's clubs had been around long enough to shape their communities, the country, and the world. Without these clubs emerging in the Progressive Era, women would not have won their rights to enter the ballot boxes.

Now a century old and permanently settled in Washington, D.C., the GFWC celebrated with a centennial theme: "A Past to Remember–A Future to Mold." Hundreds of woman's clubs across America were busy on "GFWC Centennial Day" or

"Federation Day," celebrating on their own with luncheons, fashion shows, teas, and even birthday cakes. Bobby Bjork in Virginia City, Montana, invited her Madison Valley Woman's Club members to her home for a potluck dinner. The Woman's Club of Paducah in Kentucky shared its clubhouse with sixteen district clubs for an old-fashioned Victorian tea reception and a "period fashion show" in which models wore outfits from 1890, the year the GFWC was established. Jeri Winger, the former GFWC president in Utah, recounted the organization's lifetime at the Provo Women's Cultural Center, and the celebration ended with lighted candles and music.

So, on April 24, 1990, the world heard the cheers of woman's clubs in fifty states and other countries, applauding Jane Croly for founding the "world's oldest and largest nondenominational and nonpartisan women's volunteer service organization." That same day also celebrated the successful launch of the Hubble Space Telescope on the shuttle Discovery for a five-day mission to deploy the massive stargazer into orbit. Indeed, both the GFWC and NASA shared a special celebratory day, one on the ground and the other in the universe.

However, all these women across the country quieted and settled in their seats at precisely 7 PM to watch the GFWC's video teleconference, "Women in the 21st Century," held at the U.S. Chamber of Commerce in Washington, D.C., and sponsored by the Proctor & Gamble Company. First, President George Bush greeted the viewers with his opening remarks from the Oval Office. Then, a brief video tour of the GFWC headquarters was shown, just over a half mile from where Bush spoke. Next, Dr.

Joyce Brothers led a panel discussion moderated by Judy Woodruff, a correspondent for the *MacNeil/Lehrer NewsHour*. Along with Dr. Brothers, the other panelists, including Bonnie Guiton, presidential advisor for consumer affairs, and Dr. Richard Berendzen, the American University president, explored the issues identified by the GFWC members in "Agenda for the 21st Century," a nationwide survey conducted in the previous spring. The key topics were education, elder care, environment, health, world peace, adolescent pregnancy, and daycare. In addition, selected viewers across America participated in the two-hour-long discussion via phone interaction with the panelists.

The Virginian-Pilot did not specify how the Woman's Clubs in the Hampton Roads area celebrated the GFWC Centennial; however, it did state that "local club members gathered at Tidewater Community College on Federation Day, April 24, to view a GFWC Centennial celebration televised from Washington, D.C." And the minutes from the Woman's Club of Norfolk did not give any account of what its club members did on that day. It is believed that the new WCN president in her seventies, who had taken this job when no one else would, did not make plans for the centennial day, but she encouraged the club members to "celebrate longevity with a cheer!" If the highly social and motivated Mrs. Frantz Naylor were the club president in 1990, she would have invited the entire city of Norfolk to celebrate the GFWC. And oh, yes, she would also make that week extraordinarily special because the annual pilgrimage to Cape Henry was on April 26, two days after GFWC Centennial Day!

The GFWC did not end its centennial celebration after

April 24; it had its National Convention in New York City during the week of July 4 of that year, followed by the sensational Centennial Gala with a musical extravaganza. But first, before the NYC Convention, there was a memorial service for Jane Croly, long buried in her grave. Two years earlier, the members of the New Jersey State Federation of Women's Clubs had found her two-foot-tall gravestone atop a two-tiered pedestal at Evergreen Cemetery in Lakewood. The words plainly read:

Jennie Cunningham Croly

Wife of

David Goodman Croly

Born Dec. 19, 1828

Died Dec. 23, 1901

Still, the New Jersey State Federation members felt that an additional marker of smaller size was needed to describe Jane more personally than just her name or "wife of," so they raised sufficient funding for one. Fortunately, they had enough money for roping around the gravesite and wrought-iron gates to the cemetery as well. Thus, a graveside ceremony was held on June 30, 1990, with the current GFWC president, Alice Donahue, speaking. A good-sized crowd, including some men, surrounded the new, flat, thirty-by-twelve-inch, on-the-ground grave marker in front of the original stone. That new marker has plenty of words to describe Jane. The top features her pen name, "JENNY JUNE," in bold letters, followed by the next line, "PIONEER WOMAN AND FOUNDER OF," over the second line,

"GENERAL FEDERATION OF WOMEN'S CLUBS." Finally, Jane's famous quote is shown on the marker above: "DEDICATED GFWC CENTENNIAL 1990." It reads:

"I HAVE NEVER DONE ANYTHING THAT WAS NOT HELPFUL TO WOMAN SO FAR AS IT LAY IN MY POWER."

That quote was powerful enough to inspire the attendees of the graveside ceremony to listen to Alice Donahue's speech about Jane's accomplishments, starting in 1850 when she cared for her family of five. Her long list included pioneering in the journalism world as the first woman reporter working in the office daily and writing for forty years about food, fashion, and home decorating, but then moving up to more sensitive issues such as equal rights for women and coeducation in colleges.

Standing by the gravestone, Alice Donahue said about Jane: "Her ambition was to implement more opportunities and equal rights for women. She wrote for all women because she cared about all women." Jane encouraged female journalists to achieve their goal of working outside their homes, fought for women's rights before they became popular, and founded the Women's Press Club of New York. Those feats were in addition to her roles in establishing Sorosis and the GFWC. She was so phenomenal that the all-male New York Press Club apologized to her years later for rejecting her at the Charles Dickens event. Jane even had a rose named after her pen name: "Jennie June" (although her grave marker spells the first name differently).

Then, in 1994, Jane was inducted into the National Women's Hall of Fame in Seneca Falls, New York, for her work in founding the GFWC. She was among the twenty-five women inducted on September 24 that year; others included Bella Abzug (a leader in the women's movement in the 1970s), Wilma Rudolph (an Olympic sprinter with a world's record in 1960), Geraldine Ferraro (an American politician, diplomat, and attorney in the 1980s), and Oprah Winfrey (a television personality, actress, and entrepreneur from the mid-1980s to present). At the induction, Jane Croly was remembered to have "set in motion the power of a vast, previously untapped and unorganized sisterhood of capable American women that would reshape American Society."

Twenty-one years after the Centennial celebration, in 2011, Jane's gravesite was rededicated with a shiny two-by-two-foot placard in front of her 1990 stone surrounded by a circular bed of small white rocks. The black placard features the GFWC logo in gold, blue, red, and gray; the gold ring around the center reads UNITY IN DIVERSITY—a motto supported by Jane. So now she has more words and colors at her gravesite instead of a bland "Wife of..."

***

The Martin Mansion has had paintings come and go since the Woman's Club of Norfolk acquired the mansion's ownership in 1925. Mr. Charles Barnett's loaned oil paintings, Bertha Fanning Taylor's donated pieces of her work, and several other paintings contributed by the club members have adorned the walls on the first floor. Of course, many of these paintings have been moved around or given away in later years. Only one painting has stayed in the same place to this day: A portrait of the WCN founder Virginia Gatewood in the West Wing Parlor. She deserves a special place that catches the immediate attention of visitors walking in from the foyer, as to say she was the founder of the current mansion owner.

Earlye Lee Miller, at the beginning of her presidency of the WCN in 1991, presented to the club a colored print of "The Woman's Club" by an American artist, David Robinson. That 1927 painting would enthrall club members and visitors with its powerful scene depicting the seated audience of the club members. It shows a variety of faces, both young and old, that showed genuine attitudes during a club meeting. Their outfits were typical formal meeting attire in the 1920s; almost all these women were still in their coats and wore cloche hats. Robinson's "The Woman's Club" resembles many of Norman Rockwell's paintings; both show the authenticity of facial and body language. Robinson depicted his work as the essential Americanism of the Woman's Club movement.

There is a unique story behind the painting. It began with Dorothy Canfield Fisher, a best-selling American author in the early 1900s, a social activist, and an educational reformer; she advocated women's rights, racial equality, and education for all. Hailing from Kansas, Fisher inherited two passions, education, and writing, from her parents that defined her career, so impressive that Eleanor Roosevelt named her one of the ten most influential women in America. Fisher's father was a college professor and president of the National Education Association. Her mother, Flavia Canfield, was a writer, the first president of the Nebraska Federation of Women's Clubs, and the first international GFWC president.

Flavia's involvement with the GFWC prompted her daughter Dorothy to publish an article in the 1927 *McCall's* magazine entitled "3,000,000 Women! How the Women's Clubs of America Are Bringing New 'Folk Ways to the Country.'" She wrote that the Woman's Club was "as native to our soil as the sugar maple." Her description of the fashions, attitudes, and mannerisms among the GFWC members touched the artist David Robinson so much that he painted "The Woman's Club." From a few sources, it is believed the heavy-set lady in the middle of the painting, tilting her head, is Flavia Canfield, Dorothy's mother. For additional information, the 1920s were a time when women, their fashions, and their interests spurred public interest, prompting magazines and newspapers to publish articles with pictures of the activities of society women. *The Virginian-Pilot* was an example at the time; it went from a seven-column of tiny prints on serious news, requiring a magnifying glass, to explosive pages on women and their portraits. Therefore, the painting "The Woman's Club" fitted the 1920s so well that its black-and-white print was shown in newspapers and magazines worldwide.

That painting was so profound that Lord and Taylor in New York City temporarily displayed it in its exhibition room in 1927. Then, "The Woman's Club" was exhibited in Nebraska, where Flavia Canfield led the state federation. Finally, her members requested that the painting be presented to the GFWC in honor of Flavia. So, the original artwork of interesting faces has hung in the headquarters of the GFWC in Washington, D.C., since 1928, while the still worthwhile print is hung in the foyer of the Martin Mansion.

***

After living responsibly at The Woman's Club for two years, my brother Harvey developed a trusting relationship with his former landlord, Ms. Edna Schweitzer. Approximately fifty years apart, they had agreed to keep wild parties out of the second floor of the Martin Mansion when he was living there. But then Harvey married a wonderful gal named Molly Hubard in 1986 and moved out. Four years later, he approached Mrs. Schweitzer to ask if he could rent the first floor and the auditorium to host a Christmas cocktail party. Harvey promised his guests would behave in semi-formal attire and reminded the older lady that they were all past beer-bashing college age and had approached the working thirties. After deliberation, Mrs. Schweitzer finally agreed to hand the mansion over to Harvey for an evening.

Knowing that a cocktail party at The Woman's Club would cost a fortune for one host, Harvey asked each of his ten friends to chip in $150 on the condition that they invite ten of their own friends and bring a dish of appetizers. That would add up to 100 guests, including the accompanying hosts. I was happy to comply, as were my other brother, Lindsay, and his wife, Koggie. So, we paid $1,500 for a Friday night Christmas party, which was quite a bit at the time. Thus, Harvey hired four bartenders, two in the library and the other two in the auditorium, and plenty of libations were lined up. The female hosts, including myself, prepared the dining room table for refreshments.

Harvey was an expert party planner, given his high school and college experience at our parents' house. He figured that our formal cocktail party—no jeans allowed—could use some holiday spirit and perhaps a bit of noise. So, he hired a choir of ten or fifteen from a local black church and had them sing Christmas carols side by side on the grand staircase in the foyer to welcome guests. People later told Harvey that being greeted at the door by a fully robed choir with loud, joyful voices was memorable. With its hundreds of Christmas parties, it would not be surprising if the Martin Mansion had experienced such a rambunctious choir before. Music had reverberated through the first floor and the auditorium numerous times since the Roaring Twenties.

Our Christmas cocktail party went so well that we hosted it again for the next two years. One hundred people or a few more never wrecked a thing in the Martin Mansion or "at The Woman's Club," as we called it. Of course, we could have continued throwing parties but stopped once we became busy with children. And if I ever get this dear book published, I will throw a gigantic party at The Woman's Club with the hip-hop choir on the staircase.

***

In the early 1990s, when the WCN had approximately 150 members, they had to keep raising money for the upkeep of their nearly hundred-year-old mansion. Thus, the WCN hosted bazaars and bake sales here and there, selling Brunswick stew. Contractors came and repaired or replaced whatever was broken. Of course, once they left, a new problem popped up. That was the norm of an ancient house. Some WCN members donated décor and furniture to spruce up the West and East Wing Parlors. The cleanliness of the interior was crucial to the members, so they took the job of wiping all the mirrors spotless. Almost every room had a good-sized rectangle mirror since this was a woman's home where lipstick needed to be checked for any smudges and where hair bows must be inspected for any asymmetry. The petticoat table with a crystal-clear mirror underneath was still in the foyer since the 1910 mansion completion, where women of the early twentieth century checked their long skirts for any wrinkles and where women of the late twentieth century examined their pantyhose for any runs. And that table is still in the same spot today.

The fireplaces in the parlors each had a sizable gold-gilded rectangle mirror perched on the mantle. But … the third fireplace should not have had a mirror all these years, likely placed there hastily without consideration of something valuable behind it. The WCN members made an astounding discovery in the dining room in 1991 when they were wiping the mirror: The beautifully carved wooden dogs on the mantle that had been unknowingly hidden behind the mirror. It is unknown how long those Irish setters and the American woodcocks hibernated in the pitch dark, but the WCN minutes noted that they had been covered "for years." Awestruck by the beauty of the three-dimensional woodwork on the mantel, the club members agreed the mirror had to go.

***

If Alvah Howard Martin had been alive today, he would have been pleased to see his historic office building on 300 Granby Street in downtown Norfolk remodeled to serve an educational purpose. In 1997, Tidewater Community College opened its fourth campus, including the Martin Building. The six-floor office building was constructed in 1913, three years after the completion of Alvah's mansion on Fairfax Avenue, a mile away. As it still stands today, having survived the bulldozer era, the Martin Building is striking with its tan-brick Renaissance Revival architecture. Alvah hired the same architects, Lee and Diehl, to design both his office building and mansion. Still, the architects concentrated on symmetry in both buildings. Their idea was to put a door in the middle and the same number of windows on each side of the door and repeat the same pattern on each floor after the first or second floor, plain and simple.

The Martin Building has an impressively designed entry. Two double glass doors beneath a flat canopy are topped with a beautiful arch window that, with its grid-pane pattern, resembles those found in The Hague neighborhood. Finally, a pointed Roman Corinthian pediment dominates at the top of the main door, supported by two smooth Corinthian columns. Words along the bottom of the pediment read "THE MARTIN BUILDING."

Donated by the Martin descendants, the Martin Building adds an attractive touch to Tidewater Community College. Inside, you'll find a library, office rooms, and a few classrooms. The students of TCC are comforted by the books and professors; however, they would likely get the thrill of shopping in those same rooms decades ago. What had occupied the Martin Building for seventy-one years, from 1917 to 1988, was the iconic department store Smith & Welton. Alvah Martin must have used his office there for only four years before he died in 1918.

Shoppers flocked to the tearoom at Smith & Welton for its world-famous chicken salad and piquant cheese sandwiches. And the lemon chess pie was everyone's favorite dessert. Guy Friddell, the beloved columnist of *The Virginian-Pilot* and one of Virginia's favorite contemporary writers, wrote in 1997 about the tearoom, first explaining that Mr. Welton installed it in his store to appease customers during the Great Depression. Friddell's humorous article reads:

Women found it first—they're quick to detect good food—and they brought along their daughters, wearing big hair ribbons, for etiquette lessons; boys came, too, when they could be pulled away from Saturday play, sometimes wearing their first long pants.

The women's chatter was that of a flock of birds settling in. Older couples with young eyes joined the medley, and employees of downtown offices began dropping in for lunch.

Young professional men joined the throng. A lawyer described the Tearoom as a ``bachelor's paradise" because it often supplied the only balanced meal of his day before he was married.

The Tearoom held forth on a broad mezzanine rimming above two-thirds of the first floor. You could, while eating, look down from your table by the balcony railing into the rectangular depth of the first floor as if peering into an aquarium and watch the shoppers—bright tropical fish, fins waving—swimming slowly around the main floor below.

As you watched, you could ruminate, with grape nut pudding at hand, on the mutability of human affairs, not dreaming that the Tearoom itself wasn't impervious to time. Oh, it was a lordly way to dine.

Fortunately, Smith & Welton stayed long after the suburban shopping strips and malls began pulling customers away from Granby Street in the 1960s and caused six department stores to leave. Only Smith & Welton refused to budge. I am glad to have been born long before it closed in 1988, as I cherish the memory of my teen years shopping and eating there. At least the Martin Building is still there, no longer to sell clothes and sandwiches but to teach. Alvah would not mind that as long as its unique façade architecture, inspired by his trips to Europe, stays intact and looks smart.

***

An eight-year-old girl with cerebral palsy looked up the eighty-four stone steps to the U.S. Capitol and thought she could climb up despite her young, frail age. Some people nearby objected, but the girl persisted and declared she wanted to climb those steps. The second grader threw her wheelchair aside and began crawling up the steps, using her arms to push up while her legs involuntarily trailed behind. About halfway up and thirty minutes later, she sweated profusely through her headband from the unusually hot spring sun beating down on her. The girl panted heavily, resting one of her knees on the step for a moment, and sipped water, followed by a few puffs from her asthma inhaler. She wiped her bleeding lip after hitting a step and scanned the countless steps ahead of her. The white dome loomed up in the distance, and that was the girl's destination—and her life-changing goal. Not one to give up, she said, "I'll take all night if I have to!" and repeated the push-up maneuver with her arms toward the next step. The crowd at the base filled up, along with onlookers and over a thousand activists, all watching her. The girl later said, "The further up the steps I went, the more I felt empowered. I felt like I had all of the other kids behind me [who couldn't be there]. I felt that it was important, not just to represent myself, but to represent them and their voices."

For an eight-year-old with cerebral palsy and asthma, crawling eighty-four stone steps to the U.S. Capitol was like climbing Mount Everest. It was an hour of brutality on a concrete mountain. But she did it.

Jennifer Keelan Chaffins, being the youngest activist at the scene, completed the "Capitol Crawl" with sixty disabled adults on March 12, 1990. When she stopped at the top of the long, arduous steps, her mother, Cyndi, hugged her in jubilation after two years of traveling as a duo team fighting for disability rights—and even facing arrest together at previous protests, one in Montreal. Holding up her arm, Jennifer indicated she was not done with this crawl and pulled out a rolled piece of paper from her back pocket and insisted that she keep crawling to the Senate door and hand the politicians the form. It was to push the long-stalled bill out of Congress and into effect. Jennifer would never forget the embarrassing restaurant episode two years earlier that sparked her activism at age six: The staff refused service to her and her disabled friends, saying, "People don't want to watch you all eat."

That was why Jennifer traveled to Washington, D.C., from her hometown of Denver, Colorado—to obtain disability rights for herself and all others. Her determination on the eighty-four steps worked miraculously. Four months after the Capitol Crawl, President George Bush signed the Americans with Disabilities Act into law. It was the world's first comprehensive civil rights law for people with disabilities. It prohibits discrimination in several areas, including employment, transportation, public accommodations, communications, and access to state and local government programs and services. And yes, in restaurants. Thanks to the new ADA bill, Jennifer with cerebral palsy would no longer be illegally refused service by any restaurant—or she could sue. Her dream finally occurred in a ceremony on the South Lawn of the White House where President Bush signed the bill, surrounded by Evan Kemp, chairman of the Equal Employment Opportunity Commission; Justin Dart, chairman of the President's Committee on Employment of People with Disabilities; Rev. Harold Wilke; and Swift Parrino, chairperson, National Council on Disability.

A few miles away from the nation's capital, the General Federation of Women's Clubs supported this new ADA bill. However, their support for people with disabilities had long existed since Helen Bardo, a GFWC member from Lusk, Wyoming, started the drive for accessibility for those in wheelchairs in 1966. It all started when her good friend, Ruth

Thomas, commented on the difficulties of her war-wounded husband Sam, getting into public places in his wheelchair, such as buildings lacking an elevator and having only a long flight of steps. Ruth said, "If people only knew how one step looks to people in a wheelchair." Helen was inspired enough to encourage her fellow members of the Lusk Woman's Club to eliminate barriers by proposing legislation to make buildings, sidewalks, and other public areas accessible for disabled people. Their club project was the beginning of the ADA's long road to becoming law. But first, that proposed law by Lusk Woman's Club passed the Senate but failed in a House committee.

Then Helen Bardo, earning the nickname "Mrs. Barriers" from her husband, convinced the Wyoming Federation of Women's Clubs with 1,800 members to adopt the elimination of barriers as a statewide project. Sure enough, the state boss accepted and wrote letters to legislators. Helen carried the tabletop display all over Wyoming to show that the "one step" was inaccessible unless fixed. With his woodworking skills, Sam Thomas had been asked by Helen to construct this display related to his mobility problems: He placed two small figures, a man with crutches and a woman in a wheelchair, at the base of a two-foot-tall flight of numerous steps winding to the open door at the top; the caption explained what "one step" looked like to those with mobile disabilities. That lightweight display, shown in person and in photos, won the hearts of people across the state—and then the nation. Helen carried it around in advocacy for accessibility and managed to have the barriers law passed in both houses in 1969, signed by Governor Stanley Hathaway of Wyoming.

Helen did not stop there. She realized disabled people faced obstacles on public sidewalks with curbs. Again, that "one step" over the curb proved inconvenient. By then, a member of the Governor's Committee for Employment of the Handicapped, Helen had the Federation of Women's Clubs lobby for their drafted "elevator-curb cut [ramp]" to be installed in public buildings and streets. At Helen's urging, they successfully lobbied legislators to make the state capitol in Cheyenne accessible to all. Finally, in 1975, Governor Ed Herschler signed the curb law, which led the U.S. Congress to pass a federal law mandating specific dimensions for curb cuts throughout the country.

Helen Bardo had made a remarkable feat, pioneering to ban barriers for people with disabilities in her Cowboy State and beyond. She was so admired by all that her husband, Dale, wrote her biography, and the book was titled *Mrs. Barriers*.

There was another pioneer in the General Federation of Women's Clubs who alerted the public to the needs of those with learning disabilities: Faye Dissinger of Springfield, Pennsylvania. She joined the Junior Woman's Club of Springfield when moving to Delaware County in 1964, achieving her dream of becoming "a community member." Then, she became president of her junior club in 1968 before joining the GFWC Woman's Club of Springfield in 1973. But not before Faye coordinated with Doris Stetler, a club member and president at the time, in founding the Deaf-Hearing Communication Centre in Ridley, Pennsylvania.

A deaf person had approached Doris about the lack of

services for deaf people and their families, including the availability of American Sign Language (ASL) interpreters. Then those two, a citizen and a woman's club president, launched a two-year community project called "Concern for the Deaf" in 1972. Hence, the Deaf-Hearing Communication Centre (DHCC) was formed to provide three types of service: education, sign language interpreting, and message relay service (MRS). All these services greatly benefited both the deaf and hearing communities when most schools, colleges, and organizations did not have such similar services. So, it was the GFWC Woman's Club of Springfield that established DHCC, led by its president Doris Stetler, with the help of April Nelson, Lillian Hoshauer, and Faye Dissinger.

At the time of the DHCC's establishment, Section 504, a part of a federal civil rights law known as the Rehabilitation Act of 1973, became effective, explicitly prohibiting discrimination against students with disabilities and guaranteeing them a free and appropriate public education. That was when I came home to attend regular school after seven years at a residential deaf school in Massachusetts so that my parents would no longer have to pay the exorbitant tuition. But midway through my time at the deaf school, my mom traveled to Richmond with seven other mothers to urge the state legislator to pay half of the tuition for out-of-state schools. They succeeded. That marked the beginning of Public Law 94-I42, which encouraged the education of disabled students in the least restrictive environment.

If Section 504 law had existed when I was five, my parents would not have had to send me six hundred miles away to the closest best oral school they could find. Instead, I would have attended regular school with speech therapy, ASL interpreting, and private tutoring provided by the state. And I would have come home every afternoon, as most deaf children do today. However, I do not regret being away from home for seven years, despite the agonizing send-off at age five, because I felt a powerful connection with my deaf schoolmates.

Faye Dissinger is an excellent example of the dedication of civic-minded GFWC members. She was a bank teller and bookkeeper for years, polishing her professional skills. Long after assisting with the establishment of DHCC, Faye became the Pennsylvania Federation president and started a program on learning disabilities. She and the Federation published a booklet called "I Can Jump the Rainbow," which raised public awareness and volunteerism for those with learning disabilities. That project was so successful that it earned national acclaim, and 145,000 copies were distributed throughout the woman's clubs and other organizations. A bundle of energy with curly blond hair, Faye also served on the Pennsylvania governor's task force on private-sector initiatives and as chairwoman of the Pennsylvania Association for Children and Adults with Learning Disabilities.

Finally, Faye served as the International GFWC president for a standard two-year term in 1996–1998. Like every other president, she lived for two years in an apartment at the GFWC Headquarters. She traveled to every state in America and worldwide to promote her unique projects, including China, Brazil, Russia, and the Philippines. Brazil at the time had twenty-one woman's clubs in its federation. The Philippines appealed to

Faye the most: The GFWC clubs raised nearly two hundred thousand dollars for her two-week Operation Smile volunteer mission in the Philippines with doctors and nurses who surgically corrected facial deformities in young children whose parents could not afford medical help. While Faye was there or afterward, the Op-Smile team performed 1,033 operations. In Russia, she studied women's issues since the fall of communism, where childcare was hardly available for working women after the closing of government-run facilities.

Imagine jetting worldwide and across the country almost daily for two short years while presiding over the world's largest women's organization. That was what an International GFWC president did and does, often with resilience and patience. It is not an easy job, but still, many, including Faye Dissinger, have pushed forward through the sun and rain toward the pot of gold with flying colors.

***

It might be laughable that the Woman's Club of Norfolk put up a tent at an event in downtown Norfolk and sold beer to the public. But the members were serious about raising money for charities; therefore, selling a plastic cup of Budweiser or Miller Lite to a college-age fraternity boy in flip-flops was understandable. If that TGIF (Thank God It's Friday) event was held at the Martin Mansion, the WCN ladies would have had to consider the reputation of their fancy clubhouse that was not built to be a fraternity house. For that reason, it was much easier to huddle under the twelve-by-twelve-foot white canopy, spray some of the keg beer foam on the grass of Town Point Park, hand a foamy cup filled up to the brim over the counter, spilling some, and take two dollars from an event attendee who did not even ask what organization the beer seller came from.

Everyone, possibly a thousand locals or more, went to a weekly TGIF party at the park overlooking the Elizabeth River to mingle with friends, talk about what a week it had been, and guzzle foamy beer. I admit I was one of them after a long week of landscaping for customers in the summer heat. At the time, I had my temporary landscape design business in between working for other companies from 1985 to 2002. I was not in the mood to discuss my job at a TGIF with friends. Instead, I asked questions about who was getting married or what was happening at the Oceanfront. No one ever desired to talk about work on a Friday evening unless one wanted to brag about a raise or promotion. Anyhow, we would all make a few trips to the beer vendor, not even acknowledging that under the tent, ten or more aproned ladies with puffed-up hairdos fresh from the salon were members of the Woman's Club of Norfolk. According to the WCN minutes, they enjoyed selling beer with their eyes on the charity funds.

In the 1990s, the WCN donated to fifty charities, some of which were the Cystic Fibrosis Foundation, Samaritan House, Norfolk Crime Line, The Dwelling Place, Veteran's Affairs, American Red Cross, Easter Seals Society, and many more. It was not only the beer sales that brought in funding; it was also the card parties, bake sales, yard sales, fashion shows, and bags of Uncle Al's Nuts. The Woman's Club of Norfolk was a money-raising machine and appeared never to run short of volunteers. The international relations department of the WCN made twenty dolls for Operation Smile patients abroad. The club members donated clothes, linens, and toilet articles to Women in Crisis (assumedly a former organization or changed to a different name). Some WCN members tutored children there with books or a few etiquette words in the daily world.

Since the GFWC sponsored a popular program, "Books for Babies," the WCN members visited local hospitals. They gave packets to new mothers that included the baby's first book and a personalized library card. Like other woman's clubs, they donated used and new baby books directly to mothers and hospitals. Since approximately 25 percent of all women, including new mothers, cannot read, the actual purpose of this "Books for Babies" program is to encourage the mother to read to her newborn and sign up for reading programs at the library. The new mother is given "the key" to the book world in which she is encouraged to engage her child. Laurinda Finn-Davis, a nurse at the Medical College of Virginia in Richmond, said in 1997, "When mothers leave the hospital with their new babies, we ask them if they have a car seat, Pampers, food, etc., but we don't ask them if they have things that are educationally appropriate." In the 1990s, the woman's clubs were not the only ones that participated in "Books for Babies"; Junior Leagues, Friends of the Public Library, and reading councils across the country were also involved.

***

The WCN members did an interesting project toward the end of the twentieth century; they participated in the Adopt-A-School program, a year-long approach to develop partnerships between schools and their network of supporters, specifically business and community organizations. Chesterfield Heights Elementary School, a few miles away, became the adoptee of the Woman's Club of Norfolk. That school, now Chesterfield Academy, received visits, donations, and volunteer services from the WCN members for years. The WCN started a reading program for the students, encouraging them to read as much as possible, and even had them choose a free paperback if they had read twenty-five books. Chesterfield Heights once had a poster contest for bike safety, and the WCN supported the National Poster Contest with U.S. savings bonds as a prize for the students. As we all know, competition is beneficial for young children so that they learn motivation to reach a goal. Poster competitions raise awareness of issues and participation programs.

When the GFWC announced bike safety for the youth as one of its objectives, the WCN members presented packets of fluorescent bicycle/helmet stickers to the students of their Adopt-A-School. The origin of this unique program is unknown, and it is believed that several businesses and organizations use the same name, Adopt-A-School, for their own purposes. The Federal Bureau of Investigation began its program in 1994 to help students stay away from drugs and gangs by teaching them core values and encouraging them to become law-abiding citizens. Special agents and other FBI employees have volunteered thousands of hours at schools in disadvantaged communities to be tutors and mentors for the students. The FBI had its own Adopt-

A-School program, wearing badges, while the Woman's Club of Norfolk members had theirs, sporting pearls.

***

As the twentieth century waned, the GFWC remained as busy as ever with projects to improve world conditions. This umbrella organization began to actively support the Violence Against Women Act and legislation supporting handgun control. Remembering its successful "Hands Up" crusade in crime reduction in the 1970s, the GFWC was determined to take the lead in preventing domestic and sexual abuse against women. And it still does today. The GFWC Florida website reads: "GFWC is a national leader in the fight to end domestic violence by raising awareness about this social issue. The goal of this signature program is to increase awareness of and help prevent the widespread occurrence of domestic and sexual abuse and violence against women in communities across the nation by working with national domestic violence networks, supporting existing activities, working with various established programs, and initiating educational opportunities for club members and local citizens. GFWC is a powerful voice for those who have no voice."

Once this umbrella organization was formed in 1890, it established a program, did the work in making its goals happen, and still stuck with that program for decades, even if the goals had been achieved. The GFWC continues working on old programs as if they are new. That is the case with their commitment to public libraries, 75 percent of which were founded by the GFWC alone in the 1930s. In 1997, the GFWC renewed its commitment to libraries with the "Libraries 2000" project. Over five years, the GFWC clubwomen raised and donated $13.5 million to public and school libraries nationwide. In addition, the affiliated clubs donated books and materials worth over two million dollars to libraries. Some clubs created their clever ways in the Libraries 2000 project by donating directly to school libraries in their areas.

For instance, the Woman's Club of Linthicum Heights in Maryland learned that Overlook Elementary School in their area needed a World Book Encyclopedia set but did not have the eight hundred dollars to purchase it. The club raised money by kicking off its tea reception with the theme "A-B-C – Adopting Books for Children," selling handmade creations and fruit cups at the Linthicum Community Fair, hosting a holiday open house at a club member's home, and collecting donations from members. Just then, a new set of the World Book Encyclopedia arrived on the doorstep of Overlook Elementary School as a gift from the Woman's Club of Linthicum Heights—with the bookplates depicting the GFWC "Libraries 2000" logo.

Book donations were fabulous; however, something had to come along with them: Literacy—for both adults and children. The GFWC had long been devoted to literacy since the 1920s when they cooperated with the U.S. Department of Education to reduce illiteracy. The GFWC members surveyed every state and encouraged reading classes, resulting in hundreds of thousands of citizens becoming literate. Then, libraries were formed. And in 1984, Second Lady Barbara Bush became the honorary chairman of the GFWC Literacy Program for six years. In the meantime, she launched the Barbara Bush Foundation for Family Literacy to help illiterate or partly illiterate parents learn alongside their young children. She called literacy the "most important issue we have," enough to have her husband, President Bush, sign the National Literacy Act on July 25, 1991. So that millions of adults would have the opportunity to return to school and earn their high school diplomas.

Unfortunately, many of those who cannot read do not speak up or admit their problem, primarily due to embarrassment. And there are some who insist they can manage without reading abilities, like those succeeding in manual labor. Therefore, Barbara Bush, her husband's act, the GFWC, and many other literacy agencies forged together to encourage people who could not read to accept their problem and learn to read. I will never forget the 1995 powerful novel, *The Reader* by Bernhard Schlink, in which the female protagonist considers her illiteracy more shameful than her Nazi crime. One may feel disgusted with her as an accomplice in locking Jew prisoners in a burning building but simultaneously sympathetic to her for a painful secret too embarrassing to disclose. One scene describes her touching books on a shelf and struggling to push back tears. It takes time and effort to encourage a person into acceptance and then action.

Thanks to a grant from Procter & Gamble, the GFWC established Youth Literacy/ASPIRE, a program that helps children learn to read with caring adults to Advise, Support, Prepare, Inform, Respect, and Encourage them. The GFWC members work with children nationwide, being a positive influence, encouraging an affinity for reading, entertaining with storytelling efforts, distributing books, tutoring, and mentoring. So, indeed, it is essential to ASPIRE children into literacy.

This shows that the General Federation of Women's Clubs has not stopped working on literacy for at least a century. Some or most of their goals have been achieved, but still, there is more work to be done. Women rarely give up, like mothers who push for their children's well-being and success in the ever-changing world. Jane Croly did not give up and has posthumously erected her umbrella in unpredictable winds.

***

Located roughly at the midpoint of the East Coast, Norfolk may be the envy of the nation with its moderate coastal climate condition. This city hardly gets four feet of snow or three-digit summer temperatures. The latter happens now and then, but not all summer. Norfolk's climate is classified as humid subtropical, which, yes, makes the area suffocate with extreme humidity in July and August. Everyone is drenched with sweat, even at a mild 85 degrees. But still, Norfolkians rarely see summer temperatures that bake an egg on the asphalt or winter temperatures that freeze the toilet water. And in Norfolk, there is hardly a tornado, severe drought, cyclone, flash flood, mudslide, forest fire, whiteout, or any catastrophic weather seen all too commonly across the country. Hurricanes do come to Norfolk occasionally; the last truly destructive one was the 1933 Chesapeake-Potomac hurricane, which submerged Granby Street in downtown Norfolk by four feet. So, by 1997, Norfolkians thought they had seen it all until a very uncommon storm appeared on May 1 of that year.

I clearly remember that afternoon when working at a garden center two miles from my house. As we watched a strange black cloud pass over us, loud noises resembling machine gun fire emerged. It even rattled my hearing aids, which had to be turned down. Then we noticed white ice balls, ranging in size from peas to jumbo gumballs, bouncing like Mexican jumping beans in the parking lot in front of us. It was a hailstorm, and we were totally unprepared. Many plants at the garden center ripped apart; the leaves tore off container trees, and spring blooms dissipated from perennial pots. I immediately drove home to inspect my house, and to my relief, only small pine branches were scattered in the yard. But when I went inside, my two-year-old yellow Labrador was uncontrollably shaking and drooling in the upstairs bathroom. Although she could handle the rough ocean or steep mountains with enthusiasm, Olive continued to shake despite my consoling pats and embraces. Whereas it would have taken several minutes for my dog to calm down after a regular thunderstorm or fireworks, it took over two hours for Olive to relax and budge from the black-and-white tile floor slippery with her drool. Never again did she see such a scattering hailstorm in her thirteen years.

Five miles away, the "Grand Old Lady" saw the worst assault of her lifetime. But still, the tan brick exterior of the Martin Mansion stood firm while the more fragile part of it did not. Eighteen windows shattered, and some parts of the old fragile roof produced holes, running up to seven thousand dollars in damage and requiring several months for repair. However, the original curved, handblown windows under the front porch roof were spared. That window type would be much more complex to replace than a regular flat window. So, the sunset scene from the West Wing Parlor was still poised to entertain the club members or party guests. As we Norfolkians will never forget, it was one mean hailstorm.

Two years later, the Martin Mansion received a new, unique kind of window in the East Wing Parlor. It was a stained-glass window that appeared to be destined for prayer meetings that some WCN members attended. Or it was meant for wedding vows. Jerry Brangan, a local artist from Colley Avenue, was hired to design the 2.5-by-3-foot stained-glass window with the colors chosen by the WCN members. It now sits in the corner under the untouched window sash next to the fireplace. Brangan's work shows the beauty of colors—and holiness that must have prevented another hailstorm in the past twenty-seven years.

***

On November 30, 1999, Peter G. Decker Jr., a prominent attorney in Norfolk, announced his fabulous idea at a breakfast with 300 business and civic leaders. He suggested that the city of Norfolk erect mermaid sculptures all around its area. He credited the idea to his wife, Bess, who visited Chicago and was inspired by the cow sculptures there, many colorfully painted with different themes, such as one adorned with patriotic flag colors. Instantly, the breakfast audience accepted that unique idea from Pete. The city council agreed with his suggestion of a mermaid becoming the signature symbol of Norfolk since this port city had long lured people to the sea. Presto, the "Mermaids on Parade" event took off in early 2000 after sculptor Kevin Gallup mass-produced 130 fiberglass mermaid castings for local businesses, artists, community leaders, and homeowners to adopt for two thousand dollars each and decorate in any way they wanted. Just then, the city of Norfolk became emblazoned with colorful ten-foot-long mermaids standing on small concrete planks; those sculptures were adorned with vibrant paints, glitter, jewels, seashells, mosaic tiles, gold fake coins, you-name-it. Every mermaid had its own theme, such as a pink one supporting breast cancer awareness or international peace with hundreds of national flags.

Norfolkians always listened to "Uncle Pete" because he was a flamboyant attorney and philanthropist, having served on numerous boards and charitable foundations. He passed away in February 2012, followed by an uplifting obituary. As I knew him personally, Pete loved Norfolk so much that he wanted to bring joy to his birthplace. He certainly did with the mermaids. And Norfolk is still colorful twenty-four years later, with some mermaids old and others new, all with female grace and the tail of a fish.

Chapter Twelve

Frances Lindsay, the granddaughter of Alvah Howard Martin, loved Thanksgiving as a family holiday and hosted a large gathering at her house in the neighborhood of Lochhaven for many years, from the 1960s to the 1990s. Frances was my aunt, married to my mom's brother, so I have no relations to the original Martin family. Most of the time, there were forty of us from four or five related families and three or four generations at our Thanksgiving dinner; we were more like a Christmas tree than a family tree with diverse ornaments of distinctive looks and personalities.

Aunt Frances always found the biggest and heaviest turkey in Norfolk; sometimes, she ordered two to feed all of us to the hilt. She was never without her professional camera and went from room to room, clicking pictures of one of us sitting on the sofa with a gin and tonic or another of us throwing a Nerf ball to a toddler of the youngest generation. Then Aunt Frances had a Christmas card in mind, so every year, she handed her camera to someone and had her mammoth family and herself pose in the living room: Matriarch and Patriarch, five children, and fourteen grandchildren. Aunt Frances and Uncle Harvey always sat in the center, surrounded by their offspring and little ones. By the first week of December, we received Frances's formal Christmas card with a glossy picture of her clan we had witnessed in person a few weeks earlier. Then, in the late 1990s, Aunt Frances had an idea: A Thanksgiving gathering of the same size at the mansion built by her grandfather in 1910. Just then, The Woman's Club became the site of Turkey Day for the Martin descendants.

The auditorium could have occupied all forty or fifty of us conveniently. Still, Aunt Frances must have considered its atmosphere too bland with its white walls and instead used the fancy first floor, even putting folding tables covered with white tablecloths in the West and East Wing Parlors and the library. And she placed herself and the seniors in the dining room including my parents. For every gathering at the Martin Mansion, Aunt Frances hired Leon, the beloved African-American caterer of Norfolk, and his staff to bring the cooked turkey and sides to the industrial kitchen. With an incredible sense of humor and endless smiles, Leon appeared to cherish his catering job in his white suit and black tie. Like Anthony the Butler, Leon was highly productive at the Martin Mansion but more with preparing and serving food, especially his famous hors d'oeuvres. He was often followed by Alice, a sweet-natured lady in her white uniform and, of course, an apron. We do not remember if she was Leon's wife or just working for him.

Then, one Thanksgiving in 2010, we were kicked out of the Martin Mansion for future gatherings because the elderly director did not like the commotion we caused on Fairfax Avenue by throwing a football. The ball must have landed on the front porch, but at least we never broke the windows. And the youngest generation, especially my elementary school-age nephews, had gotten a bit too unruly for the director, so she approached Aunt Frances and said, "No more!" We could not do anything because we did not own the Martin Mansion. However, a few years later, when the director was no longer at the Martin Mansion, we could resume gatherings with the third generation maturing from horsing around to walking behaviorally. But we, even adults, still threw a football in the spacious concrete backyard instead of on the street. Who can do Thanksgiving without America's favorite sport? A steaming turkey on a platter and a football game on TV is what we have been thankful for since the 1960s.

It took time and effort for Aunt Frances to organize a Thanksgiving dinner for so many of us, but she always had help from her husband, Harvey Lindsay, with his caring attitude. He was a bright star at our gatherings with his megawatt smile. And he accomplished a great deal until his recent death at age ninety-three. Uncle Harvey never retired officially and still commuted to his office at his commercial real estate company in downtown Norfolk. With his brilliant landmark developments, he brought zeal to Norfolk and the Hampton Roads area, including Newport News across the Chesapeake Bay. He developed the first mall in Tidewater called Military Circle in 1970.

Back in the early days, Uncle Harvey transformed from a rowdy college kid from the University of Virginia into a composed man with an enormous heart after serving in the Korean War in the 1950s. It was where he conversed in a foxhole with a black soldier who complained about the unfair treatment he had received in the infantry. That started Harvey's lifelong advocacy for civil rights. Once home from Korea, he advocated for the reopening of schools closed by Massive Resistance, an effort by lawmakers at the time to block desegregation. Harvey also helped organize and lead a temporary committee called the Urban Coalition, now the Urban League of Hampton Roads, and also served as that organization's president. He also served in leadership roles on many civic boards. Uncle Harvey was always concerned for the underprivileged and disadvantaged citywide, nationwide, and worldwide, enough to initiate a clothing drive at his church for the Korean people. When he celebrated his sixtieth year at his real estate company in 2014, Uncle Harvey won the First Citizen of Norfolk award and many other awards before and after. He was a caring uncle to me, once visiting me at the deaf school in Massachusetts when I was eight and writing me a beautiful letter when I got married.

Uncle Harvey was also good friends with the local plastic surgeon, Dr. Charles E. Horton, who established Physicians for Peace. This organization, PFP, delivers education and training to healthcare workers in underdeveloped nations worldwide. Since its launch in 1989, PFP has shared its power of "Teach One. Heal Many." The late Dr. Horton spoke a few times in the 1960s at The Woman's Club about surgical care; he was a remarkable man I knew personally and whose daughters, Nancy and Katie, are my lifelong friends. This world-renowned plastic surgeon and Uncle Harvey worked together to bring education and empowerment of medicine to the communities, as the latter stated that witnessing war wounds in Korea changed him profoundly and responsibly. For instance, before the war, Uncle Harvey threw his tennis racquet and stomped on it when he lost a point; after the war, he was more like Roger Federer with good manners. His new tennis racquet was spared from being dismantled. My mom once remarked of her brother, "The war did him good. He came home a completely changed man."

***

An ardent fan of genealogy, Aunt Frances began to dig into her grandfather Alvah Martin's biography and pictures. One day, she gathered her six first cousins, including Frank Batten, to make a family book showcasing Alvah's generation to the fourth generation (Frances's grandchildren, to be precise). Old photos of Alvah and his family spread over the table, chosen by the cousins for a dark blue coffee table book titled *Martin Family History.* Fay Martin Chandler, one of Alvah's granddaughters, agreed to take charge of the book, and the cousins began gathering photos to portray the life of Alvah's mammoth family from bygone times to the present.

The six first cousins who participated in the book project amid computer breakdowns, long-distance collaboration, and some shared emotions were Frances Lindsay, Fay Chandler, Catharine "Tryntje" Willcox, Dorothy Smith, Piney Patterson, and Frank Batten. They all were Alvah's grandchildren, who might have never met him due to his early death at fifty-nine. Each cousin provided photos and stories about their branch of the family tree. Frank Batten, being the only male in that book group, brought in numerous photos of his parents, Dorothy and Frank Sr., and then his adoptive parents, Fay and Sam Slover. As the only child descending from those two branches of the Martin family tree, Frank showed many of his own photos, including one of himself as a toddler on Uncle Sam's lap, another of him meeting with King Hussein in 1958, and the last one of him with his attractive wife, Jane.

And as the first cousin of Aunt Frances' five children, I was delighted to see the photos of them in the book. Overall, *Martin Family History* was beautifully done with stories of Alvah's six surviving children, grandchildren, and their offspring. Ever since the much-appreciated Nancy King, Aunt Frances' daughter-in-law, met me at The Woman's Club in September 2022 and handed me that book, it has been a tremendous help for my research since it tells stories of Alvah and his wife, Mary Eva, known as "Mamie." Without the family book, I would not have been able to include in this book the early history of the Martin Mansion or the Slover home next door.

***

Working as a landscape designer for A&R Diversified near downtown Norfolk, I was so engrossed in an extensive landscaping bid that I overlooked the sudden desertion of my office building. The company of two hundred employees had two separate office buildings with an enclosed truck port in between. It turned out that everyone had gone over to the other building to watch the news on TV. Finally, a quiet coworker, Aaron, came into my office and said, "There was a bomb in the World Trade Center."

I nearly fell off the seat because I thought Aaron meant the one in Norfolk, where my brother Nash had worked as an attorney for years. Yes, there is a "World Trade Center" in downtown Norfolk. Aaron corrected, "No, in New York." I immediately walked over to the other building, but not before I noticed its window, where many of my colleagues huddled together in front of the TV. Employees at A&R Diversified usually never slowed down since this was a sizable bustling company with strict rules. But that morning, everyone stopped. I thought, *This is bad*, and fearfully joined the TV audience and absorbed this horrible news after a long moment of confusion. That was before the second plane hit. I lost motivation in that landscaping bid and canceled a tennis game that afternoon.

September 11, 2001, brought a halt to everyone, just as the assassination of President John F. Kennedy did on November 22, 1963. The 9/11 tragedy, thirty-eight years later, saddened the Americans into tears and profanity but did what no other tragedy had done before. Not even World War II could unleash an emotional charge to such a greater degree than 9/11. But maybe the unforeseen attack on Pearl Harbor amounted to the same thing. Still, the 9/11 tragedy was different in one way. The terror attacks provoked Americans to quickly stir from immobilizing grief to *giving*. The morning after nearly three thousand people perished in the tower and plane attacks, Americans began shelling out money to the Red Cross and other charitable organizations for relief and recovery efforts. The $1.2 billion amount exceeded donations following any previous disaster in the nation's history, proving Americans were the world's most compassionate and generous people.

And the 9/11 tragedy did not generate only funds but also volunteers. As soon as the Red Cross initiated a relief effort at Ground Zero, thousands of people signed up to volunteer for the first time. Thus, more than fifty-seven thousand team members became involved in the Red Cross for years to come, even after

Ground Zero was cleaned up and rebuilt.

Unsurprisingly, woman's clubs nationwide and worldwide contributed money to the 9/11 efforts. The Woman's Club of Norfolk sent three hundred dollars to the New York Relief Fund and possibly more in later months. A few years later, the GFWC collected one hundred eighty thousand dollars for a fully equipped ambulance for use by the New York Fire Department to replace equipment lost in the terrorist attacks.

***

Trees, roof shingles, electrical wires, trash cans, and patio furniture were scattered all over Norfolk and nearby cities when Hurricane Isabel hit on September 18, 2003. Unlike most other storms, this Category 1 hurricane did not pass through in a brief time; it lingered around like a doodle on paper. For me, Isabel was a painfully long hurricane, rattling my nerves as I hunkered down with my dogs in the garage all day. Watching trees sway through the narrow upper windows inside the garage door, I had no clue if the hurricane had peaked. Unfortunately, my husband Steve was on his annual backpacking trek in Utah. Ironically, when he and his buddies emerged from the woods after a week up in the Wasatch Range without any phone or news, they stopped at a roadside gas station and gasped at the tiny black-and-white TV above the cashier. The TV was announcing the impending landfall of Isabel toward Norfolk. Steve and his friends fumbled for their long-unused cellphones in their backpacks and tried calling their wives. I had turned off my phone to save the battery; therefore, he could not reach me. It frustrated me when my husband was not home preparing our house for the impact and sitting with me in the garage to wait it out. But he deserved a good hike to take a break from work. Steve just got out of the woods and learned that we Norfolkians were *not* out of the woods!

Hurricane Isabel did considerable damage to Norfolk, its 65-mile-an-hour winds downing thousands of trees and torrential rains saturating the soil. A few small tornados passed through, uprooting trees in one Larchmont neighborhood. A neighbor's large mature tree lost a limb and smashed into the back corner of the auditorium at The Woman's Club, which, fortunately, was quickly repaired in preparation for fall weddings. As in my neighborhood, most areas had no power for five days or so. At least we had water, and I had the opportunity to shower for a friend's wedding in downtown Norfolk two days after the storm. Yes, I was clean, but with no blow-drying, my hair was severely matted, and that was what the female wedding guests complained about. Still, my dear friends Julia and Dave Pezza took their wedding vows among the tattered city flags with nonchalance and humor. They were fortunate to have electricity at their venue to keep the guests happy with air conditioning, heated appetizers, ice-cold beer and wine, and a wedding cake that never melted. That night, Steve came home from Utah, picked up our twenty-seven-foot-long RV at his office building, and parked it in our driveway so we could use the generator for power, albeit for my hairdryer. We generously offered to have two neighbors, each with a newborn, connect hundred-foot-long electrical cords to our generator so that the baby formulas would stay cold in their fridges.

It was no surprise to everyone that The Hague took the brunt of the storm, flooding the entire Mowbray Arch, just like it did during the 1933 Chesapeake-Potomac hurricane. The creek once again looked like a Rorschach blot instead of a neat, curved Y. Both ends of The Hague were submerged, as Stone Park on West Olney Road was nowhere to be seen, and the giant Torch Bearers sculpture in front of Chrysler Museum appeared to be close to standing on the water. Alas, the floodgates were overwhelmed during Isabel's storm impact and broke, filling the Midtown Tunnel from Norfolk to Portsmouth entirely. Indeed, it was a vicious storm that refused to budge for several hours, much to my suffering in the garage.

However, in comparison, Hurricane Isabel was a weaker storm than the 1933 one, which had sustained higher winds by 20 MPH and a higher tidal surge by two feet. Still, Hugh Cobb, the hurricane historian and forecaster in Miami, said, "In the '33 storm, the wind dropped off very quickly—and the tide drained just as quickly. But in Isabel, the region stayed on the more powerful right side of the storm for much longer, and the wind stayed from the east. That kept the water in many places—especially in the upper reaches of the rivers." That explains the submerged Mowbray Arch. Frank Batten's The Weather Channel was constantly running on one storm for two days.

***

One hundred years had passed since the Woman's Club of Norfolk originated in a hotel room at the Atlantic Hotel, so there was an anniversary celebration and a holiday tea at the Martin Mansion attended by over 125 people on December 11, 2005. The first floor was beautifully decorated in its holiday tradition, with the usual large wreath on the front door and a Christmas tree in each parlor. A lighted ice sculpture with the "100th" symbol dominated the atmosphere. Paul Fraim, the mayor of Norfolk, recognized the centennial of the WCN and honored Earlye Lee Miller for her dedication as the club president since 1991. Mrs. Miller spoke about Virginia Gatewood founding the WCN with three departments that eventually increased to nine. Then, the topic turned to the timeline of happenings at the Martin Mansion, including the Daughters of the American Revolution's rental of the first floor for their meetings at thirty dollars for the year 1924. Mrs. Miller's verbal list of events included the WCN's Community Improvement Project in 1984, using pet therapy at nursing homes and taking three puppies, a kitten, and a rabbit to entertain elderly patients. Finally, Mrs. Miller said, "There is so much to tell about our history," followed by loud applause reverberating through the Martin Mansion. If she had to list every single milestone of the WCN in the past century, Mrs. Miller would have kept the guests up until the wee hours.

When I recently googled "Woman's Club Norfolk Va 100th anniversary," *The Virginian-Pilot*'s 2016 article emerged about the anniversary of "The Woman's Club of Norfolk." However, it was not the one on Fairfax Avenue; it was the African-American club that originated in 1916 with the purpose of helping the black community. They first called themselves the "Needle Craft Art Circle"; the name "Woman's Club" would come later. The members met in each other's homes and created a friendly competition to see who could serve the best repast and dress the best table. And they attended plays and musicals. Like the WCN, this group rallied for child labor laws, sanitation in city slums, and suffrage, the last of which was made difficult by the South's progression that stripped African-Americans' power to vote. They also collected money for Norfolk State University and Eastern Virginia Medical School.

The main difference between the two Woman's Clubs of Norfolk in the past was fundraising; the African-Americans, mostly housewives of doctors and lawyers, used their purse money to help the community, whereas the one on Fairfax Avenue used events and projects to raise money. For instance, doctors' wives, belonging to the African-American Woman's Club of Norfolk, started a gift shop at Norfolk Community, the black hospital, and bought flowers for families that couldn't afford them. "This is a group that used their wealth, though it's relative wealth, to help the community," the third-generation member Cassandra Newby-Alexander said. "Working class people were merely trying to survive." Newby-Alexander teaches history at Norfolk State University and has written several books about African-American history in Hampton Roads.

Two years after the WCN's centennial celebration, Mrs. Miller, with the help of her daughters and granddaughter, collected hundreds of photos, documents, newspaper clippings, and minutes from the third-floor archive. They pored over dusty scrapbooks and listened to oral histories. With all the information they could find, Mrs. Miller and her helpers created a paperback coffee-table book with a gold cover titled *History of the Woman's Club of Norfolk, Inc., VFWC-GFWC 1905-2007*. That book has been an enormous help for my research, and I call it "The Gold Book" in gratitude to Mrs. Earlye Lee Miller for her arduous task of assembling such a vast collection of the WCN histories. I am sure it was like laboring on a thousand-piece puzzle of a Jackson Pollock painting.

However, I do not only use Mrs. Miller's book for this book's research but also the newspaper clippings, which have been extremely helpful with facts, numbers, names, and dates. I have noticed the interesting changes in *The Virginian Pilot* along the way from the early 1900s to the present, particularly when discussing the Woman's Club of Norfolk.

Until the late 1960s, *The Virginian-Pilot* printed numerous articles, primarily small and some half a page, on the activities of the Woman's Clubs in the Hampton Roads area. It may be true that public interest tapered off after most of the rights, such as voting and writing checks, had been granted to women. We understand that the woman's right to vote became effective in 1920 and that women gained the right in 1974 to write checks without needing a man to co-sign. In addition, women gained notoriety during World War II for their war efforts on and off the field. It appears to me, from collecting newspaper articles nationwide, that the peaks of women's coverage were in the 1920s and 1940s. *The Virginian-Pilot* initiated a whole Sunday section for the women, along with their classy photos, during the Roaring Twenties, often describing their fashionable dresses and weddings extensively. Then, the paper published lengthy articles on women's roles during World War II; it was strictly for business, not for entertainment, as it was in the 1920s. Fashion was rarely mentioned in the 1940s; the roles were. I would say that rolled-up sleeves were the fashion of women during wartime.

Like hundreds of other newspapers, *The Virginian-Pilot* has evolved over the years and currently seldom publishes anything about women's organizations of any kind. It is not because those newspapers have lost interest; it is just that women have achieved their goals and accomplishments in society, such as working in the corporate world and even racing on the speedway. The gender gap has drastically shrunk since the turn of the twentieth century. Women face political issues today, such as reproductive rights, and receive a great deal of media attention. Hopefully, that will be temporary. But we will not see a repeat of women by the thousands simultaneously escaping home confinement or engaging in Rosie-the-Riveter actions. Women are already in the workforce and military; it is nothing new, but it would have taken up the entire newspaper decades ago.

***

In May 2010, the Virginia Federation of Women's Clubs (GFWC Virginia) did an outstanding deed for my alma mater, Virginia Tech. This organization, whose headquarters are in Richmond, gave a rescue truck, a brand new one, to the Virginia Tech Rescue Squad. It took two years for the GFWC Virginia to raise $172,000 to purchase a 2009 E450 Ford ambulance for the forty-year-old, campus-only rescue squad run by students. This squad serves only on the 2,600 acres of Virginia Tech in Blacksburg; that is quite a large campus! The new "cut above" rescue truck was named Trauma Hawk, to the delight of GFWC Virginia. According to the school link, the Virginia Tech Rescue Squad 2010 was a nationally recognized and award-winning organization committed to providing exceptional emergency medical services on campus, all run by students and volunteers. If I had been more mature and less party-inclined as an undergraduate at Virginia Tech in the early 1980s, I would have volunteered to perform CPR or dress an arm.

***

When my mom stayed with Aunt Mamie in Ghent every school week during World War II, due to gas rationing, she never expected her aunt to have a public library in Norfolk built and named after her sixty-five years later. "Mamie" was Mary Denson Pretlow, a prominent librarian who added branches to the Norfolk library system and pioneered the desegregation of public libraries in Norfolk. Her living relatives, including myself, call her "Mary Pretlow," never just Mary. Trained at the New York City Public Library in the early 1900s, Mary Pretlow managed Manhattan's Hudson Park Library in a predominantly Italian neighborhood, where she arranged books for adults in Italian and those for "energetic" children in English. Also, a writer, Mary Pretlow, published her outstanding essay "What Teachers Read" in the New York Public Library annual report, in which she cataloged the educators' reading material and regaled with warm stories of working with immigrants. The Hudson Park branch in Greenwich Village remains open today as a busy children's library.

After a decade in NYC, Mary Pretlow moved to St. Louis in 1910 to take charge of two public libraries. It was at the time of the immigration wave, and she served library patrons who spoke Russian, Italian, Czech, and German. After seven years in St. Louis, Mary Pretlow was called home to Norfolk, which desperately needed an upgrade of its pitiful library system with only two libraries. But then, her stay was cut short by her patriotic decision to work for the YMCA in Paris during World War I, but not before she worked with the War Camp Community Service to gather reading materials for service members. In the fall of 1918, Mary Pretlow received a leave of absence from the Norfolk Library Board and sailed to Paris to serve as a hostess for the Paris YMCA. She took charge of trained workers, assisting American service members and allied troops in a city of unfamiliarity with a foreign language, such as arranging entertainment and shopping for them. During her free time, Mary Pretlow explored the French libraries, which she found catering only to academia, and visited the frontlines, including captured German trenches.

Finally, she came home for good at the end of World War I and revved up her library career in Norfolk, which needed more libraries for its growing population. During her tenure, Mary Pretlow added six branches, one of which was Blyden, the first public library for African Americans supported by a municipality in the state of Virginia in 1921. By her retirement in 1947, she had encouraged all Norfolk Public Library buildings to accept patrons of all races. As a fervent Democrat with concerns for integration and inclusion, Mary Pretlow said, "I was anxious that books should be put within reach of everyone in Norfolk. The idea of a public library is to put books within walking distance of every person."

In 1961, two years after Mary Pretlow died, a new library branch opened in Ocean View, honoring her. Built of masonry construction with a red-brick exterior, the Mary Denson Pretlow branch was dedicated with a painted portrait of "Miss Pretlow," commissioned by the Women's Democratic Club of Norfolk. In fact, Mary Pretlow was also a member of the Woman's Club of Norfolk and gave speeches about the library system there and at other Woman's Clubs nearby. Finally, in 2008, the old one-story branch was torn down after forty-seven years of serving Norfolkians, and a much bigger two-story branch was built on the same site at the north end of Granby Street with a view of Chesapeake Bay. Along with my enthusiastic cousins, Kate Moring and Maggie Bishop, my mom and I attended the opening ceremony in March 2008 at this beautiful new Mary D. Pretlow Anchor Branch with ninety public computers, a giant children's area, a 110-seat public meeting room, and even a wing for the Ocean View Station Museum.

The funny thing is that Mary Pretlow was my name for three days after birth. But then my mom decided that instead, I would take her name, Indiana Bain, which originated with my great-grandmother. Mom was called "Indie Bain" until college; then it was just "Indie." Maybe she felt bad about leaving out the middle name but gave it to me, added with a Y. Honestly, I would have been honored to take Mary Pretlow's name due to our love for books. But at least I am proud to tell her story here!

***

When Frank Batten was growing up with his biological mother, aunt, and uncle on Fairfax Avenue next to the Martin Mansion, he never imagined he would be involved in building a public library in Norfolk that would be dedicated to Uncle Sam Slover seventy-five years later. However, Frank, now in his eighties, had a plan for an available site to replace the forty-seven-year-old Kirn Memorial Library. That library was demolished to make room for a light rail station. Although the building was in bad shape, many Norfolkians were sad to see Kirn go. It was named after the German immigrants Henry and Elizabeth Kirn, who settled in the city in 1857 and ran a successful truck farming business before expanding their produce company toward New York and down the Mason-Dixon Line. According to city historian Peggy Haile Phillips, Henry Kirn shipped his produce up the James River and sold it "at a good profit" to General Ulysses S. Grant's army. Bessie Kirn donated five hundred thousand dollars in 1962 to build a two-million-dollar library in honor of her parents.

In 2008, it was Frank Batten's turn to pursue a new library in honor of his Uncle Samuel "The Colonel" Slover, who greatly influenced him in his young life. Frank credited his "newspaper doctor" uncle for his own success at Landmark Communications and for instilling morals and values. Slover contributed significantly to the city and ensured that every citizen was well-informed through his newspapers, *The Virginian-Pilot* and *The Ledger-Dispatch*. He knew that knowledge was vital to success. And he gave the newspaper job to Frank, so see how it prospered from there. Therefore, Samuel Slover, in his grave, deserved a library named after him, and his adopted nephew knew it.

Frank donated twenty million dollars toward the high-tech, 138,000-square-foot library a block from the historic Douglas MacArthur Memorial, where the World War II general is buried. With a knack for computers throughout his media career, Frank wanted the Slover Library to be one of the most high-tech libraries in Virginia. Unfortunately, he passed away after an illness in 2009, before the ground was broken for the new library. He left his wife, Jane, and three children, Frank Jr., Betsy, and Dorothy. Afterward, the Batten Foundation added another twenty million dollars to thc project. The city of Norfolk committed $22.6 million, and the remainder was collected from private contributions. Construction began in 2009 and took six years to complete.

Frank certainly had his dream come true: The Slover Library is a beautiful facility involving the restoration of the 1898 Seaboard Building, a seven-story glass-walled addition, and the renovation of the 1931 Selden Arcade. The architecture combines old and new structures, so unique that the Slover Library has won awards. As Frank wished, the entire library was wired with Wi-Fi everywhere and a digital way-finding system. It offers computers, interactive displays, video gaming, high-tech civic meeting rooms, classes for adults and children, teen services, and over 133,000 books. Every October, Friends of the Norfolk Public Library (FNPL) throw a party in the main lobby at the Slover Library, but guests can mingle on all floors. With live music, beer and wine, hors d'oeuvres, and valet parking, the FNPL's "Books and Brew Vino Too!" event always sells out. Frank and his Uncle

Sam would have been floored by the beauty of the Slover Library, which makes the community feel at home.

Upon Frank's passing in 2009, my uncle Harvey Lindsay remembered his friend of sixty years and told *The Virginian-Pilot*: "Frank could very easily have just led the good life and not dealt with the problems of the city and the state. But he chose to become very involved and do things that have helped many people. I think he was certainly one of the great Virginians of the century."

As I remember Frank Batten fondly, he was one of the great skiers on the Big Burn at Snowmass in Aspen, Colorado. He was an influential person emerging from the Slover home on Fairfax Avenue with valuable genes passed on from nearby Martin Mansion.

***

The General Federation of Women's Clubs continued various projects as it progressed toward its 125th anniversary in 2015 to help the nation and the world. Most importantly, this tenacious organization focused on the disturbing increase in domestic violence nationwide, creating a GFWC Signature Program in 2010. It is still influential today. The goal is to educate the GFWC members about awareness and prevention of domestic violence so they can participate in programs to assist families and communities affected by this type of violence. Then, the members are encouraged to educate themselves by researching resources, statistics, law enforcement, hotlines, and community assistance. Is there a shelter? How do the authorities respond to domestic violence? How many victims are there in your area each month?

The GFWC members also need to concentrate on partners, child/teen, and senior abuse. According to the statistics, one in every four women will experience domestic violence in her lifetime, and 85 percent of domestic violence victims are women. One in four teens reports verbal, physical, emotional, or sexual abuse each year, and about one in five high school girls has been physically or sexually abused by a dating partner. One in nine Americans over sixty has experienced some form of senior abuse. For every case of senior abuse reported to authorities, at least five more go unreported. Each year, women experience about 4.8 million intimate partner-related physical assaults and rapes. Men are the victims of about 2.9 million personal partner-related physical assaults.

Most of all, the GFWC Signature Program prepares members to help domestic violence victims. It seems to work well, as many GFWC Woman's Clubs created their own ways to increase public awareness and provide needs to the victims and their families, according to the GFWC Club Manual 2010–2012. Take Arizona and Florida, for examples:

GFWC Buckeye Woman's Club (Arizona) accomplished its goal to open a domestic violence shelter in its own city. The club members had raised over four thousand dollars by hosting a "Casino Night" and sponsoring a golf tournament where they sold hot dogs to the golfers. But the Buckeye Woman's Club did not stop at the opening of the shelter; the members continued fundraising so they could supply furniture for the interview room and the children's playroom. The shelter began serving abused women from the cities of Avondale, Goodyear, and Buckeye.

The GFWC Florida had its 115 members travel to Tallahassee and talk to their representatives and senators about domestic violence and child advocacy concerns. The women wore all purple, which showed the public their dedication to ending domestic violence. They were given a chance to start conversations with others about why they were in Tallahassee.

In 2012, the General Federation created a part of its Signature Program to help domestic violence victims: The GFWC *Success For Survivors Scholarship* to help those impacted by intimate partner violence pursue higher education. The scholarship provides survivors with a path to financial and personal independence. After years of success, the GFWC today awards abuse survivors $2,500 in scholarships so they can obtain a post-secondary education, which should offer an opportunity to improve their future by securing employment and gaining personal independence. Candidates must attend an accredited public or private post-secondary school, including community colleges, technical schools, and four-year universities. They should ask for financial aid from the school office if needed, as proved by the GFWC's 2023 *Success for Survivors Scholarship* document.

This magnificent program reminds me of a class I took in 2003 while pursuing a master's degree in counseling at Old Dominion University. Professor Radha Parker showed us a three-hour-long live video of a female abuse victim undergoing therapy spanning three years. It can take that long for a vulnerable person to gain self-esteem, fight back verbal and physical abuse, and achieve independence. There is no overnight cure or transformation for any domestic violence victim. The most profound part of that class video was the dramatic changes in the facial and body language of the victim. At the beginning of the video, the young woman appeared extremely fragile and nervous, with a sad face and awkward gestures. Through the course of the three-year span, the woman slowly, *very* slowly, transformed into a physically, mentally, and vocally stronger person as her face gained more strength and definition. With the help of my hearing aids, I could tell her voice was strengthening in tone and intonation. It was evident this abused victim did not only undergo therapy but also attended school and found employment, of which she did not feel capable during her former boyfriend's violence. A combination of therapy and education does the work for an abuse victim, although it can take years. The GFWC cannot assist with therapy but does a big favor with scholarships—and prevention.

One might wonder if the Woman's Club of Norfolk has produced such a scholarship program for domestic abuse victims. The answer is no, but the WCN has met with several victims and even their children at a local woman's shelter. The members have spent a day there, providing gifts to the children and making crafts with them. And the mothers have been given flower arrangements by the WCN members to take back to their rooms. Letters of encouragement have been sent to the victims as well. Over the years, the WCN has donated money, clothes, shoes, and toys to the woman's shelter whose location is undisclosed for safety.

***

The Hague still looked the same after 125 years, with attractive European-style homes despite occasional flooding episodes, some related to coastal storms and most related to extremely high tides. It appeared that climate change has ushered more coastal storms into Norfolk, raising the sea level. Prior to the construction of a semi-circle seawall in 1897, the Smith's Creek, before it was called The Hague, flowed freely into the marshes, including the Stockley Gardens and the lot of the future Christ and St. Luke's Episcopal Church. Those areas were dirt-filled, and the creek was pushed away from its former edges, possibly by hundreds of feet. That might have been a drastic mistake. It would have been beneficial to have kept the marshes, whose roots provided stability to the creek bed. Instead, the water creeps over Mowbray Arch and both ends of The Hague. Or maybe the creek today is weary of the formality of the Y-shaped Hague and wants to ebb and flow with the tides.

The water even creeps beneath the massive Christ and St. Luke's, as described in a lengthy article in *The Virginian-Pilot* in 2017. Win Lewis, the rector at the time, stated that even a run-of-the-mill tide on a clear day could cause the water to "come up through cracks in the floor." And the pools of water in the boiler room kept the dehumidifier humming without a break. With all its weight, Christ and St. Luke's are sitting on a creek bed. Win Lewis and his parishioners realized that denial about the rising water was no longer the answer and that it was time to prevent further damage rather than try to correct the water level, albeit at high costs. Therefore, Win Lewis planned to remove all the activities from the lowest level of the church and leave the stored containers off the first floor. Aside from praying for the best, he knew he and his parishioners would have to "live with it, manage it where possible, and fortify and make the most out of the church's higher spaces."

Fortunately, most stylish homes on Mowbray Arch remain safe from flooding because they were built high, thanks to their clever contractors in 1890. Only the street skirting The Hague faces such unfortunate submersion, bad enough to cause drivers to detour. However, Mowbray Arch is exposed most of each year, inviting locals to sit on benches, picnic on the grassy area, and gaze at the calm Hague.

***

Other than the depressing sea level, the residents at The Hague faced publicity twice in four years, one event controversial and the other beneficial. First, Drummond Bridge, now called the Hague Bridge, has seen quite a bit with its numerous makeovers over the years. Andria McClellan, a Hague resident, wrote an impressive essay about the history of the bridge that extends across the creek from Brambleton Avenue to Mowbray Arch, closer to the Chrysler Museum than Christ and St. Luke's at the other end of The Hague. Before the construction of the neighborhood in the 1890s, the bridge was merely wooden, with people and horses traveling between Norfolk and the plantations on the Mowbray Arch side. The unknown storm demolished the bridge, which was replaced with a steel structure in 1891. By 1912, the Hague Bridge became much wider, transporting Ford models and streetcars. The bridge saw some renovations in the next four decades. Finally, by 1963, vehicular traffic was stopped overall, and only pedestrians and cyclists could use the Hague Bridge. Thirteen years later, in 1976, the bridge was demolished and replaced by "a new, narrower pedestrian bridge that incorporated parts from the older bridge and maintained the bridge's historical general appearance," as described by McClellan in her essay.

Thus, the metal handrail on both sides of the new pedestrian bridge was built to resemble the 1891 one. As the 1976 replica of the handrail still exists today, the pattern exhibits the "quarry tile" with curves and straight lines. The Chrysler Museum has the original 1891 handrail in one of its storage rooms, which is fragile with age but delightful to see. So, the Hague Bridge stood elegantly in late 2013, and then a padlock mysteriously appeared on the handrail. It would spark a four-year controversy in Norfolk. More locks showed up here and there on the handrails; they were the so-called "love locks." Two lovers would take a lock, write or carve their names or initials on it, and attach it to the bridge—it happened worldwide, mostly famously in Paris. Some lovers tossed the key into the water as a symbol of their eternal love, or at least they thought so.

Hence, a hundred locks of all colors were attached in 2014 to the metal balusters of the handrails on the Hague Bridge. Then, the number increased to over eight hundred locks in the next two years, much to several Hague residents' dismay. They felt that this historic bridge was being abused and neglected. I was initially charmed by a few love locks early on, but as time passed, there were so many that they looked like graffiti. Yet, the city of Norfolk refused to remove the locks, insisting these metal objects were legal everywhere, just as bike locks were, and that the bridge was not prone to be weighed down by a thousand locks.

Then, "private citizens" removed 95 percent of the locks themselves. A group of Hague residents took the city to court, citing the locks as a public nuisance. The judge had no choice but to summon a grand jury, which never happened. Finally, without a decision from the grand jury, the city workers arrived at the Hague Bridge to remove all the locks. Later, the handrails, badly scratched from the locks, were painted glossy black, and then the bridge became a historic attraction again.

***

While the love locks were newly emerging on the bridge in 2014, another strange object appeared only several yards away on The Hague. It did not invoke controversy as the love locks did; it brought smiles to the entire Norfolk community. The Dutch artist Florentijn Hofman placed his inflatable, forty-foot "Rubber Duck" in the water in front of the Chrysler Museum, which had a reason for this surprising exhibition. The museum had undergone a major expansion along with makeovers and wanted to attract people to its grand reopening. Sure enough, the giant yellow Rubber Ducky was a hit for ten days, as it made The Hague look like a playful bathtub. People took pictures of the duck from the seawall. Steve and I posed with our bikes, with the towering yellow bird behind us. The creator, Florentijn Hofman, had designed it for his "Spreading Joy Around the World" tour and inflated the duck in the waters of Amsterdam, Hong Kong, Sydney, São Paulo, and other cities. He stated that the "Rubber Duck knows no frontiers; it doesn't discriminate against people and doesn't have a political connotation. The friendly, floating Rubber Duck has healing properties: it can relieve global tensions as well as define them." He undoubtedly brought the Norfolk community together for smiles and laughs over those ten days.

There was one building that benefitted the most from the Rubber Duck: The Chrysler Museum. This facility has experienced record attendance since it opened in 1971. The Rubber Duck was a welcome mat to about forty thousand visitors, luring them to view paintings, glass art, and sculpture at the museum. In addition, its Facebook page saw a spike in views from 20,000 to 1.6 million. The art director and president, Bill Hennessey, was approaching retirement and had succeeded in overlooking the renovations/expansions and inviting the Rubber Duck to host the reopening. He said, "The happiest thing for us is a great many of the people who came to see the duck also tried out the Chrysler Museum for the first time and seemed to have a wonderful time. So, we've connected with a whole new audience that we hope will become regulars."

***

Despite occasional flooding, The Hague was still in great shape, with a new view of Harbor's Edge in the distance. This high-rise retirement facility with seventeen floors opened in 2007 on the bank of the Elizabeth River and next to the historic Fort Norfolk, which helped protect the city during the War of 1812. Then, during the Civil War, the Confederate army seized and used the fort to defend Norfolk and Portsmouth across the river. Whenever I visited my parents, who moved there in 2007, at Harbor's Edge, it was always a treat to view from one of the top floors the perfect semicircle of The Hague this way and the white Fort Norfolk the other way.

The medical community next to The Hague was booming with a new heart hospital, the renovated Children's Hospital of King's Daughters (CHKD), and several new facilities. In the next few years, there would be significant additions to the medical area: The CHKD's fourteen-story Mental Health Hospital with its Children's Pavilion and the Waitzer Hall, an eleven-story education and academic administration building for EVMS students.

Colley Avenue still enlightened with restaurants, gift shops, and coffee cafes. Stockley Gardens was green as ever, with live oaks providing cool shade in the summertime. Medical students, long-time Ghent residents, artists, and young college graduates filled the apartments surrounding The Hague neighborhood. People entered and out of religious buildings such as Ohef Sholom, Ghent Methodist, and Christ and St. Luke's every weekend. Joggers and dog walkers crowded Ghent Square and Colonial Avenue. So, the entire Ghent Historic District was as lively as ever. 2014 seemed like a good year for Ghent residents, further enhanced by the Rubber Duck and a pre-controversial display of love locks on the bridge.

But one part of the Ghent Historic District was not lively. Silence had enveloped this place for a while. Neighbors noticed that hardly anyone entered or departed anymore. There was no longer animated noise or chatter inside. Maintenance or repair trucks had not arrived for a long time. The grass in the front yard had not been mowed for a while, but the neighbors next door took notice and began doing the job themselves. They did it quietly, without disturbing anyone inside. These neighbors knew the place could not look any worse outside with the uncut wilting grass, so that was all they could do to make this historic mansion look normal on their block. But the inside fared the worst: Water stains, pipe leaks, unclean rooms, overloaded electrical cords, musty smells, and peeling paint. The Martin Mansion was being neglected. And the Woman's Club of Norfolk was near extinction. That house's 104 years of rich history seemed to dissipate to oblivion. Even the wooden carved dogs on the mantel faced something worse than being accidentally covered by a mirror for years; they were surrounded by an air of dereliction, not darkness.

Tea And Toil at The Woman's Club

Chapter Thirteen

Susanne Ott looked at the mansion with exasperation and experienced a fight-or-flight response. Could it really be saved? Should it be saved? The work to be done was overwhelming, to say the least. This would be a time-consuming, messy, and expensive endeavor. The easy way out was to throw in the towel and just give up. Surely, everyone would understand. Many passers-by, dog walkers, kids on bikes, and nosey neighbors have curiously looked up to the porch and said, "Who lives there? What do they do?" No one really knew, and did anyone really care? Should this dilapidated, formerly loved home just sink into disrepair? The most accessible thought always comes to mind first. Just sell it. Explain to everyone that you tried your best, but it was too much. Everyone would understand. But as Susanne stared at the mansion with a thousand questions racing in her mind, she thought, *Or maybe, just maybe, with a few volunteer members, Walt my supportive husband, Richard the electrician who came with the house, and a few well-meaning neighbors, just maybe something could be done?*

As they had been members of the Woman's Club of Norfolk and grew to love the Martin Mansion since the early 2010s, Susanne and Paige Rose miraculously saved the mansion from dilapidation and bankruptcy in December 2014. This rescue occurred long after the elderly director began to have cognitive decline, failed to maintain the mansion, and ignored the mounting bills. Sarah Petroske and her husband Ken had lived next door on the right since 1981; for the first fifteen or twenty years of their residence on Fairfax Avenue, Sarah had witnessed the vibrancy of the WCN under the presidency of Edna Schweitzer. But then she noticed in the first half of 2010, the club's activity, under the elderly director, had slowed down almost to a halt. Lastly, the mansion fell into neglect, and the club seemed nonexistent.

After the director left for good during the 2014 holiday season, Susanne and Paige took on the enormous task of cleaning up the mess in the mansion and calling for repairs. And they had to beat the two-month deadline of correcting the failed house and fire inspections. At the time of the mansion rescue, the bank account held only nine thousand dollars, far below what should have been in five or six digits. Indeed, Susanne and Paige were left in a colossal mess despite some quick repairs and had to deal with the existing tenants on the second floor – while their families stayed home with the holiday décor. Those two women were not asked to do the work; they did it themselves. Of course, Susanne and Paige were exhausted and even considered letting the mansion go. It had to be the most stressful holiday they had ever had in their lifetimes.

Much like one of the former WCN directors, Edna Schweitzer, Susanne was drawn to the challenges, the naysayers, and the very large obstacles that lay ahead of her for years. The locals wondered why anyone would ever volunteer their time to this house, much less align their names to it. In so many moments, this forgotten mansion, now with Susanne tied to it, felt like a lost cause. Once when she was pondering if she had made the right decision, she was working in the cluttered attic on the third floor. As it might have been God's purpose, the afternoon sun gleamed on an oblong portrait in a gold frame, several feet away, where Susanne could have missed it—and given up the mansion altogether. But the sunlight led her to the portrait of Mary Eva and Alvah Martin, obviously taken in the late 1800s and long ago stashed away. As she incredulously stared at Alvah and Mary Eva, Susanne knew with an inner drive that she had to lead the effort to revitalize, repair, and renovate this historic mansion. She was not going to give up.

So, at the beginning of 2015, Susanne decided, *Yes, the mansion is worth saving, it will be worth pulling the club back to its bygone glory.* With years of experience in business management at previous jobs, Susanne knew she and her helpers needed to double the income of the property immediately, just to keep it from falling into further disrepair. Thus, it was time to bring it back under favorable conditions for events such as weddings, which would generate revenue much needed for repairs. And thankfully, Paige was able to resolve the eight-thousand-dollar property tax bill, long ignored by the previous director, with a nerve-racking eight-hour-long phone call to the Internal Revenue Service; they agreed to give the Martin Mansion a clean slate.

Determined to save the Martin Mansion, Susanne created a short-term plan. She recruited Sheila Kilpatrick, Sarah Petroske, Wendy Auerbach, and Polly Jones into the Woman's Club of Norfolk as members. So, they could use their hands to help clean and discard unwanted items such as outdated TVs down in the basement. Polly and the rest of the members would later join and help with the physical work. Paige became the club president, Susanne the vice president, and Sarah the secretary. With all these women now at the helm, the Woman's Club of Norfolk sprang to life, just slowly. And, there would not be tea for a while; instead, there would be toil, a lot of it, to revitalize both the club and the mansion back to where they were thirty years earlier. Members worked long and hard on the side of the Woman's Club of Norfolk to keep their club running, but the other enormous side of the puzzle was to bring revenue into a quickly disappearing bank account. Susanne would figure it out with her management skills.

***

After launching a neighborhood magazine in the Ghent community, Sheila Kilpatrick joined the Woman's Club of Norfolk in 2015 to meet new people and give back. With untiring motivation, she would delve into many community projects in the next eight years and become the valuable WCN president, as she is today. Sheila helped petition the Virginia legislature to help local victims of human trafficking and encouraged the club to donate clothing and food worth ten thousand dollars to human trafficking victims. She also leads the WCN in sponsoring women in war-ravaged countries and teaching them trades so they can provide for their families. Furthermore, Sheila is an avid supporter of the Susan Komen Breast Cancer Walk each year, hauling the club members to join and wear all pink for the long walk. The Woman's Club of Norfolk would not be here as a reinvigorated organization if not for Sheila's dedication to the community.

***

Beginning in Spring 2016, Susanne had been asking Polly Jones to help her restore the Martin Mansion as well as the Woman's Club of Norfolk; however, the latter was not ready since she had a lot on her plate at home. Approximately eighteen months after the

December 2014 mansion rescue, Susanne had successfully created three streams of revenue: Special events, tenants, and fundraisers. Many members arrived for the WCN meetings, but what Susanne really needed was someone who could be physically present on a daily basis to meet the challenges coming from every direction. She needed another dedicated full-time member at the mansion, daily, who could help her conquer problems that a team would usually encounter. If only Susanne had the budget for a few salaried positions like other organizations, she would be able to hire employees to fill many different positions. Instead, Susanne and the full-time member would fill these positions mostly on volunteer hours. She knew Polly would be a reliable partner. Along with her business acumen, Polly had a professional background, determination, and contagious optimism, which could help Susanne save the mansion.

But it would not be until a year and a half later when Polly finally entered the scene. Susanne maintained her patience and continued to do the work, about ninety percent alone, around the Martin Mansion. While Paige was busy raising her small child and managing school activities, she came by to help Susanne at the mansion once in a while. But she did speak with Susanne often on the phone, while her daughter was at school, to discuss business for the mansion and the club.

***

The Garden Club of Norfolk and the Harborfront Garden Club, as a duo team for the annual Garden Tour, chose The Hague neighborhood for the 2017 event. I had been a member of the first club, as were my mom and grandmother for decades. I must give a brief history of the Garden Club of Norfolk (GCN), which originated in 1915 with a roster of forty charter and two honorary members, all garden and nature lovers. The GCN was only the third in the state and the first garden club in Tidewater. In 1920, the GCN became a part of the Garden Club of America (just like the Woman's Club of Norfolk is a part of the GFWC); each has the chick-under-the-umbrella effect. The GCN is also a member of the Garden Club of Virginia, just as the WCN belongs to the state federation.

The Garden Club of Norfolk's first activities, back in the early days, were flower shows where the members encouraged amateur gardeners and exhibited and judged floral varieties. Next came the first Historic Garden Week held by the Garden Club of Virginia, in which several cities hosted their garden tours of private homes and gardens. Norfolk had its first garden tour in 1928, organized by the GCN, and it has continued every year except during World War II and the 2020 pandemic. During Historic Garden Week, the GCN has raised significant funds through its annual tour that go to the Garden Club of Virginia's Restorations of Historic Gardens across the state.

Thus, The Hague neighborhood drew publicity for its upcoming garden tour on April 27, 2017. Six homes, one on Mowbray Arch and five others in the semi-circle grid pattern, would enthrall people with their interiors and gardens. And The Woman's Club would show only its garden, although it was not much. This mansion was chosen for the tour because of its grandeur and historical look, and it had been a considerable part of The Hague for a century. Unfortunately, the front bed looked pitiful, with misshapen plants as old as the mansion itself. It was mostly pyracanthas unprofessionally pruned like shrubs, whereas they should have been treated as espaliers (pruned and tied to a flat plane like the fence or lattice). These pyracanthas looked like poorly shaped bonsai, leaning this way and that.

Connie Kellam, the chairman of the 2017 Garden Tour intended to take place five months away, called me to The Woman's Club and asked what on earth we could do about the sad landscaping destined to be shown on the tour. I took one unblinking look at the front bed, which had two long, narrow sections with a walk in the middle. My mind was made up. I declared that all the disfigured pyracanthas and non-flowering plants had to go. They were too old to be shaped with pruning. With that being said, the bed had to be cleared entirely and started anew. We had only a few months before the garden tour to turn the forlorn landscaping into one as pretty as the inside of the Martin Mansion. I knew it would be feasible with the help of others.

I met with Susanne and Paige outside with my suggestions to remove everything from the front bed and offered a landscape plan free of charge. It was immediately agreed that the Woman's Club had the worst landscaping on Fairfax Avenue and could use a massive makeover. And Susanne concurred on having the WCN pay for the demolition and installation of the front bed, measuring sixty feet long and eight feet wide, cut in half by a wide walkway toward the porch. They would find someone to do the work while I helped with setting up the plants.

Because of the symmetry and formality of the Martin Mansion, I drew a symmetrical layout of the formal plants adapted to the hot southern sun. The same plants would be on both sides of the walkway leading to the porch steps. And I chose plants that would not grow too fast or hide the iconic arch openings under the porch. Two forty-eight-inch-tall spiral junipers abreast of the walkway would be the focal point of the landscaping, inviting people to step in from the sidewalk. In addition, those spiral junipers would exhibit the elegance of the Martin Mansion. Then, for more color, annuals would be installed just in time for the Garden Tour.

It was about time the Grand Old Lady received a significant facelift on her front landscaping, with the four-foot-tall spiral junipers acting as elegant earrings. Soon enough, a drone was used to film the Martin Mansion to promote wedding events. The drone first flew over the new landscape and then snaked into the front door to show the foyer in a panoramic view before entering the parlors, auditorium, and upstairs into the bridal room. And that drone video is still on the Martin Mansion website. Every time I watch it with the background music, I am thrilled to see the spiral junipers, round Japanese hollies, and other agreeable plants instead of misshapen pyracanthas. More critically, landscaping shows the value of the home inside and out; once you see the pretty exterior, then you expect the pretty interior as well.

***

One evening in the late fall of 2016, I arrived at The Woman's Club for a meeting with Susanne and Paige to explain the steps of landscape maintenance and prepare for the 2017 Garden Tour. Unexpectedly, I had a strange sensation in the foyer for the first time in forty-five years. I had been to the mansion numerous times in my lifetime, from Christmas choruses in my preteens to Thanksgiving gatherings in my fifties. This time I experienced shock and surprise at the beauty of the foyer as if I had never seen it before. Every time I was in the Martin Mansion, many people were around, enough to cause distraction from the woodwork, landscape mural, grand staircase, and even the chandeliers. Parties, school skits, science projects, and other noisy events took my attention away from the unique interior design of the Martin Mansion. But that evening was quiet with only Susanne and Paige, which made the mansion almost empty. While I stood in the foyer surrounded by mountains, lakes, cabins, boats, and an assumed figure of Alvah Martin, the bird hunter, in the mural, I thought, *This is The Woman's Club I've been to hundreds of times, and it's beautiful!*

My eyes then turned to the coffered white ceiling with dark oak trimmings over the foyer, where a simple crystal chandelier hung in the middle. What enraptured me about the ceiling was the circular lacelike plaster design, a foot in diameter, around the chandelier's hanging hook. I realized that the West and East Parlors had those larger attractive plasters over their chandeliers as well. Then I scanned the woodwork around the first floor, including the staircase and wall paneling, all the same dark oakwood. The entire floor showed the hidden corners of history, and I was appalled by my ignorance for so many years. I finally realized there was much more to "The Woman's Club" than parties, school plays, and weddings.

Dumbfounded, I turned to Susanne and Paige, remarked on the century-old beauty of the interior, and said, "Why haven't I noticed it before?" My new friends gave a knowing look, as they had witnessed this awestruck reaction from others daily in the past two years of their revitalization of the Martin Mansion. And Susanne and Paige had appeared in *The Virginian-Pilot* in 2016 for their dedication to the mansion and restoring it as a wedding venue.

While standing in the foyer and gazing around in long overdue admiration, I realized it was not only the character of the mansion so absorbing, but also the unknown history of such magnitude. It seemed like I was only on page one of the history schoolbook, possibly a thick one. A sudden urge to learn the history of the Woman's Club of Norfolk and its clubhouse swept over me. Then an idea entered my head. Something had to be done to give The Woman's Club the recognition it deserved. Susanne and Paige raised their eyebrows when the nine words came out of my mouth:

"I am going to write a book about it.

***

Luckily, five months after the landscape installation at the Martin Mansion, the 2017 Garden Tour was a huge success, with hundreds of people strolling the streets of The Hague. The warm, sunny weather helped tremendously, encouraging ladies to wear colorful outfits and broad hats. The front beds at The Woman's Club, freshly mulched and colored with annuals, joined the other gardens in garnering admiration. And by the end of the Garden Tour at 5 PM, the members of my garden club celebrated with wine and cheese—on the front porch of The Woman's Club, overlooking the spiral junipers in the front bed. The Grand Old Lady sure had a fabulous day, being admired by people on one of her many tours in a century.

***

Polly finally agreed to take her first step in the fall of 2017, not realizing exactly what she was in for. She walked into a buzz of wedding guests, planners, vendors, and a huge hum of anticipation with the Bride and Groom trying to avoid each other until the big moment. In those days, it was "Venue Only," meaning Susanne and Polly were on patrol to protect the house. They discovered a guest trying to nail blue Dollar Store plastic sheets to the hundred-year-old wooden walls for photo ops. Others wanted to plug three times the electricity into an elder two-plug outlet, blowing all the fuses in a room lovingly referred to as the romantic setting. Of course, candles were lit to make up for the loss of light, while Susanne and Polly scrambled to the basement with a flashlight. These two women would hit every switch until the mansion lit up like a Christmas tree. Only Susanne and Polly knew they had hit pay dirt when the surprised guests upstairs started cheering. Ah, success.

From the word *GO*, Susanne and Polly felt like chasing after a race car and never quite catching it. Before Polly arrived on the scene, Susanne was single-handedly fielding phone inquiries, running the events, doing the setup and breakdown, organizing the parking, and creating budget reports for each event rental for the accountant with a profit or loss. And aside from events, she was scheduling the landscape maintenance, dealing with plumbers and yearly inspectors, running the property rentals for the tenants living on the second and third floor, fighting abhorrent water bills, cleaning out closets, and running interference with guests wandering throughout the house and property. But now Polly was working with her, and never again would Susanne hold the reins by herself. Early on, they both knew this house needed to be run as a business or the house would fail and thus, the Woman's Club of Norfolk would fail.

***

Susanne and Polly's first stop was to visit two clubs in Richmond that had highly successful business models to better understand how to revitalize a severely shrunken club and lay out the framework for the foundation that would be tasked to create development for the mansion and the support of the WCN. Founded in 1894, the Woman's Club of Richmond inspired Virginia Gatewood to establish the Woman's Club of Norfolk in 1905. Executive Director Diane Beirne was extremely helpful in making recommendations to Susanne and Polly, who admired the Bolling Haxall House, which, like the Martin Mansion, is rich in history and a popular event venue. The next stop was Colonial Dames, a national society that has its own foundation promoting its heritage through statewide historic preservation, patriotic service, and educational projects—especially at the Wilton House Museum in Richmond. The staff at the Colonial Dames gave Susanne and Polly insights on how to develop a foundation. Better yet, Polly is a lifelong member of the Colonial Dames; no wonder she brings her passion for history to the Martin Mansion.

These meetings with the Woman's Club of Richmond (now called The Woman's Club at The Bolling Haxall House) and the Colonial Dames were the beginning of Susanne and Polly's creation of a foundation to preserve, restore, and educate about the unique history of the Martin Mansion. It was also a vehicle to apply for grants and accept donations. Their first step was to find a name for the foundation that would support the Woman's Club of Norfolk. How very difficult it was to rebrand this old grande dame that held such a solid, sentimental place in Norfolk's collective history. Many generational families regarded it as The Woman's Club which it is and always will be. However, Susanne and Polly chose to name it "The Gatewood Martin Mansion Foundation," or GMMF. It was an obvious nod to Virginia Gatewood, who started the Woman's Club of Norfolk, and to Alvah and Mary Martin, who built and completed this beautiful home in 1910. Susanne and Polly developed a strategic plan for the next five years. They tasked themselves with preserving the mansion; managing tenants, repairs, and improvements; directing events, fundraising; and writing grant proposals.

These two women set up an office on the third floor of the Martin Mansion and went to work. Susanne took the lead while Polly helped create timelines, goals, projects, and budgets. She also explored marketing options and reviewed types of insurance. These women shopped event management software platforms, updated the website, and learned how to interface forms related to the WCN through their computers that can be shared with members and guests. And when Susanne and Polly were not booking events, they were continuously repairing, renovating, and upgrading the mansion. They painted, hung pictures, cleaned out the basement, secured locks, and cleaned rugs. And they hired independent contractors to upgrade the wiring, fix outdated plumbing, install security cameras and new lighting, and refinish the auditorium floor. Now the Martin Mansion had been much improved for a wedding venue or any kind of event, particularly in its auditorium which Susanne and Polly call "The Event Hall."

***

Susanne exceeded her goal of increasing the revenue by 5,000 percent by 2023, which is fifty times more income than was available the day she began saving the mansion in early 2015. Polly's arrival in 2017 was instrumental in realizing this goal. That is astronomical in only eight years, including the hit they took from COVID! Susanne and Polly applied for many grants, succeeding with one that was earmarked to defray the costs of renovating and improving the outdoor space. It turned out that many brides and grooms want outdoor space for their ceremony, reception, or both. Hence, the large, bland parking lot in the back of the Martin Mansion became a courtyard with Italian flair. As of now, the courtyard is almost fully done with the new brick wall, an antique wrought iron gate, altar columns, and outdoor décor. It has already hosted a few weddings and WCN meetings with success, and there are more events lined up. The satisfying part of the courtyard is the view of the Ghent Historic District skyline over the back brick wall, dominated by the 113-foot-tall bell tower of Christ and St. Luke's.

Susanne and Polly work amazingly well as a duo power team. These two women are vastly different in personality and management, yet somehow complementary. Susanne is an introverted business manager with excellent leadership skills and an ability to create structures and systems where there are none. Whereas Polly is a leader in her own right, an extroverted entrepreneur with the utmost motivation to complete long-term goals. They brainstorm ideas daily, set goals for fundraising and projects, and continuously resolve surprise problems that inherently come with older houses. With plenty of humor and God leading the way, Susanne and Polly both swear their collective faith is what guided them through the hardest of times.

***

By 2018, the WCN membership roster had increased from near extinction in 2014. Unfortunately, COVID-19 appeared two years later and affected the organization severely. Events at the Martin Mansion were canceled, drastically reducing the finances. Susanne had previously ensured monthly operational costs were covered by rental incomes, which saved the day. To this day, Susanne and Polly continue leading the special events department, restorations and repairs, tenants, and the development team.

The General Federation of Women's Clubs took notice of the WCN's rebound and honored the club by bestowing national, state, and district federation awards for its service, education, and membership projects that changed the lives of Hampton Roads residents and beyond. Ever since she rescued the mansion and the club with Susanne in December 2014, Paige Rose has done the WCN an enormous favor by successfully organizing community partnerships and organizing an enormously helpful night for

Yazidi refugees at a packed Naro Theatre. In addition, she ran a tutorship program for third graders for three years. However, that was not all Paige has done for the community, as there would be more of her work toward 2023 explained later in this book.

***

One winter evening in 2018, I helped Susanne, Paige, and Polly clean out the attic. However, it was impossible to remove all the unwanted things at once. The attic was unusually narrow, with a few nooks, not the typical kind that sits over the entire floor or even half of it. Considering the size of the Martin Mansion, you would expect its attic to be enormous as well. But no, it was surprisingly small, with a strong, dusty smell. Christmas decorations, costumes, and other long-unused items crammed the space, and as we carted things out, our arms full of former treasures, we had to pass one another cautiously in that tiny space.

As I turned back toward the attic's tiny door, the eyes in one of the nooks appeared to follow me, and I yelped. It was an antique, three-foot-tall female doll in a lacy, off-white dress with red ribbon trimmings. Standing with a basket of rose petals in one of its hands, the doll looked up at me with a strange smile and a slight cock on its head. Its posture was unlike any other doll I'd ever seen; it looked atypically relaxed, not rigid. The face was eerily lifelike, not even possessing a smooth, pasty, porcelain feel, and it had dimples. The doll was made to look like a human being as if its blue eyes with lifelike brown lids could pierce through me like a preying eagle. And its wavy blond hair looked real, too, flowing over its shoulders. The sight of that doll spooked me, all right. I remarked to the girls we should get out of the attic, which was becoming spookier by the minute. Those doll eyes continued to look me over, and I swear I saw a smirk on its human-like face. Where did that doll come from? Did it land here at The Woman's Club when the house was completed in 1910 and then lived in the attic for a hundred-some years? We left the doll in its place looking comfortable, ready to chat with any other ghosts lurking in the attic. After the attic door closed, I declared I would never return to the attic again.

Several months later, I remembered the doll and asked Paige if it was still in the attic. She gave a surprising update: When she and Polly prepared for a yard sale to get rid of things found in the attic, they pondered over the doll and looked under its dress and found a tag stating the year it was made: 1990, not 1890, as we had expected. How the doll ended up in the attic, obviously unused or never played with, we had no idea. But I later learned it was placed in the women's bathroom on the first floor years ago, scaring all the visitors, and then relocated to the attic. So, it would have to go to the yard sale. No one bought it, despite the reduced price. Finally, Polly gave the doll away. So, the attic ghosts lost a companion.

And there may be some ghosts in the basement as well. Over a hundred phone numbers were written all over two walls in one room with an inked pen. Polly showed them to me, and it was spooky enough because none of these numbers, in normal scribbling size, were local. We wondered if Anthony the Butler wrote them down since he spent his bathroom breaks and resting times in the basement over his thirty-eight years of employment at The Woman's Club. But why would he do that, if he lived in Norfolk and the scribbled phone numbers on the walls did not contain the local area code? And Anthony was too kind to pull a mysterious prank, much less waste his time making up phone numbers and plastering them on the walls. He had enough problems with the dank basement, an occasional stopped-up toilet, or a messy bathroom left by male party guests, some of whom were likely inebriated. The phone numbers seem too foreign to put the responsibility on a human being, so it might have been ghosts wanting a phone chat. The seven-digit numbers are still on the walls; at least they don't have prying eyes like the doll that scared me half to death.

However, Anthony the Butler seems to be a strong presence as a friendly ghost throughout the Martin Mansion. When we sit in the West Wing Parlor for our WCN meetings, we often sense him standing at the entryway in his suit and bowtie and making sure we are mighty comfortable in our seats. And when we have cocktails in the East Wing Parlor, we feel Anthony adjusting the gas fireplace. When we are selecting appetizers off the table in the dining room, we sense him looking over our shoulders to ensure we are thoroughly enjoying cheese biscuits or meatballs. Well, if we are in the basement, it is unknown what Anthony would do, because we never go down there!

***

The Woman's Club of Norfolk found an intriguing partner to help the Norfolk community: Sam the Lasagna Lady. A Chicago native who relocated to the area in 2018, Samantha Peavy found her calling by making lasagna in the wake of tragedy. On Valentine's Day 2006, she lost her eighteen-year-old daughter, Amanda Skye Gallon, to a crosshair shooting. Because homemade lasagna was one of Amanda's favorite foods, Sam developed a passion for baking these dishes and bringing them to homeless people living under bridges in Chicago. She published a few books, one of which was titled *Life Through Lasagna's Eyes*, containing her journal writings and recipes that she created as she coped with her daughter's death.

I witnessed Sam the Lasagna Lady's outstanding contribution at The Woman's Club on April 18, 2019; she, along with WCN club members, baked lasagna for nearly a hundred hungry firefighters, cops, and paramedics from the city of Norfolk. In the event of the "Lasagna Luncheon," the industrial kitchen was abuzz with Sam and WCN volunteers preparing and baking their favorite Italian food. And to my amusement, those burly first responders in their dark blue shirts and pants paused in the foyer with looks of astonishment, dropping their muscular arms and gazing around at the mural, woodwork, and coffered ceiling. They appeared shocked, as they had expected the Martin Mansion to be like a bland church hall or recreation center. We helped direct those awestruck gentlemen to the auditorium through the dining room doors. It was a delight to serve hot plates of Sam's lasagna to them sitting at round tables. One remarked that it was the best lunch he had ever had in his years of fighting fires.

However, the Lasagna Luncheon caused panic among the neighbors and locals who happened to be driving by. They stopped and asked if the Martin Mansion was all right. A good number of fire and paramedic trucks were parked in the driveway and on the street, and they feared a fire. The concerned people were reassured the mansion was just fine and that hungry first responders were simply having lasagna for lunch.

The pandemic could not even stop Sam the Lasagna Lady from doing what she loves best in the kitchen at The Woman's Club, beginning in November 2020. The WCN and the Norfolk Fire Department partnered with Sam to give more than a thousand lasagnas to people in the community before the end of December. Donning a mask and gloves, like everyone else in the kitchen, Sam told *The Virginian-Pilot*, "There are some people who are just struggling with a meal, so we just want to share in the good spirit by giving lasagnas to families and people in the business community because a lot of them have suffered. We're doing it so everyone can have that warm—I call it a warm shape of love, a warm square of love—on their dinner table."

***

During one of our WCN meetings one evening in November 2021, Polly wanted to show me a few things around the mansion, as she knew I was going to write a book about it. She rubbed the wall paneling in the dining room and said she had figured out how the oakwood was cut without a power saw in the early 1900s. She pointed out the "tiger marks" in the wood and explained the woodcarvers back in the old days cut against the grain, resulting in a beautiful tiger pattern. It was done by quarter sawing, which means cutting at a 90-degree angle from the growth rings on a log to produce a vertical and uniform pattern grain. In the early twentieth century, quarter-sawn oak became one of the hallmarks of the arts and crafts style. Undoubtedly, Alvah Martin's wall paneling and other woodwork, such as mantle posts, radiate elegance and traditional beauty, even improving with age. The extra work put into it without a power saw is admirable, and the tiger marks truly stand out. I thanked Polly for giving me a bit of Woodcutting 101.

She then ushered me into the auditorium and pointed to the hardwood floor line several feet from the left wall of the large room. That line is a contour of the former porch on the right side of the mansion. That was before the 1920 addition of the auditorium; hence, the porch floor is slightly darker and, of course, older than the rest of the floor. I could not believe my eyes and imagined the Virginia Club men partying on that side porch and leaning over its rails in a jubilant mood. Polly explained that there was an attractive large window over the porch that was covered up with the solid wall at the time of the auditorium's construction. The contour of the former side porch under the large round tables and Chiavari chairs is not obvious; therefore, people do not notice it unless it is pointed out. Indeed, the Martin Mansion has numerous hidden surprises, possibly in every nook and cranny.

***

Paige Rose developed the first WCN scholarship program in the club's history. Jamyla Turner Parker, a graduate of Norview High School in Norfolk, was the recipient of the 2022-2023 Amanda Skye Gallon Scholarship, named after the deceased daughter of Sam the Lasagna Lady. Jamyla's teachers at Norview High School sent a glowing report of her leadership abilities in the classroom and overcoming a difficult home situation. Jamyla had a roof over her head, but her father and stepmother made her buy her own food and even pay them to drive her to the grocery store. She had a mountain to climb just for basic survival and is trying to lead a productive life such as attending college.

The Woman's Club of Norfolk is now working on two additional scholarship programs for the years 2023-2024, one of which will include a partnership with Sentara Health.

Paige also arranged the Ukrainian Tea at the Woman's Club on January 22, 2023, which I attended, along with over a hundred people. It was a touching community panel featuring nine female Ukrainian refugees who had fled the war through Poland and settled in Hampton Roads. Dressed in their embroidered tops and flowered headdresses, these women told heartbreaking stories of leaving their loved ones behind. They expressed fear of losing their visas after expiration and did not know what would happen to them in the future.

Kenny Alexander, who was elected in 2016 as the first black mayor of Norfolk, was present and assured the community would try to figure out how to help the refugees who still needed jobs, housing, language training, medical support, donations, and even social opportunities for their children. Money was raised for these panel refugees, some of whom were tearful, and Paige did an excellent job of initiating the Ukrainian Tea in an overfilled auditorium, in partnership with the Tidewater Ukrainian Cultural Association, Tidewater Ukrainian School, and the city of Norfolk.

After a few hurdles, Paige received great news two months later: The U.S. Citizenship and Immigration Services finally approved her family as a host for two Ukrainian refugees, Ivanna and Igor. She was determined to help her new friends launch a peaceful new chapter, while they waited for the horrors of the Russian invasion to end.

***

Now that they had created the Gatewood Martin Mansion Foundation (GMMF), Susanne and Polly assembled their foundation board comprising eight professional women, each with lengthy experience in the non-profit sector. The GMMF mission is: "Rebuilding lives while rebuilding the Martin Mansion." After many long nights, Susanne and Polly finally incorporated the GMMF into a 501 c3, which renders this non-profit foundation tax-deductible.

The long-term plan was to observe how other historic properties in the area could maintain and grow their hundred-year-old business models. The Hermitage Museum and Gardens was one. The other was the Hunter House in downtown Norfolk, built in 1894 and designed in Romanesque style with Victorian decorations and arts. Forward-thinkers, Susanne and Polly included a plan to ensure the continuation of a leadership team long after they were gone.

Polly showed me the sinking foundation under the porch. I was dismayed to see a significant crack on the left side of the aging brick foundation. Susanne and Polly recently hired an engineer to inspect the foundation, which needs to be repaired with underpinnings. That was another reason Susanne and Polly established the Gatewood Martin Mansion Foundation. The foundation's preservation goals include continued roof repairs, kitchen renovation, a restored courtyard, mural repair, and most importantly, the foundation underpinning project.

The foundation's program goal is to set up a Veterans' educational program in the courtyard, which should be a perfect non-clinical setting for those who have served our country. The Art for Veterans will use the courtyard for a peaceful respite for painting and other art programs led by college students studying art therapy. Susanne saw this model-based program at Walter Reed National Military Medical Center in Bethesda, Maryland, and witnessed its huge success in a courtyard away from the hospital. And she spoke with the veterans participating in the Art for Veterans program, and they felt that it tremendously helped with their healing from war wounds, PTSD, and other mental issues. Indeed, that is what the Woman's Club of Norfolk needs in its new courtyard. The suicide rate in the veteran community in Norfolk is extremely high, and hopefully, the WCN's upcoming program will help our veteran friends.

Of course, it will take time for the foundation to raise sufficient money to host art therapy sessions for the veterans and do all the repairs and renovations for the mansion. In addition, a large part of the royalties of this book will go to the Gatewood Martin Mansion Foundation.

***

I decided to do something before finishing this book: Visit the General Federation of Women's Clubs in Washington, D.C. Joanna Church, the organization's librarian, had agreed to meet with me to ascertain everything I wrote about the GFWC's activities in the past 133 years. And I wanted to explore the GFWC Headquarters and get a feel of this world's oldest and largest volunteer woman's organization.

After traveling over four hours on Amtrak from Norfolk, I checked into the Courtyard by Marriott and settled in a fifth-floor room with a window view of the GFWC headquarters across the street. When I first noticed this splendid panorama, I thought with amusement, *That's what I am here for—a job to do.* The headquarters occupies the historic Miles Mansion on 1734 N Street, NW, built in 1875 and designated a national historic landmark in 1991. Connected with other buildings in between, its Renaissance Revival architecture is impressive with white stone. Minutes later, I greeted Joanna at the front door under the iconic splayed glass-and-iron marquee. She gave me a breathtaking tour through the first and second floors, connected by an attractive oak staircase. I saw a pastel portrait of Jane Croly in the same pose similar to the late 1890s photo shown in this book. The colored portrait of Jane in a gilded frame by Roy Gregory was created for the GFWC's hundredth-anniversary celebration in 1990 as a gift from the Rhode Island Federation in honor of Alice Donahue, the GFWC president at the time.

Joanna showed me around the music room, the long social hall, and the dining room, all of which would hold a large crowd of women. The Miles Mansion was built to be fancy with French taste, not as heavily wooded as the Martin Mansion, but it does have impressive dark oak crown molding. The rooms are beautifully decorated and furnished with enormous mirrors, vintage paintings, statues, marbled fireplaces, gilded mantles, and historic collections, enough to enthrall visitors into feeling like they are in a palace.

On the second floor, a large square yellow room displays fifty-four portraits of past GFWC presidents, giving an air of authority. Joanna explained that each of the past presidents lived in a third-floor apartment during their two-year service. And she regretted to say the current international president, Deb Strahanoski, was not in since she was in New Mexico at a conference. It did not surprise me since a two-year term presiding over such an extensive organization does not give a president ample time to work in her headquarters office if she has fifty states and several foreign countries to manage!

I was delighted to view in person the original 1927 painting, "The Woman's Club," more spellbinding than the print version at the Martin Mansion. The middle-aged and elderly women look slightly up in one direction, apparently listening to the speaker. Their faces show a mixture of civility, curiosity, and awe, which makes the painting eerily lifelike. For me, it was the same kind of feeling anyone would have at a museum featuring historic paintings, like the billboard-sized "Washington Crossing the Delaware" by Emanuel Leutze, which draws the viewer into the drama of the American Revolutionary War.

Finally, Joanna showed me her task room: The Women's History and Resource Center (WHRC), where she works as a librarian. The elongated room reminded me of a seed bank with thousands and thousands of small boxes, neatly lined in rows from floor to ceiling. The volume of processed records in the collection is humongous, spanning the years 1889 to 2023, the bulk of which date from 1890 to 1990. Most of the records are bound volumes or paper files, but there are also photographs, audio-visual material, and artifacts. These collections are cataloged and preserved for use in research, exhibitions, and loans. They consist of the GFWC archives, special collections, and the research library. Joanna was the right person to read my entire manuscript except for this last chapter and correct any writings about the General Federation of Women's Clubs. Indeed, she was a huge help with her list of corrections and suggestions.

I asked her for information on the demography of Women's Club members, since race and religion are a bit sensitive these days. It is true the woman's club movement during the Progressive Era was started by white, middle-class, Protestant women. Then a second phase of the movement was started by African-American women; however, these women already had their clubs dating back to the Civil War, mostly through their churches, which promoted anti-slavery and advocated Frederick Douglass' newspaper, *The North Star*. Hence, African-American woman's clubs and the general woman's clubs were independent of each other. Throughout the twentieth century, the General Federation of Women's Clubs and its affiliated clubs stayed predominantly white, although they welcomed diversity along the way. For instance, Roberta Campbell Lawson, a half-Delaware Indian born in Oklahoma, was the GFWC president from 1935 to 1938. She led the GFWC's two million members in goals of "uniform marriage and divorce laws, birth control, and civic service," according to the Encyclopedia of Oklahoma History & Culture. Ms. Lawson also published books on Native American music, as well as transcribed Lakota chants.

Joanna also stated that woman's clubs across America have welcomed Jewish members over the years, as has the Woman's Club of Norfolk. However, there is a large Jewish woman's organization that has been in existence since the Progressive Era. The National Council of Jewish Women (NCJW) has the same purpose as the GFWC and African-American clubs: The empowerment of women and community involvement. Founded in 1893, the NCJW is the oldest Jewish women's grassroots organization in the country, continually guided by Jewish values that call on its members to improve the lives of the most vulnerable women, children, and families. Israel is involved in this organization as well. Even during World War II, when they faced the anguish of Holocaust reports in Europe, members of the NCJW participated in war relief efforts, including an affiliated section in Hampton Roads. And more poignantly, the NCJW rescued Jewish children from Germany and worked to reunite thousands of displaced persons with family members.

Since the Progressive Era and onward into the twenty-first century, all the women's organizations, including the GFWC, have been independent of each other, each with its own federations. Yet, they all have fought for women's rights, regardless of their race or religion. And they have engaged in volunteering and community improvement. The biggest similarity of all the women's organizations is their focus on the power of women. They form a collective strength to work, advocate, protest, resolve, volunteer, contribute, and enhance, even during a crisis. It indicates that women in a group fight and stand up for what they believe in. And they form a team to help the unfortunate, contribute to society, and improve the community.

The General Federation of Women's Clubs has always insisted on keeping politics from infringing on the equality of women since it has long been a nonpartisan, nondenominational organization. Clubwomen may advocate for policies or legislation but are NOT allowed by law to endorse candidates or engage in partisan politics.

I had a lingering question for Joanna about one woman, as I had heard rumors of her visiting the Woman's Club of Norfolk more than a half-century ago. *The Virginian-Pilot* and *The Washington Post* yielded nothing about her, despite my arduous search on several newspaper links. Maybe the visit was a secret for security reasons, or it might have been just an impromptu pop-in for a minute or two. Susanne stated she was told by a late member of the GFWC that the woman did step into the Martin Mansion, but it was not exactly confirmed. And I had read that in 1922, the woman recommended this mansion on 1734 N Street NW #1 as the headquarters for the GFWC, even before she became a huge celebrity and an ultimate hero for women worldwide.

My question was, Did Eleanor Roosevelt ever visit the Woman's Club of Norfolk? As most of us know it, Eleanor was a First Lady, social reformer, columnist, teacher, political activist, and a tireless advocate for the poor and disadvantaged. She served on the first U.S. delegation to the United Nations and drafted the Declaration of Human Rights while chairing the Human Rights Commission for that body. An active member of the Chautauqua Women's Club in Upstate New York, she maintained a close relationship with the GFWC by holding meetings at the White House, hosting teas for the members, and speaking engagements. Coincidentally, my husband Steve and I travel to the Chautauqua Institution almost every August, where there is a historic moderate-sized white house with four tall columns. Surrounded by flower gardens, the house sits on top of a hill facing the majestic Chautauqua Lake. That is Chautauqua Women's Club (Yes, an e), on whose elegant porch Eleanor sat for many years.

Joanna answered my Eleanor question with a look of uncertainty and said, "How can we find out if there were over 16,000 clubs?" She explained that many other clubs had asked the very same question since they wanted to prove that the phenomenal First Lady had graced their clubhouse. I accepted that unsurprising answer and would never want Joanna to dig into thousands of records to see if Eleanor ever stepped into the Martin Mansion. So, maybe she did not. Or maybe she did it on the spur of the moment without alerting a drove of reporters. We will never know the answer. But still, I left Washington, D.C., completely satisfied with the outcome of Joanna's valuable involvement with my book. She deserves deep gratitude for pointing out miscalculations and real facts about her employer, General Federation of Women's Clubs.

Jane Croly, the founder of GFWC, would have agreed with one of Eleanor's many inspirational quotes: *A woman is like a tea bag; you never know how strong it is until it's in hot water.*

Look how far the women of the GFWC and affiliated clubs nationwide and worldwide have come, making this world a better place with women's rights, national parks, libraries, cleaner and safer cities, war relief efforts, crime prevention, car safety, accessibility for the disabled, animal welfare, and much, much more. What a difference they have made in 155 years since Charles Dickens visited America and unknowingly stirred such a mighty fighting spirit in the rejected women and their leader, Jane Cunningham Croly.

And then that fighting spirit ended up for a good long time on the doorstep of the Martin Mansion on Fairfax Avenue, earnestly owned by the Woman's Club of Norfolk.

Made in the USA
Middletown, DE
05 February 2024

49140673R10225